# FAMILY MENTAL HEALTH

## Theory and practice

# FAMILY MENTAL HEALTH

## Theory and practice

**RAE SEDGWICK, R.N., Ph.D.**

Psychologist, Family Therapist, Private Practice,
Bonner Springs, Kansas

*illustrated*



**The C. V. Mosby Company**

ST. LOUIS • TORONTO • LONDON 1981

Printed in the United States of America

The C. V. Mosby Company
11830 Westline Industrial Drive, St. Louis, Missouri 63141

**Library of Congress Cataloging in Publication Data**

Sedgwick, Rae.
Family mental health, theory and practice.

Bibliography: p.
Includes index.
1. Family psychotherapy. I. Title. [DNLM:
1. Family. 2. Mental health. WM105 S456f]
RC488.5.S42 616.89'156 80-20160
ISBN 0-8016-4447-X

C/M/M 9 8 7 6 5 4 3 2 1 05/B/611

To

**MY FAMILY**

# PREFACE

The family is the most important social organization and emotional environment that individuals encounter in the process of growth and development. Within the family system, individuals are shaped by and learn to shape the world around them. Family effectiveness is influenced by the individuals within the particular family, by the history that those individuals bring to the contemporary unit, by the dynamics that occur within the unit on a day-to-day basis, and by the events and situations that surround the family. How well the family operates as a social organization and how successful the family is in creating an emotional environment conducive to group interaction as well as individual growth and development are measures of the family's effectiveness, or mental health. Family mental health is the result of interactions within the family system and between the family system and other social systems.

This book is presented in three sections. The first section is an overview of concepts and principles related to the family as a system. The second section is an overview and discussion of clinical involvement and the clinical process. The third section discusses clinical application and presents case illustrations. Family is defined and described as a system; additional concepts are discussed throughout the text to familiarize the clinical student with those concepts that have been helpful to me as a clinician in working with families. Mental health is defined in terms of psychological and social effectiveness; clinical intervention is viewed as a process of change in which attempts are made to enhance the level of effectiveness of the family system. Although the text was originally prepared with the clinical nursing student in mind, it is believed to be appropriate to the practicing clinician in health-related fields, such as social work, psychology, and counseling in which the primary focus is on the family as a unit. Thus all chapters will be useful to the clinical student, and certain chapters can be read and used selectively by the more experienced clinician. Both groups, the beginning and the more experienced clinician, will find the study questions and exercises at the end of each chapter helpful in testing and applying their own understanding of the material provided.

The material presented is the result of my academic exposure to and clinical experience with nursing and psychology, as well as the result of working with families in and out of therapy. Thus the text contains both the ideas of others and some of my own original thinking. Permission has been granted by Charles B. Slack, Inc. and The C. V. Mosby Company to use work that has appeared elsewhere.

Like many endeavors, this textbook is the result of the efforts of several people, to whom I am deeply grateful: Beth Lee and Dr. Nancy Elsberry, Clinical Nurse Specialists, for their critical reviews and constructive comments; Linda Reynolds, for her diligent and careful preparation of the manuscript; and Susan Hildebrand, Clinical Nurse Specialist, for her support and critical reviews and for maintaining a sense of order in our clinical practice, particularly during the final stages of manuscript preparation.

Since many of the ideas and clinical tools presented in this text are developmental and are still in the growing process, I welcome comments and suggestions from students and clinicians as they work with and further develop the ideas and clinical tools presented here. One of the exciting aspects of a text of this nature is the knowledge that clinicians and practitioners will be using and critically testing the concepts and practices presented. Their ideas and comments will be useful in the further refinement of these particular tools and in the development of new ideas and new clinical intervention strategies. To the above-named people and to the clinicians who use this text, I am grateful and look forward to a long and productive relationship.

**Rae Sedgwick**

# CONTENTS

# PART I

# Theory

## Chapter 1

# OVERVIEW

This is a book about families, mental health, and the contextual factors that shape both. The text is presented in three parts: The first is an overview of concepts and principles that I find helpful in working with families. The second part is an overview of clinical involvement and clinical processes in general. The third part focuses on specific clinical application and case illustrations. Themes that appear early in the book reoccur throughout the text: family as a dynamic process; family as a system with unique social and psychological characteristics; mental health as a composite outcome of the family's system effectiveness; mental health as an outcome of individual, family, and society interaction; stress and change as the natural outcomes of daily living in a highly organized, technologically sophisticated society; change as the natural by-product of the interaction within the family and between the family and external systems; the clinician as participant observer; the clinician as change agent; and clinical involvement as a mutual responsibility of the client and the clinician.

### FAMILY OVERVIEW

Family is chosen as the central focus of discussion primarily because of the powerful influence it demonstrates in shaping individual mental health and because, in our clinical practice, the family as a dynamic unit is a basic concern. To effect change within individuals, it is often necessary, even mandatory, that changes occur within the larger family unit. The family can be one of the most demanding as well as one of the most supportive and influential systems with which individuals must learn to cope. Within the family system, individuals are shaped and, in turn, learn to shape the world around them.

The family is a social and psychological arena in which individuals learn values, take on beliefs, absorb attitudes, initiate and imitate actions, and practice ways of behaving. Members of the family watch and learn from one another. Within this arena, generations pass on ideas, attitudes, habits, and practices down through the years as a legacy on which future generations build. Family members from previous generations can be as powerful in their absence as they were as living members of the family unit. Through the processes of naming, unfinished tasks, and centrality of place and purpose, family history presents itself to the contemporary family unit and plays a part in shaping the social organization and psychological environment of the contemporary family.

The family is a social organization whose purpose is to develop in its members sets of skills necessary for productive membership in a larger social system. The family is often evaluated by the ability of its members to learn, produce, create, exercise sound social judgment, adhere to social norms and expectations, and otherwise actively participate in meaningful community life. As a social organization, family has a pivotal purpose: linking the family members one with another and bringing the family as a group into contact and interaction with other societal networks, for example, school, church, government, and work. The family's embeddedness in a larger social network helps the family to set goals, derive expectations, and make future plans. The interaction of the various networks forms the context in which family occurs. Through its network, the family processes information, makes decisions, engages in productive and expansive activities, and provides for individual growth and development in light of demands that will be placed on individual members in the future. Patterns of communication and styles of relating reflect the social context of any particular family unit. As a social organization, the family is responsible for teaching social, intellectual, and physical skills. Although the family has many characteristics of social organizations, it is also an emotional environment.

As an emotional environment, the family is imbued with the responsibility of creating an atmosphere conducive not only to group living and cooperation but to individual development as well. As a psychological environment, the family has the ability to fashion its members in a variety of ways. The family may, in light of its history and its contemporary social context, engage in emotionally honest or emotionally dishonest forms of communication; shape its members through acceptance and approval or through disapproval and rejection; and use the spaces within its boundaries judiciously or misuse physical, emotional, and environmental resources within and outside the family limits. As a psychological environment, the family may provide its members with a sense of connectedness and belonging or may fail to provide its members with a sense of belonging, of identity. Connectedness is expressed in emotional attachment, or bonding.

Bonding, or the emotional closeness that develops in a family relationship, is integral to survival. The ability to touch and be touched, to care and be cared about, to unite with yet retain a separate identity, to know another and be known intimately, to express commitments and obtain them from another human being, and to work toward similar goals are all qualities of positive, growth-inducing bonding. To establish an emotional climate of trust, warmth, concern, and acceptance; to expect group commitment yet provide for individual uniqueness; to encourage conflict and disagreement as readily as harmony; and to adapt in light of changing needs and demands are all within the realm of possibility for the healthy family.

## FAMILY DEFINED

The family is made up of people who have a shared sense of history, experience some degree of emotional bonding, engage in directionality and goal setting for the future and whose activities involve group issues as well as individual concerns. Group issues may include physical survival, social protection, education, and development of skills. Individual concerns may involve protection, acceptance, nurturance, approval, belonging, identity, support, and growth. The bonds that unite family members are powerful and persist, through time, in significance and impact on individual members. Family members may or may not be biologically related; the bonds that unite them may or may not be legal. This definition of family encompasses the social and psychological features of the relationships that form the primary core of the family experience. Most family units contain at least some members who are biologically related or engaged in some form of binding legal contract. However, some family units whose commitments are firm, whose goals are defined, whose sense of history shared, whose members are interdependent for physical, emotional, and social needs may not be legally or biologically related. Single parent families, aged who pool their resources, communal groups, religious orders, and blended families are all families by definition as well as by commitment. In a recent interview with a young child, I asked her to name her family. She began, "Karen, Linda, Susie, Jason, and Billy." I thought that the family consisted of two siblings and a single parent. "Who are all these people?" I asked her brother. He replied, "Kids at school." The small child smiled and said, "That doesn't matter, we can be family, too." Her comments show the importance of knowing who is considered family by the various members of the immediate family or the family being interviewed. If one member perceives the network to be more extensive than other members, the operating family unit will be different depending on who is being interviewed. It is important to be able to identify family members; in order to do so, the clinician must be able to see family from the perspective of those who consider themselves to be family. Family members often have a broader definition of what constitutes family than the clinician does, especially if the clinician has been raised in a traditional two-parent, three-sibling, middle class family setting. Each member brings to the family system a unique history, individual needs and wants, expectations and skills, and ideas of what will contribute to good family relationships. Success will depend on individual and family ability to fulfill social and psychological needs of the group as a whole and of individual members.

## FAMILY MENTAL HEALTH

*Mental health* is used in this text interchangeably with *effectiveness:* it is a measure of the family's ability to successfully execute activities essential to meeting family and individual needs and satisfying societal demand and expectation. These activities include (1) gathering information; (2) making and implementing decisions; (3) resolving conflict and providing for individual growth and development; (4) creating an emotional atmosphere conducive to self-disclosure, trust, cooperation, and acceptance; and (5) engaging in productive and adaptive activities with regard to internal family needs and external societal demands. These activities are essential to effective family life. The ability or inability to successfully engage in these activities is related to individual ability, family organization, environmental conditions, and sociocultural constraints.

The less able a family is to engage in the above activities, the less effective the family will be as a system and the greater the probability that individual behavior will reflect that lack of effectiveness. Individual mental health is considered a reflection of the state of affairs within the family system at any given time, thus removing from any one individual the entire responsibility for failure, sickness, or ineffectiveness. In this book, the identified patient is considered to include the family, the social structure of which the family is a part, and the contributions that the individual family members make to the overall process.

Mental health, then, is a multifaceted outcome of the interaction between the family unit and larger social systems and between the social systems and individual family members. To judge mental health, it is necessary to identify the family in its given context. The context includes cultural, social, economic, and community background. What is effective in one setting may be less than effective in another. What is typical for one culture may not be typical in another. The environment, or physical surroundings, with which a family must cope plays a significant role in that family's ability to be productive, to withstand stress, and to make changes.

### Change

Change and the need for change are components of daily living for families. A rising cost of living, fluctuations in the market value of the dollar, discrepancies in health insurance plans, and rapid technological advancements all operate to force the family to make constant changes and to undergo stress for prolonged periods. Management of stress and ability to participate in change are essential and influential factors in the mental health of a family. Lack of mental health can be a transitory situation that is the result of too much stress, too much change, and too few resources. Individual members within the family unit are often the red flags that signal that the family is about to succumb or needs help in coping with change. Because of the situational, overlapping nature of effectiveness and ineffectiveness, it is possible to help family units to alter patterns, to exchange old habits for new ways, and to become more effective.

Helping families to change is not always an easy task; it can be complicated and fraught with difficulties. The family often comes to the clinician because a member has been identified by the school, police, community, or family as a source of trouble. The identified individual is labeled and often begins to act out the assigned label. Not only must the family be helped to see the interlocking nature of individual behavior with family dynamics, but the individual must often be assisted in giving up the "sick patient" identity. It is sometimes easier for families to consider one member sick than to realize that the entire unit is engaging in ineffective practices. The clinician acts as a change agent, one who often pushes the family in the direction of self-awareness and self-determination. In so doing, the clinician may become a focus of energy that unites the family and brings members to an awareness of their group abilities to make changes in their daily lives. The clinician is a participant, active and involved; an observer, passive and data-gathering; and an agent, directing and facilitating.

Changes that come about are the joint endeavor of the clinician and the family unit, each with a set of rights and responsibilities. The contract, written or informal, serves as the meeting ground on which the clinical process is constructed. As illustrated in the following example, it is important not only for the clinician and the immediate family to be involved, but distant and influential family members as well. In the example, a significant family member was overlooked and his influence underestimated.

**Example.** Larry was brought to my office because of repeated school failures. Present in the household at the time were a father, mother, and two older sisters. His siblings were doing well in school, and, although the parents were minimally educated, there was no apparent reason for Larry's progressive lack of success. Larry was puzzled by his failure but not apparently distressed. Following the initial interview, which took place in my office, a home visit was made, largely because of the lack of tangible clues to Larry's poor performance. During that visit the mother happened to mention that Larry was looking forward to an upcoming visit to his grandfather in a nearby community. In later visiting with the grandfather, I became aware that the man had little, if any, positive regard for formal education, being a self-made and rather successful farmer. His emotional attachment to Larry was evident in his frequent visits, gifts, and comments. He was unaware, however, that he was conveying to Larry a general lack of interest in Larry's school performance, that he had communicated his rather low opinion of formal education in general, and that he was serving as a model for Larry. As we explored his influence during the sessions that followed, the grandfather became sensitized to and influential in changing Larry's attitudes toward school.

During the initial interview, the grandfather was not mentioned except in passing. His influence was not considered important, chiefly because he did not live in the same household and because his farm was some distance away. His impact, however, was powerful and real. His participation was essential, not only in gathering a complete family profile but, more important, in helping the family members to make changes in their style of interacting with each other and with the school system. Larry was a link between his grandfather and his parents; between his parents and the school system, and between the school system and my office. Through Larry's efforts, all were somewhat changed in the encounter.

Larry's family situation demonstrates the powerful yet often overlooked impact of the so-called distant, or extended, family member. It also points out the changeable nature of relationships. These relationships were temporarily ineffective but, with assistance, reached a level of effectiveness. There was a strong bond between Larry and his grandfather, one that affected everyone it touched, including Larry's classmates who later made educational visits to the farm.

Larry's case can be used to summarize a number of points about families in general:

1. Family membership involves not only members residing together but distant members as well. In Larry's case, this was a living grandfather. In other families, members may include aunts, uncles, deceased but influential grandparents, close friends, retired school teachers, ministers, school nurses, or professional colleagues. A family member's relationship to the family unit is often a matter of emotional attachment and social influence as well as economic support and physical proximity. Family pets and individual members' hobbies, jobs, and responsibilities are often so demanding that, in a sense, a membership role is created for that job, pet, or demand.

2. Family consists not only of people but of what happens between those people as well. Relationships established, patterns organized, and habits that family units develop are as much a part of the family as are the people

themselves. *How* a family goes about organizing itself and catering to the needs of its members is as important as *who* does it and *what* is accomplished in the process. The process underlying family organization is reflected in statements like the following: "It isn't what he does that bothers me, it is the way he goes about doing it," or "We really care about each other, but we just can't seem to show it," or "The way we make decisions? Who knows? I guess they just happen." Process is also revealed in actions and patterns that characterize a particular family unit: some arise out of social expectations, some have origins in family history and culture, and some emerge from interactions of the present family unit. One of the keys to change is being able to identify the patterns that form the basis of the family process in any specific family unit. What happens within the family is influenced by what is going on around the family as well. These surrounding features can be referred to as the "context."

3. Family occurs within a context: community, schools, jobs, churches, culture, race, social class, and religious beliefs. The context, or environment, shapes and, in turn, is shaped by the families in that environment. The context forms a larger interlocking network around the family, a network of which the family is an integral part. Some families are more actively involved in their environments, whereas some families are relatively isolated. The degree of involvement or the extent of isolation affects the family's ability to exchange ideas, to incorporate norms and expectations, to receive support, to be challenged and stimulated, and to change. Larry's family was an involved family, seeking out help, reaching out to one another, and acting on new information provided through contact with outside resources. Such a family has a high probability of maintaining an effective level of operation and of regaining effectiveness following a crisis or period of stress. Both the isolated and the involved families are influenced by their environments, but the involved family has a better chance of being as influential in changing the environment as the environment is in changing the family. The interchange between the family and the environment is important for family and also important for the environment. Norms, expectations, attitudes, and even directionality of family goals are often greatly shaped by the settings in which the family resides—socially, psychologically, and physically. At the same time, in order to make norms relevant, to keep expectations within the realm of possibility, to modify attitudes with regard to social or technological developments, and to alter goals as necessary, the family's active involvement is essential. In order that the environment be maintained in ways that serve human needs, human beings must be actively involved and decisive. Such behavior is learned primarily in the family setting.

4. Individuals within the family play a vital part in the way the family

interacts. Larry's grandfather was a strong figure in the unfolding of events in Larry's family. Just as the family had an interlocking relationship with the school, the members within the unit had an interlocking relationship with one another. Individuals make their contribution in a variety of ways. I have identified and discuss in a later chapter several ways in which individual family members participate in family dynamics: (1) as links, or essential units, that connect people, events, and situations; (2) as translator-interpreters who bring wishes, expectations, and desires to realization through performance; (3) as source-resources who serve as prototypes of behavior and generative forces of energy; (4) as agents responsible for their own actions; (5) as victims shaped to fit the needs of others; and (6) as indices, or barometers, of the dynamics within the family unit. Each member may contribute in any or all of the above ways. However, in many families individuals develop and family units encourage patterned ways of behaving. The less effective the family, the more likely the family is to have limited avenues of individual contribution to the family interaction. In determining family effectiveness, the individual's ability to contribute and the family's ability to provide avenues for individual participation must be assessed. The overall assessment of family effectiveness must include an examination of more than one facet of behavior, belief, or emotional expression and must take into account the environment, individual ability, family history, and social context.

5. Family mental health is the outcome of a series of interactions within the family and between the family and the physical, social, cultural, and emotional environments. No one factor can be held responsible for the mental health of families or individuals. Effectiveness is the outcome of cumulative interactions among several factors: namely, the family as a whole, inidividuals within the family, and the social network of which the family is an integral component. Larry's individual abilities—intellectual, verbal, social, and physical—were certainly factors in his school performance. However, his grandfather's attitudes, his parents' relationship with the grandfather, and Larry's relationship with his grandfather were also factors in that performance. Larry's own father's relationship with the grandfather had a bearing on the strong emotional bond that developed between the grandfather and his only grandson. The fact that the community was a farming community had a bearing on the expectations and needs of the family as a unit. The school's relationship to the members of the community served as an aid to the family's resolution of their problem. The grandfather, the school, the community, and the relationships among these social networks were all part of the complicated profile of Larry's "problem"; they were all involved, to some degree, in the resolution of the immediate situation.

Larry's grandfather, the farming community, his parents, his siblings, and the school system were also part of the completed profile. The family's openness and information gathering, their ability to make and carry out decisions; their having created an emotional atmosphere conducive to change, and their willingness to work with school and mental health personnel were all integral to effective problem solving. Their ineffectiveness was transitory. There was a temporary decline in the level of mental health within this particular unit; the decline itself was the result of a number of factors. These factors must be taken into consideration not only in gathering data about families but in order to help the family unit to be more effective in future situations.

## SUMMARY

Family life is a composite of people—their behaviors, thoughts, feelings; the rules that govern group interaction and individual contribution; individual ability and skill; and sociophysical environment, composed of other people, agencies, cultures, institutions, and physical spaces. To understand and effect change in family dynamics, the clinician must take a broad view that places the family in its particular context, operating according to a particular set of rules, being influenced by sociocultural demands, performing according to formal and informal expectations, and being successful according to standards established prior to its own existence. How effectively the family performs its functions depends on the interrelationships among a variety of factors that make up the family's environment and the internal sets of dynamics that operate in the family system itself, including individual ability, clarity and flexibility of individual contribution, remnants of the family's past, and unfinished tasks.

The discussion that follows and the examples that have been selected illustrate more fully the multifaceted and interdependent nature of family mental health with family history, society, environment, and physical health of individuals. They also illustrate the clinical process as a means of studying, learning from, evaluating, and facilitating change within the family system.

**Chapter 2**

# CONCEPTUAL FRAMEWORK

The family is a network, composed of people, their relationships, and the interfaces between the family network and society. A network of people and relationships, the family operates as a system of interdependent components bound together by mutual needs and goals. The family as a system may be characterized by the following: (1) components, or subsystems, that are interdependent and mutually interactive; (2) boundaries or constraints that surround the system and serve to filter and translate the flow into and out of the system; (3) existence within a larger network of systems; (4) openness, or permeability, of boundaries that allows for exchange between the system and other systems; (5) proximity of subsystems within the system and proximity of the system to larger networks of systems; and (6) having patterns of organization, or structure, that strongly influence function.

## CHARACTERISTICS OF SYSTEMS

1. *A system is defined as being made up of components, or subsystems, that are interdependent and mutually interactive* Berrien (1968). The family is composed of both people and what happens between them. Individuals within any given family share similar goals and have mutual needs, as described briefly in the preceding chapter. The basis for the relationships between individuals and among family members can be economic, legal, social, physical, or emotional. Because of common goals and the shared basis for relationships, what affects one member will affect another; what affects the relationship will have an impact on individuals within the family as well as on the family unit itself. What one family member does, for example, occupationally, affects the economic status of the family and more often than not the social and emotional status as well. How members decide to use individual leisure time influences how much time is left for group endeavors and family pursuits. Goals set by adults determine actions taken by children. Actions taken by children may change goals that adults or family leaders have selected.

Although family may be generally characterized as made up of subsystems, or individuals, and their relationships, how any one family operates is determined by the abilities or persons within that family, by the nature of relationships established within the family, and by the contacts that the family maintains with other systems. Loving and being loved, protecting and being protected, growing and helping others to grow, making decisions and being part of decision making differ somewhat from family to family. As a system one family shares characteristics with another family, but the unique qualities of individual members—physical attributes, intellectual ability, emotional make-up—and the special features of culture, religion, and ethnic background of the family add a particular, definable dimension to each family system.

2. *Systems have boundaries.* These separate one system from another system and filter or translate information that comes into and flows out of the subsystem. Families have boundaries—rules, sanctions, communication patterns, attitudes, and values—that bind them together and guide their beliefs and practices. A family is bounded by its beliefs about human behavior, about social expectations, and about individual performance based on age, sex, or experience. Boundaries that surround the family are social (norms, expectations, myths), physical (space, territory, housing), emotional (feelings), historical (legacy, belief, expectation), and individual (ability, need, desire). Each set of rules evolves in part from the family's contact with society, in part from the family's history, and in part from the contemporary life of the family.

Beliefs about human behavior, that is, about what makes people behave in certain ways, partially determine how family members behave—toward one another, their children, members of the opposite sex, and members of other ethnic, cultural, or racial groups. These beliefs prompt use of various modes of behavior (for example, discipline or punishment), shape interaction patterns with people who differ from the family, influence sociosexual interaction within the family, and influence the development of behavioral guidelines used by various family members.

Rules evolve that members are supposed to acknowledge in practice. Communication patterns (who talks to whom about what) and interaction patterns (who does what with whom for what reasons) reflect unspoken rules that guide the family. Special uses of language—phrases, gestures, family jokes, and nicknames—and ways of behaving peculiar to a family establish boundaries around the family that unite it in a shared identity and common practice and keep outsiders and non-family members at a reasonable distance. Family boundaries are buffer zones, cushioning the family from external forces and distinguishing information as useful or irrelevant to the family system. Family boundaries are often closed enough to gain the family a reputation of being "close-knit," "cliquish," or "clannish." Such labeling reflects the psychological, social, and physical nature of boundaries that the family has established. Examples of rules and practices that serve as boundaries are: (1) a ten o'clock curfew—a time boundary, (2) not dating someone of another race or culture—a cultural or ethnic boundary, (3) not having premarital sexual relations—a sociosexual boundary, (4) working at specific occupations—an occupational boundary, (5) verbal and nonverbal expressions unique to the family—communication boundaries, and (6) participation of particular family members in decision making—a boundary of the social organization. Boundaries come in part from family history, handed down from generation to generation, because "That's the way we do things"; in part from social contact with other systems, "People are expected to. . ."; in part from religious beliefs, because "People are supposed to act certain ways," especially to others; in part from tradition; and in part from the ongoing experience in the contemporary family setting.

Boundaries come from within the family through history, belief, and expectation as well as from outside the family through social contact. The physical environment, including the family's house, neighborhood, and community, sets limits on behavior that is expected, appropriate, and necessary for any given family. External expectations regarding family life and individual behavior, as well as constraints placed on the family unit, are indicative of the family system's position in a larger network of systems.

3. *A system is characterized by existence within other systems.* A family does not exist in isolation but in an intimate and mutually influential position with regard to a larger network of systems. Individual members provide the interface between the family and other social systems. The worker connects the family and the economic system; the student connects the family and the educational system; the consumer connects the family with social systems geared to meeting basic needs; the activist connects the family with political systems; the church member connects the family with religious systems; and the physically ill, emotionally distressed, or chronically disabled connects the family with the health care system.

Individual family members are often intensely involved through jobs, careers, personal ambition, individual needs, and family goals in one or more systems outside the family but connected to it through the individual. The larger set of systems is often referred to as the suprasystem, whereas the network of individuals is referred to as the subsystems. Through such contact, exchanges take place that involve energy, information, and products. The suprasystem is dependent on family members for energy to run the system, for consumption of the products of the system, and for ideas and links back to the family. The family depends on the larger system for goods and products, education, health care, recreation, cultural opportunities, individual growth and development, basic survival, and meeting of social needs. The family system and other social systems are dependent on one another for maintenance as well as for growth and expansion. The individual family member serves as a link between the family and the larger system. The family itself serves as a connector within the suprasystem.

Just as the individual family member is the subsystem that contributes to the overall social and psychological profile of the family, so the family unit is a subsystem that contributes to and influences the overall profile of the larger social systems. Churches, schools, neighborhoods, and communities depend on the family system for input, energy, information, and physical labor: individuals to people the systems. Social policy, political movements, and religious activities are geared toward and are dependent on the family as an ongoing, integral component. Individual members need not be a physical part of a political, social, or governmental system for the entire family to be influenced by and have an impact on those systems through voting, consumption, and approval. The exchange process and the degree of influence between the family system and other social systems reflect the permeability of family boundaries as well as the nature of proximity in the network of systems.

4. *Systems are characterized by openness.* An open system is capable of being influenced by and having impact on other systems beyond its boundaries. An open system is maintained through interchange with other systems: sharing of information, physical contact, shared responsibility, mutual goals, shared territory, common language, and so forth. The family system itself is rarely closed to or unaffected by the larger network of which it is a vital component. Avenues of accessibility and influence include individual family members' physical and social presence in other systems; mutual goals related to occupation, education, and health care that necessitate contact and interaction with other systems; reciprocal needs for energy, information, and physical and emotional support. The family is extensive, and complicated needs necessitate reliance on other family systems and other social system. The suprasystem's exclusive and complicated organization causes its reliance on the family system.

The degree of mutual influence possible depends on the family's openness to new ideas, their willingness to try new ways, and the flexibility of longstanding family rules. There are families who find new ideas and different practice stimulating and challenging. Families with open boundaries display an interest in learning through education, exposure, and experience. Outsiders are seen as welcome avenues for broadening beliefs, ideas, and attitudes. Such a family generally has a well-developed social network that includes an array of people with differing beliefs and attitudes as well as divergent cultural, ethnic, racial, and religious backgrounds. Active exchange among the differing groups takes place. Social systems outside the family system are generally viewed by such families in a favorable light. That is, other systems are believed to exist to help the family, to facilitate the family's growth, and to assist individual development. Mutually beneficial relationships tend to develop across the respective boundaries.

Members of a family system whose boundaries are less permeable tend to have ideas that are rigid, demonstrate a reluctance to try new ways, and exhibit a general resistance to change. Because change is an inevitable and natural part of living, rigid families experience frequent difficulty. Strangers with new ways and new ideas are seen as threats; unbendable rules are believed to be essential to survival; exposure to new ideas or differing backgrounds is avoided; and the potential for acquiring social support is rarely actualized. Learning is viewed with fear and mistrust, and other systems are considered threats to the sanctity of the tightly woven family system. Schools, community groups, and social agencies are viewed as unwelcome intruders into the family system. Counterproductive relationships, founded on suspicion and mistrust, are often established between the family system and the suprasystem. Prejudice, isolationism, and authoritarian views are associated with systems whose boundaries are inflexible.

The more involved the family system becomes with other systems, family and nonfamily alike, the more support and encouragement are available to the family through social networking. It is difficult to be part of a larger system and remain unaffected by the dynamics that occur, not only because of the family's interdependence with the larger system for self-maintenance, input into other systems, regulation and maintenance of system function, and meeting individual needs, but also because of the physical and social closeness (proximity) involved.

5. *Systems exist in proximity to other systems.* They are affected by that proximity. A system is subject to influence by those systems that are adjacent to its boundaries. The distance between the boundaries of respective systems also has a bearing on the nature of the interface between the systems and the interactions that develop as a result of proximity. Although proximity alone does not determine the formation of a system, it is a necessary condition for interaction between systems to occur.

The family's proximity to other systems influences both the internal working of the family system and the relationships that the family establishes with other systems that lie adjacent to the family's boundaries. The family system occupies physical space: rooms, houses, apartments, and yards, over which the unit has primary control and responsibility for maintenance. The regulation of activities within the space brings into contact those systems that have some investment—financial, social, physical, or emotional—in the space.

Space that is occupied by or belongs to a particular group or person is referred to as "territory"; the behavior exhibited in relation to maintaining, protecting, or defending the space is referred to as "territoriality." As a system, the family's territory often overlaps with that of other family systems. Apartments in which families live are located in apartment buildings where tenants may share entryways, elevators, laundry areas, fire exits, and so forth. Family homes are located in neighborhoods where physical boundaries are adjacent and often psychologically overlapping. Families within communities live close together and share much of the same territory: banks, grocery stores, drugstores, hardware stores, schools, and churches. Each of the subsystems that constitute the community occupies a physical, social, or emotional space that lies close to or overlaps that of other systems. Regions of overlap require that those systems involved be active in setting goals and determining policies for the care of and responsibility for the areas. Laws, ordinances, social edicts, and community expectations influence and are influenced by the use of space by family systems.

Subsystems within the family are in close or intimate contact: living in close physical space, engaging in psychosexual interactions, expressing and meeting socioemotional needs, sharing similar beliefs, and working toward mutually defined goals. Within the space provided or acquired, individuals must find personal territory, over which control can be exerted and within which privacy can be maintained. The acquisition of space—a room of one's own, a cigar box filled with private treasures, a project, an idea, or even a belief of one's own—and the caretaking responsibility associated with its preservation are vitally important to the family system as well as to the individual, or subsystem, as will be pointed out in detail in a later chapter.

Although closeness does not in itself determine system interaction, closeness is necessary for system interaction to occur. Bringing two people together will not make a family out of them, but, in order for a family to evolve, proximity, or closeness (physical, emotional, or social), must occur. The physical and emotional proximity of family draws it together; emotional involvement, shared communication styles, mutual expectations for the future, and existence within a given physical and social space are evidence of family proximity. Proximity involves physical closeness, emotional intimacy, and social identity. Proximity is a powerful shaper of family interaction. Family interaction is influenced not only by the physical and emotional closeness of the system but by patterns of organization within the family as well.

6. *Systems are characterized by structure, which exerts a regulatory influence over function.* The manner in which a system functions depends to some extent on how the system is designed to operate: a two-wheel bicycle operates differently from a three-wheeler; a water fountain is generally designed to provide water; and a business is geared toward the production of salable products. Each system functions according to certain principles, to its basic design, and to how closely the actual system approximates the original design.

Family structure regulates function. Family structure is to function as a staircase is to a step. If the staircase is winding, the steps will form a circle and lead the traveler in a circular pattern. If the staircase is long and narrow, the steps will form a straight line and will lead the traveler down a straight path. If the staircase is sturdy, the steps will support those who walk on them and will serve the purpose for which they were designed. "Family structure" refers to the overall organization that characterizes communication and interaction within the family, including (1) information processing, (2) decision making, (3) conflict resolution and individuation, (4) emotional climate, and (5) productivity and change. "Function" refers to the individual actions taken within the framework of the larger organization, each reflecting the other.

That family function is related to structure is reflected in the manner in which: (1) egalitarian structures produce democratic members; (2) warm, accepting structures facilitate tolerance and acceptance of others; (3) self-disclosing, open structures encourage authenticity and emotional honesty; (4) rigid structures produce rebellious or rule-dependent members; (5) loose structures produce permissiveness; (6) abrasive structures engender abuse; (7) emotional coldness encourages alienation, and (8) family disorganization promotes individual dysfunction and emotional distress.

At the same time that family structure regulates function in the form of individual interactions and relationships, individual members act in ways to influence or alter the patterns of interactions within the family system. Each new family member is a source of energy, ideas, and information, the addition of which requires adaptation on the part of the family organization. Adding new members, like losing members, affects the social organization and exerts an influence on the family's emotional environment. Individual growth and development—birth, death, aging, change—alter the family's communication patterns, modify interactions between original or remaining members, change the nature of demands on the physical environment, and transform emotional attachments within the family system. The more integral the member is to the family organization, the greater the changes within the system when the member is lost or leaves the system. Addition or loss of a wage earner, for example, changes the economic structure of the family; addition or loss of an emotionally supportive member alters the emotional atmosphere. Loss of a very sensitive or articulate member alters the communication structure. Individual members do not have to be lost to the system to exert an influence on social organization and system effectiveness: they exert influence through personal changes, physical presence, and individual growth and development.

## SYSTEM EFFECTIVENESS

The ability of a system to function is related to the internal organization of the system, to the nature of the event or situation that the system is confronting, and to the ability of the individuals within the system. Coping with change is related not only to skills and preparedness of the system but also to the severity, familiarity, and timing of the change itself. The survival of the system depends on its ability to prepare for and manage circumstances that confront the system and to adapt when management alone is insufficient to alter the circumstances.

Survival of a system depends on its ability to incorporate change, to produce useful and valued outputs, and to produce positive outputs that outweigh unwanted or useless products. Outputs, like inputs, are defined in terms of energy, information, or products. What is useful is largely determined by the suprasystem. Exchange within the suprasystem is essential in order that sytems know what is expected, appropriate, and useful. To the extent that the suprasystem has total control over determining value and usefulness of products, interaction is mandatory. To the extent that systems are dependent on the suprasystem for permission, approval, or acceptance, self-determination within the system is limited.

Family effectiveness is related to the internal organization of the family, to the nature of the events with which the family must cope, and to the abilities of individuals within the system. Organization refers to the structure of the social organization and the nature of the emotional atmosphere that has been established. The family's level of effectiveness can change as circumstances, individual ability, and internal organization change. The more experience a family has, the more able the family may become in coping with change, aiding individual members with growth and development, and interacting productively with other social systems. Experience alone is not always sufficient, however; frequently, advice, counsel, or training is necessary.

Family effectiveness is related to productivity, to social interaction with other systems, to experience with change, to the family's history of success or failure with change, to individual members' experience with and ability to confront change, and to the ability to incorporate changes into ongoing patterns and interactions. The more experience a family has and the more involved a family system is with other social networks, the better prepared the family may be in terms of managing continual change, a natural by-product of system functioning. Family survival depends on productivity, flexibility, experience, and commitment.

## PATTERNS OF EFFECTIVENESS

The effective family, as I identify it, is essentially a family whose ways of relating have developed into patterns that are basically conducive to and supportive of change, whether that change is as basic as normal growth and development of individuals or as complex as coping with massive advancement in social technology. Ineffective families, however, develop styles or patterns that are not conducive to or supportive of change. Dynamics that form the basis for patterns are essentially the same for effective and ineffective functioning; that is, basic requirements for family functioning include the ability to (1) seek and process information, (2) make and carry out decisions, (3) resolve conflict and incorporate differences, (4) create positive emotional environments, and (5) be productive as well as flexible with regard to change. These dynamics are influenced by contributing factors: family history, medical problems, health status, social connectedness and environmental contingencies, critical incidents, and individual differences among family members. The organization or patterns that evolve underlie effective or ineffective functioning: that is, a family that demonstrates faulty decision making will generally also show lowered productivity and poor adaptability; a family whose emotional atmosphere is nonsupportive will also tend to have problems coping with conflict. No one index (information processing, decision making, and so forth) can be used to describe or evaluate effective functioning, for it is the composite of patterns of interaction that most accurately describes family mental health.

Family mental health is strongly influenced by contributing factors that may change with time. A marginal family faced with repeated stress and relying on inadequate historical and emotional skills may quickly develop into an ineffective, even abusive family. Patterns of effectiveness can be altered by establishing a supportive, connective social network; acquiring social and psychological skills lacking in the family legacy; gaining self-worth and confidence through emotionally supportive environments; and otherwise building strengths where weaknesses exist. Every family has the potential for effective functioning, just as every family runs the risk of ineffective functioning through faulty practices, neglect of emotional and personal needs of members, or through priority setting that puts family lower than social status, material gain, or personal ambition.

Divorce, separation, marital discord, behavioral management problems, inability to live with an aged parent, recurrent and irreconcilable differences between family members, attempted suicide, child abuse, nightmares in children, bedwetting, learning disabilities, chronic illness leading to depression, and blatant "crazy" behavior on the part of one or more members are all reasons, conditions, or situations that prompt people to seek help. Among the families and individuals who seek help, there are differences but also patterns of similarity; patterns are both the result and the cause of poor human relations, faulty family history, garbled communication, mixed messages, and contradictory actions in families. Factors that contribute to these patterns include: family history, societal and cultural pressures and expectations, individual makeup and ability, and environmental contingencies. These patterns are manifested in the family's information processing, decision making, emotional tenor, conflict management and individuation, and productivity and flexibility.

These are the same functions in which healthy, or effective, families are involved. Effective and ineffective families engage in many of the same practices, hold many of the same beliefs, set many of the same goals, and belong to many of the same organizations and groups. What differs is the way in which and the extent to which these behaviors, beliefs, and goals are organized into maladaptive, ineffective patterns in unhealthy families. The patterns can be summarized as follows.

### Information processing

Effective families demonstrate patterns of flexibility in seeking information and using resources that generally fall somewhere between two extremes.

The patterns of information processing in the ineffective family, however, are of two kinds: limited and supportive of what is already known, or diffuse and entirely reliant on outside resources for guidance, advice, and control. Neither extreme contributes to overall autonomy, interdependence, self-reliance, or ability to change. At one extreme is the limited use of information and resources, with the exception of one or two family members; a fairly isolated social system with no apparent organizational or community ties; and little or no tolerance for challenging or divergent opinions. At the other extreme is the excessive use of and reliance on a widely divergent set of resources, extreme dependence on outside authority (law, mental health professional, physician, school teacher, neighbors), and the demonstration of minimal autonomy. Either extreme in information seeking or reliance on family resources generally becomes rigidly characteristic for the ineffective family regardless of the situation or event at hand. Extremes in information seeking and resource utilization seem to occur in conjunction with patterns of decision making that are typical of the ineffective family.

**Decision making**

Effective decision making is characterized by methods that best suit the situation at hand and that use resources within the family in ways appropriate to age, experience, and ability. As the family unit progresses through various stages and confronts differing situations, decision-making patterns vary in terms of authority, assistance, and implementation. When children are young, for example, most decisions must be made and carried out chiefly by adults. As children grow older and the family system gains experience, decision-making patterns can be altered to take into consideration changes in age, experience, interest, and ability. As events occur, for example, crisis in the family, decision-making patterns may have to be modified to accommodate the situation at hand.

Patterns of ineffective decision making, like those of ineffective information processing, seem to reflect two extremes on a continuum. At one end are rigid, fixed patterns with authoritarian overtones; in this case, non-decision-making family members are often told of decisions after they are made, have very little voice in altering decisions, and are expected to follow rules regardless of the situation or the individual's ability to do otherwise. At the other end of the continuum are patterns that are so diffuse and illogical as to be illusory, in which members are often assigned roles and responsibilities that far exceed their age and experience, and in which the few decisions made are rarely, if ever, carried out.

Effective decision making is organized, purposeful, expansive, and includes those involved in implementation. Effective decision making, like ineffective decision making, coincides with the emotional atmosphere characteristic of the family.

**Emotional tenor**

Effective emotional atmospheres contain messages that are consistent and congruent; self-worth takes precedence over performance; approval is given for attempts as well as successes; and emotional attachments are based on bonding that is supportive, warm, and conducive to emotional honesty. Although the effective family makes mistakes and often has to alter overly constrictive or counterproductive emotional attachments, there is a consistent pattern of warmth, support, endurance, and ways of behaving appropriate to age, sex, and experience. Whereas there is room for cross-generational bonding, for example, between parent and child, the attachments are not exclusive, that is, do not shut others out, are not used for abusive purposes, but have room for expansion and inclusion of others. There is protection of one member by others, but each member also speaks individually and can defend the self. There is a strong sense of belonging, but there is also opportunity to try out one's wings and experience oneself as a separate entity.

The emotional atmosphere that is least effective is a fluid, ever changing, unpredictable environment in which behavior is motivated out of fear of punishment or indifference to consequences. Emotional reward or punishment is not consistent, bonding is exclusive to one or two members, and manipulative tactics are used to exploit individual members. This roller coaster atmosphere is strewn with high expectations for perfection, constant threat of disapproval, and inconsistent clues for appropriate emotional expression. The healthy or unhealthy emotional atmosphere forms one of the strongest foundations on which management of differences and tolerance of individuality are based.

**Conflict and individuation**

The effective family recognizes the need for differences, is aware that harmony is not necessarily indicative of health, encourages individual growth, and accepts that members change and grow. The life of the effective family is marked by encouragement of individual pursuits and acceptance of change as both desirable and necessary for survival.

The ineffective family either does not encourage or tolerate differences or is made of so many differing opinions, ideas, and individuals that reaching a decision or working as a group is impossible. In the first pattern, change in one member as expressed through individual opinion or action sends shock waves throughout the rigid family system. In such instances, there is a push for "oneness," "togetherness," and toward conformity that disallows any individual effort or experience. Each family member is a mirror for the other, with the resultant reflection needing to be nearly the same each time. Arguments are ignored; a frequent method of handling disagreements is through withdrawal. In the second pattern, the family is essentially made up of disconnected individuals; what happens to one has little or no significance for others except as it constricts, influences, or affects other members' individual pursuits (educational, emotional, financial). Individual members generally act out in various ways to attract professional or legal help for the fragmented and chaotic system. Such systems are often discovered by school nurses, who find children who come to school hungry, poorly clothed, or ill—in spite of the fact that many come from what is considered a "good home."

### Productivity and adaptability

Effective patterns of productivity include goal setting, priority identification, and the ability to follow through on tasks, while maintaining enough flexibility to allow for change where individual need and situational demands warrant alteration in plans.

Ineffective patterns of productivity, however, are either limited and rigid or nondirective and unpredictable. There is either a consistent rigidity or lack of a fixed direction. A general resistance to change and a reluctance to accept alterations in plans characterize ineffective patterns. Change itself constitutes stress; somatic complaints and other stress-related behaviors are often the response. Productivity is limited; reliance on outside resources is often extensive; and inability to adapt is manifested in physical illness, acting out, or withdrawal.

## SUMMARY

Whereas family organization strongly influences function, individual action has a reciprocal impact on family organization. Concurrently, the social context and surrounding environment affect both structure and function. Social involvement, cultural setting, ethnic background, financial status, and physical setting can support or place inordinate strain on the family system. Ethnic identity, cultural rootedness, social belonging, and economic independence are often positive supports to the growing, changing family. Lack of strong identity, racial and sexual discrimination, prejudice, poverty, and lack of social network support can do much to undermine and contribute to the final downfall of the marginal family.

Family effectiveness, like system effectiveness, is the outcome of interaction within the family, between the family and other systems, and between family and environment. Individuals within the family system contribute to the family system; the family system contributes to the overall effectiveness of the suprasystem; and the environment contributes to the effectiveness of both. The concept of systems aids in understanding and describing the reciprocal, mutually interactive nature of the family, society, and environment.

### STUDY QUESTIONS

1. Describe five characteristics of a system. In what ways is a family a social system?
2. What is the relationship between system effectiveness and the environment?
3. Discuss the relationship between system characteristics and system effectiveness.

### EXERCISES

The following questions are set forth as tools for helping students study their families as systems in preparation for observing, interacting with, and intervening in other family systems.

1. How best can you describe who are members of your family and what primary function each serves in the family system?
2. What function do you play in your family? Are you, for example, an initiator, a peacekeeper, a troublemaker, an organizer, a leader, a follower, a merry-maker, or a doom-sayer? If your family were an orchestra, what instrument would you be? What instruments would other family members be? Who would be the director? Who would select the music? Who would assign the seating?
3. Complete the following:
   a. My family is . . .
   b. I like my family the most when . . .
   c. I like my family the least when . . .
   d. The funniest thing that ever happened in my family was . . .
   e. The saddest thing that ever happened in my family was . . .
   f. What I fear the most is . . .
4. Of all your family members, who do you resemble the most? In what ways? Who do you least resemble? In what ways?
5. Draw a picture showing a typical evening scene in your family. You might want to draw a second picture to contrast an evening during the week with an evening on the weekend (time as a boundary).

**BIBLIOGRAPHY**

Barker, R., and others: Habitats, environments, and human behavior, San Francisco, 1978, Jossey-Bass, Inc., Publishers.

Berrien, F. K.: General and social systems, New Brunswick, N.J., 1968, Rutgers University Press.

Bowen, M.: Principles and techniques of multiple family therapy. In Bradt, J. O., and Moynihan, C. J., editors: Systems therapy, Washington, D.C., 1971, Bradt & Moynihan.

Drapier, A., and Whitker, C.: The family crucible, New York, 1978, Harper & Row, Publishers.

Laing, R. D.: The politics of the family, New York, 1972, Vintage Books, Inc.

Papajohn, J., and Spiegel, J.: Transactions in family, San Francisco, 1975, Jossey-Bass, Inc., Publishers.

Speck, R., and Attneave, C.: Family Networks, New York, 1973, Pantheon Books.

Chapter 3

# FAMILY HISTORY

In order to understand how family operates effectively or ineffectively as a system, it is necessary to take a closer look at some of the internal characteristics of the family system: history, bonding, space and territoriality, and language. These attributes not only characterize but also mold and, in turn, are molded by the contemporary family system. Family history plays a part in shaping the social organization and psychological environment of the family system.

One of the most powerful shapers of contemporary family systems is the heritage acquired from previous generations: character traits, emotional disposition, nuclear family constellation, sibling order, and goals and ambitions. Not only do people inherit money, property, and eye color from their ancestors; they acquire social and psychological heritages as well.

Drazin, in his recent guidebook on searching out family history, envisions the family as an hourglass, with the contemporary family as the stem through which lineage flows from past generations top of the hourglass) to future generations (bottom of the hourglass). Lineage flows in some obvious ways: through physical characteristics, property, and money. Some less obvious ways are unfinished tasks, naming, and centrality of place and purpose. These less obvious ways in which family is shaped by its heritage will be the subject of this chapter.

## UNFINISHED TASKS

Each generation passes on to the next unfinished tasks: goals not reached, jobs not completed, ambitions not attained. For some, completion of such tasks is a conscious decision; for others, involvement with unfinished tasks is less conscious.

The following clinical examples demonstrate the process of unfinished tasks. Harold was ten when his father lost all the family money through a poor investment. Harold's lifelong ambition became that of regaining the money that his father lost. He devoted his life to becoming a millionaire.

May came from a family with little formal education. When she married, she vowed that her children would never be without the advantages that education could bring. She became the major force behind her husband's business success and her children's involvement in dance, music, and college.

George's father was a janitor in the local high school, which George and his brothers attended. During his high-school years, George determined to join the Navy and escape the drudgery of menial labor. In later life, George became head of a business firm that contracted out services to local schools; the services provided were janitorial services.

Other examples include the woman who became a buyer in a store where her mother had been a clerk, the man who bought a car dealership where his father had been a salesman, and the man who became manager of a municipal parking lot where he had been a parking attendant as a boy. Bigger houses, better jobs, and more expensive cars are often measures of success that families use to compare their ability with that of previous generations. Festinger, among others, has demonstrated that people frequently compare themselves with others, particularly with those closest to them. Comparison with others gives us references by which we measure our own success and failure.

Such comparison attempts are not always positive: the pressure to outdo a previous generation may result in marriage failure, physical illness, emotional exhaustion, or behavioral disorder. Harold, mentioned above, died trying to make a million dollars; he left a wife and three small children. The most important drive in his life was to make the million that his father lost, even if it killed him, which it did. (Harold died testing a machine, the patent of which he had hoped to acquire and thus make his million.)

The compelling nature of the unfinished task can be partially explained by what social psychologists refer to as the "Zeigarnik effect." In a research study conducted many years ago and since documented on several occasions by others, Zeigarnik demonstrated that assigned tasks which are interrupted are more readily recalled than those tasks that subjects are able to complete. That is, not allowing the experimental subject to finish a job made that job more easily remembered weeks later than a job that the subject was allowed to finish.

In Lewinian terms, unfinished tasks create tension within the individual: in this sense, within the system. This tension acts on those people in which it has been created and seeks its release through task completion. The tension remains until the job is complete. When the goal is reached or the task complete, the tension created by the previous lack of completion dissipates considerably. The dissipation of tension following task completion is often referred to as "letdown" or "postevent depression."

The Zeignarnik effect helps to explain the drive behind unfinished tasks and the letdown that accompanies job completion. The tension created by getting ready for the task dissipates once the task is completed or the goal reached. Individual family members often report a feeling of relief when a success is obtained. Following the achievement, sadness, depression, or boredom often occurs. The finished task no longer has the pulling power, is no longer a challenge. Without such challenges, family members may seek new goals, new unfinished tasks. What compels a person to complete a partially finished task? Part of the answer may be in the human tendency to close gaps, to bridge great distances, to create perfection out of imperfection, to make whole that which is fragmented. Just as the human mind creates phantom pain for the lost limb, the unfinished task creates psychological pain in the family system.

Psychological experiments reveal people's tendency to perceive objects in "wholes," even when the perceptual object is presented in parts. Fragments of a line are often perceived as an unbroken line; parts of a circle are perceived by many to be a completed circle; words are often perceived correctly even when one or more letters are missing. It is not unlikely that this need or ability to see "wholes" where only parts exist and the enhanced ability to recall incomplete tasks are related to the pressing drive within some families to complete that which was left incomplete by generations before them.

Precisely how the tension created by unfinished tasks weaves its way into the present and future of families is unknown. Word of mouth, actual involvement, reading the family scrapbook and looking at family photograph albums, or being shaped by similar events and circumstances may all be avenues whereby the influence of unfinished tasks is passed from generation to generation.

Alex Haley's *Roots* has made us become quickly aware of the connectedness of the past with the present; how revenge and search for freedom are passed from generation to generation; how religious belief and family loyalty are passed from member to member; and how superstition and verbal symbols are used to transmit family and cultural history. Family and cultural history live on not only through unfinished tasks but also through "special" people. Such special people are often designated by the family through the process of naming.

## NAMING

Identity, power, influence, and expectation are passed on by previous generations through naming. The power and influence that accompany a name are associated with the real and symbolic meaning that tradition, history, culture, and family have ascribed to any particular name. Symbolic meaning may be culturally ascribed, as in *Roots* in the case of

Kunta's daughter Kizzy (meaning "to stay put"); historically ascribed, as in the regal names of Henry, Charles, and Elizabeth; or socially ascribed, as in names associated with movie stars, presidents, or other famous people. Similarly, contemporary families have names that are passed from generation to generation in the hope of carrying on the family tradition.

The process of naming is an extremely important vehicle for the transmission of family legacy: those who carry the name are often assigned the responsibility of fulfilling the family destiny. Naming symbolizes an offspring's relationship to a larger network of people, to whom the child belongs, from whom the child receives support, and toward whom the growing individual is expected to feel a sense of responsibility and loyalty. Naming creates a sense of identity, carries a certain amount of influence (good or bad), and is imbued with a certain set of expectations.

The expectations may be for performance, intellectual development, artistic achievement, or personal virtue and greatness. Names that carry the greatest expectations are those given in hopes of carrying on tradition: names of famous people, influential relatives or noted scientists. George Washington Carver was named for a great president; he became a great scientist. Children are often given family names with the hope of recreating or maintaining bonds with a deceased or distant relative: for example, a grandparent, brother, or cousin. It is often hoped that the child will in some way resemble or become like that missing person. Naming a child after a famous person or dead relative places on the child the burden of carrying out an unfinished task, of completing a broken circle, of restoring a lost relationship.

Names carry image as well as expectation. One's image of a Daisy Bell, for example, differs from that of a Barbara, as does one's image of a Hortense from that of a Jonathan. Similarly, one expects different behavior from a Chuckie than from a Charles, from a Mickie than from a Michael, from a Lulu than from a Louise. Chances are those individuals will see themselves differently as well.

Naming supplies a special identity and a sense of belonging to people who share the same name. Whereas such connectedness creates familiarity and security, it may limit an individual's ability to develop a new and personal identity. Individuation, or the development of a personal identity that fits simultaneously with group identity and family network, is a lifelong process; naming can either aid that process or make it more difficult.

Nicknaming has the effect of creating a special identity: Shorty, Fatso, Pinhead, Sissy, Boo-boo, String Bean, Pee-wee. Such names grow out of a special set of feelings but may develop into a special set of problems as the child grows older. Naming creates what psychologists refer to as "self-fulfilling prophecies": that is, the person becomes what he or she is set up to be regardless of the qualities that the person might actually have. Calling a child "dumb" may create a dumb child; telling a boy he is a coward may create a fearful person; expecting a child to get hurt may create an accident-prone individual.

An experiment was conducted in which teachers were given bogus reports about students. The teachers were told certain students were less bright than others. In the final teacher rating, the students with bogus reports were judged to be less bright, and they actually performed below their potential. The performance was irrespective of any real talent that the student might have had. The *expectation* of lower performance is believed to have created the final outcome.

Naming may create an identity and shape an individual in ways that may or may not suit the personality characteristics and motivations of the individual to whom the assignment is made. As studies have shown, expectations are not based solely on actual qualities and performance of the one perceived but on the image that outsiders give to that person, thus setting up a self-fulfilling prophecy in which the individual is shaped in expected directions.

The process of naming is similar to the process of labeling, in which patients become the disease category that best describes their condition at any given time: the "gallbladder" in room 229, the "depressive" in room 116, the "problem" patient in room 667. One characteristic becomes the total identity of the person or family: troublemaker, stubborn, lazy, bright, exciting, hyperactive, crazy, deceptive, manipulative, and so forth. The one characteristic overshadows other qualities and characteristics of the individual or family. "His father was an ex-convict." "His mother wasn't married when he was born." "Her sister is a thief." "That family is shifty": the label becomes the primary identity of the family for others. Unfortunately, labeling, like naming, has the ability to foster and perpetuate the image created by the label.

The ability of one powerful characteristic to overshadow other qualities that might be reasonably attributed to an individual or group has been demonstrated by Asch and his followers. By placing the word *hot* or *cold* in the middle of a set of adjectives, Asch was able to manipulate the overall impression formed. The only variable was the one word, *hot* or *cold;* all other adjectives in the descriptions remained the same. The overall judgment differed when the central, or core, word was changed.

Naming is a labeling process that provides a person, as in the case of a first name, or a family, as in the case of a last name, with a core identity around which other aspects of development are shaped. This is particularly true where the name, or label, has powerfully positive (for example, Einstein) or powerfully negative meaning (for example, Booth) associated with it. The process has positive outcomes: it provides identity, security, familiarity, and embeddedness. It also has negative outcomes: the constraint of the individual's freedom and the creation of a powerful set of expectations that may or may not be in line with abilities and desires of the family or individual involved.

The identity and sense of belonging that a name provides undoubtedly form a powerful psychosocial component of family life that shares with centrality of place and purpose the ability to shape the future in accordance with past expectations and experiences.

## CENTRALITY OF PLACE AND PURPOSE

Like naming, centrality of place and purpose provides identity, security, and connectedness. "Centrality of place" refers to physical and geographical location of families, particularly of families who live in the same area for several generations. There is a "place" from which people originate and to which people can return if need be. "Centrality of purpose" refers to the "reason for being" that each family gives itself: to raise children, to be physicians, to farm, to sing, to write, to be good people. Each family has a theme around which the family rallies, in a sense of purpose for being.

Centrality of location gives a family a sense of belonging in time and space, influences to some extent members' relationships with each other and those around them, and helps to shape the family purpose.

Jane Howard, journalist and author of *Families,* refers to location as being psychological as well as physical. A person without a physical sense of place must create a psychological sense of place, that is, a sense of belonging, of rootedness. Families without a physical sense of origin or rootedness often find their sense of place with one another. Many families feel a centrality of place and purpose when the family system is together in one unit. When the family system grows and members break away, the sense of place is often lost and the family feels at loose ends in terms of its purpose or group identity.

A sense of place, or centeredness, can be found within a person as well as a place. Many families have a person—mother, grandfather, sister, or aunt—who serves the function of "keeping the family close." Either through letters, telephone calls, visits, or verbal reminders, the designated person serves as the information funnel through which family members keep in contact with one another. Much of what goes on in a family is subject to this person's awareness and approval. Other people serve vital "target positions" in relationship to a family's place and purpose.

For example, many families have within their systems a person who serves the vital function of family "historian." The family historian is privy to more information than any other one family member. The family often feels a sense of place with such an individual. Historians have a sense of family secrets, family origins, and often family destiny. They are, in Drazin's terms, the "stem" through which much family legacy is passed.

Most families have such a person—or persons—who keeps track of births, deaths, weddings, love affairs, lost children, and shattered dreams. Major changes within the family are noted and recorded in the pages of family history by historians, without whom the family sense of location and place in time is often lost (as may occur at the death of the historian).

The importance of feeling a "belongingness" in place and time cannot be underestimated, as evidenced by the following example.

The Davis family lived in the same house for more than 30 years and in the same town for three generations. The house was an old one, hard to heat and hard to cool. The yard was big, rambling, and difficult for the Davises to maintain as they grew older. The Davises decided to sell their old home and buy a newer one in a better neighborhood in a nearby town. Not long after the move, the trouble began: arguments, irritability, and a sense of "floating around." What the Davises gained in terms of efficiency, they lost in terms of familiarity, identity, and a sense of rootedness. The family grieved over the loss of the old house, much as a parent would grieve over a lost child, or as a child would grieve for an absent parent. They yearned not only for the old house and yard, but for the old neighbors as well. They were "lost" without the feeling of rootedness that they had worked long and hard to establish. To give up location can be to give up part of self.

Another example is a young woman who related her experience in moving from her first home, which she had lived in during the initial years of marriage, to a newer and bigger home in the family's more affluent years: Feelings of grief and resentment developed because the "best years" of her life had been spent in the first house. She refused in her "heart and mind" to ever leave that house. Her loyalty to her first home is not unusual; it is an experience frequently reported by members of mobile families. Many people can describe in vivid detail their childhood home, their first room, and their first yard. They report the loss of such rootedness with a feeling of sadness.

Centrality of purpose, like centrality of location, is passed from generation to generation. Each family has a theme, or themes, around which the family is organized: for example, social mobility, educational achievement, personal success, business ambition, or artistic development. These themes are passed from generation to generation, much as the unfinished task is passed. These themes in some ways resemble Berne's scripts, which he maintains an individual is given at birth and around which individual destiny is shaped. Similarly, each generation in a family receives a theme, or a script, that it is responsible for fulfilling and passing on to the next generation.

Scripts or themes become part of the legacy that each generation gives to the next. However, not all subunits within the family system are capable of carrying out or willing to carry out the family theme. The person may decide to write his or her own script or to organize his or her own theme. The possible outcomes of this situation are: (1) conflict with the larger family system, (2) compromise with the larger family system, or (3) withdrawal from the family system. In order to remain within the system, the subunit (individual or couple) may elect someone to get sick in order to justify not carrying out the family theme. The basis of the "sickness" will be discussed in Section two.

Common themes in families are to have and raise children, to be successful, to make something of themselves, and to acquire wealth. If a subunit decides that having children or being successful is not his or her theme, open conflict with the larger family system may result. Subtle messages are sent to the person or couple to indicate the family's disapproval. If compromise is not reached, for example, not accepting the couple without children as a viable family unit, then the subunit may choose to "get sick," as evidenced by marital discord, or to withdraw from the system. Many choose to withdraw.

Another family theme might be to "educate the children." This is basically a good theme except in the case where an individual decides that college is a theme without appeal. Again, unless compromise is attempted, for example, working at a job that one enjoys is as important as a college degree, conflict ensues. Conflict alone will not lead to family disorder. Inability to support difference or resolve conflict, however, will contribute to difficulty in other areas of the family system.

Like naming, centrality of purpose provides family a sense of directionality. "Directionality" refers to a movement in a defined direction and carries with it the pressure to move in that direction. Whether that directionality involves farming, raising children, perpetuating the family, having a son or daughter become president, being the first family in space, or simply being the best of whatever you are, it is a theme around which the family is organized and shaped. Families without a legacy of direction and place are often families without a sense of contemporary purpose. Their direction in life may be to discover what that purpose may be for themselves and for subsequent generations.

## SUMMARY

Family systems, like other systems, begin somewhere and if the system is to survive, go somewhere. The direction or organization of any system is related to the design and implementation of the systems that preceded it.

Part of any design involves tasks that do not get completed and the selection of special people to be in charge of and carry on various aspects of development. Design supposes a particular location and provides direction and purpose for the system.

The family system is shaped by the design of previous family systems with regard to unfinished tasks, naming, and centrality of place and purpose. In the contemporary family unit, the effects of the past are brought to bear on the kind of relationships that the family experiences (bonding), the means whereby interactions are carried out (message system), and the ways in which the family uses its current space (territoriality). These characteristics of the contemporary family system will be the focus of discussion in the following chapters.

### STUDY QUESTIONS

1. Discuss Lewinian tension, the Zeigarnik effect, and their relationship to unfinished tasks.
2. In what ways can the process of naming be compared and contrasted with labeling, self-fulfilling prophecy, and Asch's theory of core concepts?
3. What is centrality of place? How does it affect family connectedness?
4. Discuss ways in which family history provides directionality, identity, and otherwise serves as a link with future family units.

### EXERCISES

The following exercises are provided to help students identify their families of origin.

1. Where did your family begin? Who is credited with being the initiator of the family?
2. Is the family basically traced through matriarchal or patriarchal lines or a combination of the two? *Note:* It is typical for a family to "know" more about and be more "connected" to one side of the family than to the other.
3. What family constellations seem to predominate? For example, some families are typified by two parents and three children and some by two parents and four children. These constellations have a tendency to be repeated in families.
4. What sibling orders are repeated? For example, eldest son marries youngest daughter of a three-sibling family; only child marries only child.
5. What names are common in your family? What characteristics do you notice among people who share the same name? In what ways do people with the same name differ? What was the purpose of naming in your family?
6. What unfinished tasks can you find in your family history? In whom and where did you find the tour guide to help you unfold the pages of your family history?
7. Where is your family's sense of place, or location?

*Note:* A technique for unraveling some of the above information is to write each family member's name on an index card. Lay all the cards out on the floor. Select three cards at random and ask two basic questions: (1) In what ways are these three people alike? (2) In what ways are these people different? The information can be recorded and then categorized according to the series of questions that you may want to ask about your particular family. Be sure to include all family names, beginning with parents and siblings of contemporary family and working back through as many generations as possible. Later the cards may be separated into groups: similar occupations, those who broke away, those who never married, those who moved around most often, those with similar constellations, those with similar sibling orders, those with common names, those with incomplete tasks, or whatever categories emerge from discussions with other family members. Be patient; this process may be very time-consuming.

**BIBLIOGRAPHY**

Asch, S.E.: Forming impressions of personality, J. Abnorm. Soc. Psychol.**41:**258, 1946.

Berne, E.: What do you say after you say hello, New York, 1974, Bantam Books.

Drazin, Y.: The family historian's handbook, New York, 1978, Jove Publications.

Festinger, L.: A theory of social comparison processes, Hum. Relations **7:**117, 1954.

Festinger, L., and Thibaut, J.: Interpersonal communication in small groups, J. Abnorm. Soc. Psychol. **46:**92, 1951.

Haley, A.: Roots, New York, 1976, Dell Publishing.

Howard, J.: Families, New York, 1978, Simon & Schuster, Inc.

Lewin, K.: Field theory in social science, New York, 1951, Harper & Row, Publishers.

Rosenthal, R.: Experimenter effects in behavioral research, New York, 1966, Appleton-Century-Crofts.

Schaeter, S., and Singer, J.: Cognitive, social, and physiological determinants of emotional state, Psychol. Rev. **69:**379, 1962.

Schaeter, S., and Wheeler, L.: Epinephrine, chlorpromazine, and amusement, J. Abnorm. Soc. Psychol. **65:**121, 1962.

Zeigarnik, F.: Uber das behalten von erledigten und unerledigten handlungen, Psychol. Forsch. **9:**1, 1927.

## Chapter 4

# CONNECTEDNESS

## bonding within the family

Family bonding can be discussed in terms of the kinds of relationships that characterize any one family, particularly the emotional relationships that are found in the contemporary family system. The contemporary family unit, "the stem through which family legacy flows," will reflect the nature of family bonding in previous generations. Parents who are close to their children will probably be close to their grandchildren; parents who are close to their children will in all probability have children who are close to their children, whereas parents who are distant from their children may have children who are distant from their own children. Unless someone actively breaks the patterns of bonding—close, warm, and supportive or cold, distant, and competitive—the kinds of relationships established by previous generations with their offspring will tend to be repeated in future generations.

The nature of bonding in the family system sets the stage for the kinds, quality, and quantity of relationships that family members will establish with others inside and outside the family system. Where bonding in families is strong and positive, family members will grow up believing that people can be trusted and relationships are worthwhile. Where family relationships are characterized by coldness, suspicion, or distance, family members will grow up cautious of other people and tentative about commitments to others, particularly where the nature of the relationship involves intense emotions. Security in family relationships leads to self-confidence; instability leads to uncertainty and lack of self-confidence.

Bonding between people is the basic fabric out of which the family cloth is woven. If the relationship is solid, communication and interaction will reflect that solidarity. If the relationships are negative, communication and interaction will be troubled and confusing. Good solid relationships, based on emotional honesty and positive regard, serve as attractant forces that bind the family system together. Weak, cold, or distant relationships or relationships based on emotional dishonesty and disregard for others serve as repellent forces that weaken the connective tissue of the family system.

## DEFINITION

Bonding is the psychological glue that unites the family system. Bonding involves depth of emotion and breadth of attachment within the family system. The psychological attachment that unites family has strength, direction, and sentiment.

The strength of a relationship refers to the degree of attachment in subunits (dyads or triads) within the family system. This degree of attachment is usually qualified simply as weak or strong. The direction of a relationship defines who is involved in the relationship. The sentiment (positive or negative) refers to the feeling that characterizes the involvement. For example, the following illustrates how the bonding relationship in a three-person family unit might be diagramed:

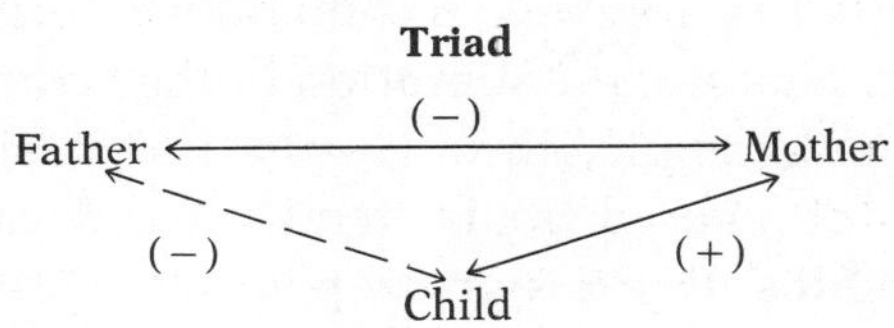


*Sentiment:* Positive (+) or negative (−)
*Direction:* Toward (→) or away (←)
*Strength:* Weak (− − − − − − − −) or strong (————)
*Dyad:* Two people
*Triad:* Three people

In this example, there is a strong (strength), positive (sentiment) bond between mother and child (direction). There is an equally strong, but negative, bond between mother and father. There is a weak, negative bond between father and child. Strength is indicated by solid or dotted lines, direction by arrows, and sentiment by either a plus or a minus sign. When the direction (between father and child) and sentiment (positive or negative) are the same, a single line and a single valence (plus or minus sign) can be used, as shown in the above example. However, if the direction and valence between two people or within a triad do not correspond, each person is represented by a line and a valence, as shown in the following example:

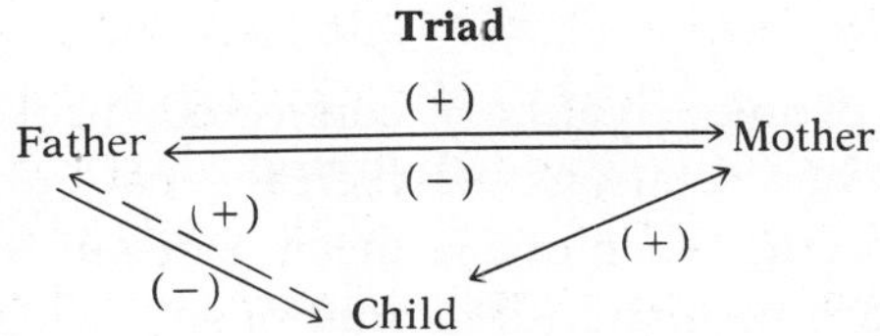

## CHARACTERISTICS OF BONDING

Bonding relationships are characterized by (1) intensity of emotional involvement, (2) strength of emotional commitment, and (3) degree of internal consistency, or harmony.

### Internal consistency

According to Heider, the nature of relationships (bonding) is to tend toward balance or consistency. Jim likes Alan; Alan likes Mark. It is expected then that Jim will also like Mark. The relationship among the three boys is said to be consistent or balanced. Bob does not like Rex; Rex does not like Bob. The relationship between the boys is consistent; mutual dislike is a balanced situation. Since all three in the first example feel positive toward one another and both boys in the second example feel negative, there is no pressure to change.

Heider defines a balanced state as one in which the components (entities, elements, or people) fit together harmoniously and in which there is no pressure to change. His basic assumption is that components or people that are connected, for example, through proximity, similarity, common fate, past experience, or shared goals, tend toward consistency, or balance, in their relationships. Entities or people that (1) live together, (2) are somehow similar or share similar interest, (3) are involved in a mutual endeavor, or (4) are subject to the same consequences are perceived as belonging together and thus are connected. In Heider's terms, such people form a unit and have a unit relationship and will therefore tend toward balance in that relationship. The family readily fits the definition of a unit; family members are perceived as belonging together.

People have sentiment relations along with unit relationships; that is, people are connected by feelings and opinions. Sentiment relations, according to Heider, involve evaluative judgments and are either negative (rejecting, disliking, and condemning) or positive (liking, admiring, and approving). In order for a sentiment relation to be a significant factor, there must first be a unit relationship. If there is no unit relationship, or sense of connectedness, sentiment is generally incidental or unimportant. Heider maintains that unit relationships and sentiment relations tend toward balance. People who belong together and form a unit will tend to like each other; people who do not form a unit may feel indifferent to one another. Lack of balance causes tension within the system and creates pressure toward change.

In general, if two people (dyad) are connected through a unit relationship, balance exists when relations between the two are all positive or all negative. Imbalance occurs when one relation is negative and the other positive. Alan and Jack are brothers (unit relationship); Alan likes Jack (positive), but Jack does not approve of Alan (negative). There will be disharmony in their relationship and some pressure to alter the relationship. Alan and Jack might, for example, grow distant (weaken the unit relationship); Alan might change his ways and gain Jack's approval; Alan might change his opinion of Jack (alter positive to negative). Any of these alternatives would balance the relations. Where the unit relationship is weakened, the sentiment becomes less important. If Alan gains Jack's approval, positive feelings are mutual; if Alan alters his impression of Jack, negative evaluations are mutual.

Triads (relations between three people) are balanced when all three relationships are positive or when two relationships are negative and one is positive. When one relationship is negative and the other two are positive, imbalance occurs. Mark and Betty are married (unit relationship) and have a baby (unit relationship). Mark loves Betty (positive); Betty loves the new baby (positive); however, Mark discovers that he does not like babies (negative). Disharmony (two positive relations, one negative relation) in the family will cause tension and pressure the family members to strive for change and, hence, balance. Balance will occur if (1) Mark and Betty grow distant (sever the unit relationship); (2) Mark develops a dislike for Betty (negative sentiment); or (3) Mark develops a positive bond with the new baby (positive sentiment). Hopefully, Mark will develop a new interest in and a positive bond with the child.

In order to examine bonding relations within family systems, it is helpful to isolate a dyad or triad unit relationship (for example, father-daughter, mother-father, mother-daughter or father-daughter-mother, mother-son-father, mother-son-daughter, father-son-daughter, or grandfather-son-grandson) and then to establish the sentiment relation that typifies that unit. In addition to balance, one might want to examine strength or direction of the relationship.

The previous example consists of a three-member, contemporary family unit: Mark, Betty, and baby. The example can be expanded to include either or both sets of grandparents. This bonding network might appear as follows:

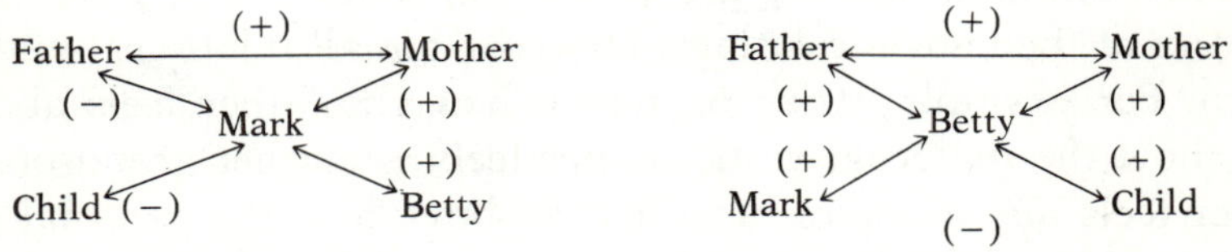


**Mark's perception** **Betty's perception**

In observing bonding within families, particularly as one begins to make judgments about the balance, or harmony, of such bonding, one must exercise caution. One must know, for example, in whose perception the bonding relationship is being evaluated. In the example, Mark does not perceive a balanced relationship between his father, mother, and himself and describes a negative bond between his father and himself. Mark is unclear about how he feels about his father. His perception will influence the perception he develops about his present family and may contribute to the negative feelings that he has for his own child. However, it is possible that Mark has misperceived the father's feelings. Mark's father's evaluation might serve to clear up misconceptions and help Mark to develop a more positive relationship with his own child.

The following example illustrates the importance and complexities of examining bonding that involves several generations. Relationships can be examined for strength, direction, and sentiment as well as consistency. The example is from a clinician's view of a two-parent, three-child, primary family that includes the widowed mothers (*Y*—mother, *X*—mother) of the spouses (Father—*y*, Mother—*x*).

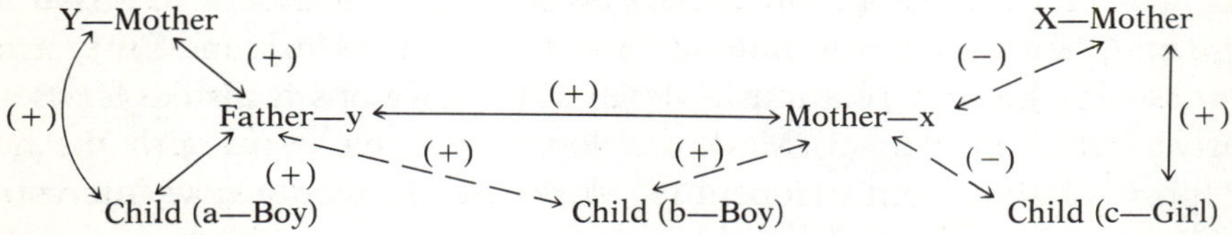


*Y*—Mother has a strong, positive, relationship with her son (Father—*Y*) and grandson (*a*—boy). The father has a strong positive relationship with his mother, his wife, and one son (*a*—boy); a weak positive relationship with his other son (*b*—boy). *X*—Mother has a weak negative relationship with her daughter (Mother—*x*) and a strong relationship with her granddaughter (*c*—girl). Mother—*x* has a weak negative relationship with her daughter (*c*—girl), a weak positive relationship with her son (*b*—boy), and a weak negative relationship with her own mother (*X*—mother).

In Heider's terms, all triad units are balanced (all positive or two negative and one positive), with the exception of the sibling relationships (two positive, one negative). Predictably, there will be disharmony in the sibling relations. Shifts in bonding are unlikely to occur easily, given the balanced nature of the known relations. *However,* not all relations (sentiment) are known. For example, it is not known how the father feels about his daughter; how the maternal grandmother feels about her grandsons; how the mother feels about one of her sons (*a*—boy), how the paternal grandmother feels about the other son (*b*—boy); and how the paternal grandmother feels about her granddaughter. Each of the unknown dyads or triads can be isolated and studied, with the resultant information providing a wider range of possible alternatives for predicting and facilitating shifts in bonding. One can readily see that until one knows all relations, those that are known serve as a base on which to build as additional information is available. As the family becomes more involved in the unlayering process, their perceptions will also help clarify the nature of bonding and balance within the family system.

When relationships between dyads, among triads, and within the family system are observed and evaluated for consistency from a clinician's standpoint, it is important to remember that such evaluations may or may not agree with participants' evaluations of their own experiences. Balance theory is a conceptual tool that, along with other tools and additional clinical information, aids in understanding and working with family systems. It is not a tool to be used alone, without feedback from the family involved.

Basically, balance theory describes relationships that belong together and provides a way of looking at disharmony, or the press for change, in those relationships. Other theorists, such as Newcomb (1963), Osgood and Tannenbaum (1955), and Festinger (1957), have further elaborated the idea that consistency, or harmony, is a desirable and pleasant psychological state, that lack of consistency results in tension within the system and works to press family members in that system to make changes in the relationships. Although the actual use of each model can be complex, knowledge about family relationship is enhanced by the application of one or more models. Whereas the nature of relationships is to tend toward balance, it is the emotional involvement and commitment that underlie those relationships that makes consistency important, possible, or difficult to achieve.

## Emotional honesty and emotional dishonesty

The emotional tenor of relationships, like the tendency toward harmony or disharmony, tends to be repeated in families. Weak bonding generates weak bonding; negative sentiment usually generates negative sentiment. Strong parental ties generally lead to strong parent-child attachments in the next generation. Similarly, weak parent-child attachments often lead to weak parent-child attachments in later generations; inadequate parenting generally leads to inadequate parenting. Sibling rivalry or imbalance in sibling relationships usually reflects difficulties in the adult or parent relationships; that is, weak parent-spouse attachments, negative parent-grandparent bonding, or overattachment between one parent and one child.

Although there are many aspects of emotional attachments in family relationships that may be examined, one of the most influential factors in shaping involvement and consequent commitment is the degree of emotional honesty that is possible and practiced.

Emotional openness is, in Jourard's terms, the knowing of one's self through the process of disclosure to another individual. According to Jourard, one can only fully experience oneself to the extent that one is willing to reveal oneself to another. Knowing and being known are, according to Jourard, the most essential ingredients of mental health.

In order to fully experience ourselves and others, there must be emotional honesty: telling the "truth" as we experience it.

Emotional honesty entails experiencing the world through the senses (sight, sound, touch, feel, and smell) and reporting those experiences as accurately as possible. Reporting, describing, and being open to the reports of others constitute being emotionally honest. Emotional honesty gives permission to feel, to express, to speak, to disagree, to explore, and to experience a variety of human emotions. Emotional honesty involves risk taking and self-disclosure: bringing to the outside reports and descriptions of what is going on inside the person. Emotional honesty lays the groundwork for positive, strong bonding relationships within and outside of the family.

Conversely, emotional dishonesty means feeling one way and acting another. The behavior or verbal report does not accurately reflect the internal experience that the individual is having. Emotional dishonesty means telling others what they want to hear, describing for others what we think they want to see, and using our sensations to get others to do what we want them to do. Emotional dishonesty grows out of fear of disapproval, fear of rejection, and fear of failure; that is, fear of being unable to attain the love and recognition that are necessary for growth. Emotionally dishonest families may create individuals who learn to manipulate in order to get what they need in terms of personal recognition, acceptance, and approval.

Emotional honesty and emotional dishonesty are ways of relating to others that are experienced and learned in the family system. Essential to emotional honesty is an atmosphere in which honesty and openness are encouraged. Such an atmosphere is characterized by mutual respect and concern. Individual growth, as well as group conformity, is valued and encouraged. Self-worth is based not on what one is able to do but is a natural extension of one's being. Atmospheres in which interpersonal respect is based on one's importance as a person are characterized by what Fromm calls "unconditional love" and Rogers refers to as "unconditioned positive regard." Unconditional love is warmth and respect toward others based on their worth as persons, not on their abilities to fulfill certain expectations or perform certain tasks.

Unconditional respect and acceptance can be contrasted with conditional respect and acceptance; that is, love and recognition dependent on something that one does, says, or attains. Performance and ability—to do what one is told, to follow rules, to perform well in school or work—determine whether or not one gains approval and acceptance. If the rule is not followed or the goal is not attained, then love and regard are withheld. One must perform according to expectation in order to gain approval.

Conditional love lays the groundwork for emotional dishonesty and lack of emotional commitment. Individuals are encouraged to perform (rather than feel) for others in order to achieve personal recognition. Development and actualization of self are secondary to achievements, success, and gaining recognition. The catch in conditional love, however, is that one is not always sure of the conditions that must be fulfilled before the praise or recognition is forthcoming. Second-guessing another's expectations becomes a way of life in families in which the atmosphere is one of conditionality. Rather than being attuned to inner feelings and interactional needs, family members learn to heed cues from others in order to gain recognition and approval. One becomes emotionally dishonest, not only with others, but with oneself as well. Authentic needs and feelings become subordinate to social and manipulative skills aimed at getting attention. An individual will become reckless, abrasive, and negative if that is what is necessary to obtain attention and recognition: in Erikson's terms, a bad boy rather than no boy at all.

Families vary in their ability to provide an atmosphere of acceptance and emotional honesty. Much of what has characterized family life in previous generations will be found in current family situations. Parents who are distant and emotionally closed off from their children do not provide models of openness. Parents and significant others who use rewards and material incentives do not provide models of love and recognition based on self-worth. Two ideas that may underlie a family's attitudes about unconditional love and emotional openness are: (1) conditional regard is necessary to get people to do what is best for them; and (2) love comes in finite amounts that must be doled out cautiously lest the supply be exhausted. In both beliefs, it is the responsibility of the adult to offer the reward or provide the love; parents are providers and children are recipients. The first belief is reflected in the "carrot and donkey" syndrome and the latter belief in the "pitcher" syndrome; both are partially based on myth.

**Carrot and donkey syndrome.** In the carrot and donkey syndrome, the underlying belief is that it is necessary to offer small rewards, such as money, praise, or affection, to get people to perform in desired ways. However, when the person achieves the desired goal or fulfills the expectation, the significant other or parent moves the carrot just a little ahead. Reward or praise is never totally given, and expectations are subject to unannounced changes. Comments like "Keeping them reaching," "Never quite enough," "Just short of the goal," and "Not quite perfect" describe the emotional tenor of such families. Although such comments are seldom actually used within families, members often use them to describe the atmosphere that dominated family life or one aspect of family interaction, for example, parent-child expectation.

The fear that apparently underlies the carrot and donkey syndrome is that, if people are praised too much or too easily, praise will be meaningless and fear of punishment or failure can no longer be used as a motivating factor. Such beliefs are based on principles of negative learning: that people learn in order to avoid punishment, as well as to receive reward. The result of practices based on these beliefs is that individuals (1) get tired of reaching for the unattainable and give up, (2) learn devious ways to obtain praise and recognition, (3) decide that praise and recognition are not worth having anyway, or (4) go somewhere else or to someone else for praise, acceptance, and recognition. Emotional ramifications are (1) anger, which grows out of the frustration of futile reaching; (2) manipulation, which develops from strong needs and the even stronger determination to obtain recognition and acceptance; and (3) depression, from the abandonment of desirable goals or of the family system that was unable to provide recognition. The inability of families to supply recognition, praise, respect, or personal regard for others is based not only in the belief in holding out a carrot to move the donkey but also in the belief behind the pitcher syndrome.

**Pitcher syndrome.** The pitcher syndrome is a product of the belief that love comes in finite amounts that must be doled out cautiously by designated persons who themselves must not take from the pitcher's contents. There is a sense that love must be shared equally among family members and a fear that it can possibly be exhausted. Rather than given preferential treatment to any one family member or risk running out of love, pitcher syndrome families withhold love all around. That is, rather than give any one member too much, all must go without. Emotional deprivation characterizes such families.

In the pitcher syndrome, one person is generally designated by the family system to be the "provider" of emotional needs. The designated person is usually the mother, eldest child, or grandparent. The emotional provider may be seen as the emotional pitcher, whose responsibility is to provide love needs (recognition, approval, acceptance) for all other family members. Family members may be seen as having emotional cups into which the pitcher pours love and affection. Not all cups are the same size: some individuals have greater needs than others; some seem to have insatiable needs; and all forget that the pitcher has needs. Within a short time, because the pitcher has no way to replenish its contents, the emotional reservoir runs dry. An empty pitcher cannot supply others, let alone fill the self.

An example is the 41-year-old housewife with three teenage children who has spent so much time caring for others that she has forgotten how to replenish her own emotional reserves and has neglected to teach her children how to replenish the supplies of others. She has been so busy supplying the emotional needs of her family that they fail to realize she also has needs. Because she sees the pitcher as entirely her responsibility, she has difficulty relinquishing it long enough to let family members learn how to fill each other's needs. She wonders why no one sees that she has needs; she wonders why her teenage son spends so much time sending flowers and writing poems to his girlfriend (who is teaching him to give); she wonders why her husband thinks she is so self-sufficient. She feels "drained" and "used"; she finds it easier to give than receive but wonders why her children and husband never give her emotional support or recognize that her supply is low.

The error in the pitcher syndrome, evident in the previous example, is the belief that love needs are the responsibility of one person. Where responsibility for emotional support and recognition is shared or passed around from time to time, each individual has the opportunity to learn to give as well as take, to restore the low emotional reserves of others.

Emotional reserves vary from time to time in families. Relaxation, pleasant times together, open discussions, and mutual endeavors tend to fill emotional cups. Emotional crises, physical illness, loss of a family member, or adding new members causes emotional reserves to dip a little. When support is valued and considered an important component of family living, each family system finds ways of its own to replenish emotional reserves and supply the family system with emotional support.

Where family systems assign the responsibility to one person, particularly the mother or parent figure, the significant adult may experience the empty pitcher syndrome: giving all to others who give little in return and having none left for the self. As the pitcher empties, family members will seek emotional support and social recognition in other families, with other individuals, or through other activities. The giving and receiving of emotional support must be learned. Emotional involvement based on unconditional regard and mutual respect will more often than not generate emotional honesty.

Being emotionally honest or dishonest is not always a conscious choice that one makes. Circumstances often create a need to be self-protective and only partially open with others. However, when one is unable to be open within the family system, one does not learn the ability to accurately assess emotional needs and honesty of others. Where emotional involvement is not possible in families, it is doubtful that the individual will ever see the value of emotional commitment to others outside the family.

The family provides the emotional backdrop against which individuals assess relationships with people outside the family. If emotional involvement and emotional honesty have not been practiced in the family, it may never occur to family members that such relationships are possible. Should such relationships become possible, the individual may lack the tools to shape the relationships into emotionally honest, psychologically balanced encounters founded on unconditional love and positive regard.

Family experiences that are consistent, honest, stable, and predictable contribute to feelings of self-confidence and self-worth. A family background of positive bonding, in which individuals are valued for their human worth, in which emotions are legitimate modes of experience and expression, and in which love is given out of concern and respect for others, provides family members with a better chance for growing into emotionally honest adults than a family background characterized by conditional love and tentative acceptance based on performance or ability to adhere to rules.

## SUMMARY

Bonding, the emotional connectedness between family members, has direction and intensity. In a positive sense, bonding provides identity, security, protection, and a sense of belonging. The emotional attachment that underlies bonding tends toward consistency. It may be conditional (based on performance) or unconditional (based on self-worth), emotionally honest or emotionally dishonest. In order for emotional honesty to be possible in a relationship, unconditional love is a basic requirement. The responsibility for meeting the emotional needs of family members must be taught and shared throughout the family system.

The nature of bonding in which one is involved as a child influences in part the ability of the grownup individual to love and be loved in return. Bonding has shaping ability: it shapes people within the family boundaries and the kinds of relationships that family members have outside the system and determines whether a person enters into another family system with a full pitcher or an empty cup.

**STUDY QUESTIONS**

1. Discuss Heider's balance theory and its usefulness in understanding human relationships.
2. Discuss the concepts of emotional honesty and emotional dishonesty. How do emotional honesty and emotional dishonesty affect family relationships and individual development?
3. What does unconditional love have to do with human behavior and family interactions?

**EXERCISES**

Exercises are provided to assist students in examining the bonding relationships in their own families. Much of our experience with patients and clients reflects the nature of experiences within our own families. That which is unresolved in family experience as well as that which is most valued in one's own family may be superimposed on other family systems in hopes of working out the problem or recreating a desirable state. Such superimposition is often unintentional and is less apt to occur when one has a good grasp on the dynamics of one's own family system.

1. Which of the adjectives in each set best describes the bonding in your family: close or distant; warm or cold; genuine or artificial; open or closed; conditional or unconditional?
2. In your family, to whom do you go for:
   a. Recognition
   b. Direction or guidance
   c. Sympathy
   d. Approval
   e. Love?
3. What similarities in bonding do you observe between your parents and their parents (or brothers and sisters)? What differences do you observe? *Note:* Give particular attention to the conditional or unconditional nature of the bonding and emotional honesty or emotional dishonesty.
4. What aspects of your family bonding will you try to avoid in the family you will create? What aspects will you attempt to retain?
5. In what ways is your family emotionally honest? In what ways is it emotionally dishonest?
6. Complete the following:
   a. When I was little I wished my father . . .
   b. When I was little I wished my mother . . .
   c. When I have my family I will . . .
   d. Love should be . . .
   e. Five years from now I want to . . .
   f. The one thing that I wanted but did not get from my parents was . . .
7. Diagram the bonding relationship within your immediate family (direction, strength, and sentiment). *Note:* Give particular attention to your involvement.

Father Mother

You

Sibling Sibling Sibling

Add additional family members as you learn about them.

8. To what extent do your family members share characteristics of unit relationships?

| | *Proximity (geographical location)* | *Similarity (physical, psychological)* | *Common fate (illness, occupation)* | *Past experience* | *Goals (college)* |
|---|---|---|---|---|---|
| Mother | | | | | |
| Father | | | | | |
| You | | | | | |
| Sibling | | | | | |
| Sibling | | | | | |
| Sibling | | | | | |
| Maternal grandmother | | | | | |
| Maternal grandfather | | | | | |
| Paternal grandmother | | | | | |
| Paternal grandfather | | | | | |

9. To what extent are positive sentiments (approval, liking, admiring) evident in your family relationships? To what extent are negative relationships evident in your family (dislike, disapproval, rejection)? Continue with as many family members as you can, following the example in the chart below.

| *Between* | *Positive sentiment (like, approve, admire)* | *Negative sentiment (dislike, reject, disapprove)* |
|---|---|---|
| Mother-father | | |
| Father-mother | | |
| Father-son | | |
| Son-father | | |
| Mother-daughter | | |
| Daughter-mother | | |
| Father-you | | |
| You-father | | |
| Mother-you | | |
| You-mother | | |
| Mother–maternal grandmother | | |
| Mother–maternal grandfather | | |
| Father–paternal grandmother | | |
| Father–paternal grandfather | | |

10. What events (divorce, death, accident, injury, handicap) have occurred in your family that have resulted in weakened unit relationships?

## BIBLIOGRAPHY

Brooks, J., and Lewis, M.: Attachment behavior in thirteen-month old, opposite sex twins, Child Dev. **45**(1):243, 1974.

Brooks, J., and Lewis, M.: The effects of time on attachment as measured in a free-play situation, Child Dev. **45**(2):311, 1974.

Cohen, L., and Campos, J.: Father, mother, stranger as elicitors of attachment behavior in infancy, Dev. Psychol. **10**(1):146, 1974.

Erikson, E.: Childhood and society, New York, 1963, W. W. Norton and Co., Inc.

Erikson, E.: Conflict, decision and dissonance, Stanford, Calif., 1964, Standford University Press.

Festinger, L. A.: A theory of cognitive dissonance, Stanford, Calif. 1957, Standford University Press.

Frankl, V.: Man's search for meaning, New York, 1969, Washington Square Press.

Fromm, E.: The art of loving, New York, 1963, Bantam Books.

Harper, L.: The scope of offspring effects;

from caregiver to culture, Psychol. Bull. **82**(5):784, 1975.

Heider, F.: The psychology of interpersonal relations, New York, 1958, John Wiley and Sons, Inc.

Jourard, S.: The transparent self, New York, 1964, Van Nostrand.

Newcomb, T. M.: Stabilities underlying changes in inter-personal attraction, J. Abnorm. Soc. Psychol. **66**:376, 1963.

Osgood, C. E., and Tannenbaum, P. H.: The principle of congruity in the prediction of attitude change, Psychol. Rev **62**:42, 1955.

Rinkoff, R.: The effects of distance of mother and a stranger on attachment and stranger exploration behavior in ten month old infants, Dissertation Abstracts International, Ann Arbor, Mich., 1974, Univ. M-Film #75-10948.

## Chapter 5

# TERRITORIALITY

## physical and psychological space within the family

The nature of interaction within the family system is integrally related to the family's involvement and exchange with the space around it. Just as bonding describes emotional relationships within the family system, territoriality describes the social relationship between the family system and its environment.

### DEFINITIONS

Generally, "territoriality" refers to an organism's characteristic behavior in a setting in which the organism has membership and status and on which the organism lays claim. Laying claim or having ownership is, according to Bakker and Bakker-Rabdau, a major factor in determining whether or not the space one occupies is also one's territory. "Territory" refers to space over which one exerts ownership; "territoriality" refers to the behavior one exhibits within that space.

Space within the boundaries of a given territory, according to Hall (1969), provides protection and identity, assures physical survival, facilitates communication by closeness, and offers a source of group membership that is not possible outside the setting's boundaries. Territoriality has both physical and psychological dimensions: physical protection and psychological identity, physical security and psychological belonging, and physical survival (food, warmth, clothes) and psychological prosperity (love, recognition, reward).

A family's territory is generally expressed in its home, yard, cars, material possessions, and even family members. A family system exerts ownership over its territory, people as well as objects. The nature of ownership can vary: from a vague sense of belonging to a particular clan to outright possessiveness on the part of the family. The intensity or vagueness of family ownership can be understood more fully if one is able to determine where the majority of family interaction takes place. As will be seen, family interaction that takes place in intimate or personal spaces will tend to be more intense than family interaction that takes place in social or public places.

## CHARACTERISTICS OF TERRITORY

According to Hall, there are four dimensions to the space that surrounds an individual: intimate, personal, social, and public. The area defined by each of these dimensions is referred to by Hall as a "zone." A person may be envisioned as being at the middle of four concentric circles that delimit zones, with the intimate zone being closest to the person and the public zone being the most distant. According to Hall, each zone can be measured in terms of physical distance: intimate, 6 to 18 inches from the individual: personal, 18 inches to 4 feet; social, 4 to 12 feet; and public, 12 to 25 feet and beyond. In a sense, the individual projects a sense of self outward through the zones, with control over each zone dissipating as the distance grows. Thus, personal influence over others should become less as the distance between the persons involved grows greater. However, the telephone, television, and mass media make it possible to contract large spaces into spaces of manageable size, thus making it possible to maintain influence across large distances and social and public spaces.

Each zone is characterized by actions and feelings that are particular to that space. Intimate zones are characterized by intimate behavior: touching, smelling, feeling, and physically responding to sensation and stimulation. Personal zones are characterized by closeness, as in personal discussions between family members. Social zones are characterized by social distance: for example, in business transactions, casual greetings, impersonal interactions, and general discussions. Public zones are characterized by public transactions: political rallies, church meetings, classrooms, or general public meetings are examples. The unwritten expectation is that behaviors and transactions that belong within a certain space will take place in that space and not in others. One does not expect business transactions to be conducted in intimate spaces, nor does one expect to find intimate behavior occurring in the public zone. How people feel about each other and the nature of their relationships are decisive factors in determining the distance that occurs between members within the family system. In turn, the distance kept influences the relationship that can be established and the interactions that are possible.

Family interaction is highly personal and intense. Much of family behavior takes place in intimate and personal zones. Where family interaction is less intense, the relationship may have more of a social or public nature. The more intense the relationships, the more ownership the family system will exert over family members. Ownership in this sense implies identity and protection as well as expectations of commitment and loyalty on the part of the family members.

## CHARACTERISTICS OF FAMILY TERRITORIALITY

Territoriality in the family system may be characterized by interactions that reflect the zone within which any particular interaction takes place. That is, in families where relationships are close, interactions may take place in a face-to-face manner, within the confines of the family home; family territoriality and the behavior that characterizes it will be intimate and personal. In such a family, there will probably be a sense of closeness such as might be used to describe a clan. There will be mutual ownership, with the belief that family members "owe" something to the system and that the family system owes something to its members.

Conversely, where the majority of family interaction takes place in social or public spaces, there will be less territorial behavior, and use of space will be characterized by social or group behavior common to nonfamily systems. There will be less of a sense of ownership of family system as well as less commitment to family members as individuals. The sense of family kinship will be much less in family groups who do not exhibit or participate in intimate and personal interactions. In a sense, relationships established within the family system are partially determined by where those interactions take place.

### Design and use of space

Although most individuals take pride in the amount of influence they can exert over events and other people, there is little doubt that events and environments may be more powerful in shaping individual and family destiny than any one person or group of persons. On a very simple level, in a house without individual bedrooms there is very little opportunity for individual privacy. In houses where there is no social space, such as an entertainment or recreation room, there will be scant opportunity for social interaction. In a house where the largest space accommodates three to five people, there will be little opportunity for gatherings of the entire family if family size exceeds five. In many modern homes, with the advent of formal dining rooms and small, eat-in kitchens, there is little opportunity for the family gatherings that typified the large, spacious kitchens in older homes—kitchens in which the entire family gathered to discuss the day's activities and personal problems and to learn social expectations. Small rooms, thin walls, narrow hallways, and fenced yards are characteristic of contemporary houses. A sense of privacy, the opportunity for intimacy, and available space for personal, informal gatherings are often hard to come by in contemporary homes.

**Example.** The Anders family is a middle-class, two-parent, three-sibling family that lives in a four-bedroom home in a moderate-size city. When the last child reached school age, it was time to add on another bedroom. The Anders family altered the basement of their modern home from a family room (social space) into a bedroom (personal space) for their eldest child, who was about to graduate from high school. However, the bathroom for the lower level of the house (where the converted room was located) could be reached only by going through the boy's bedroom. When the family room had been a social space, walking through to get to a private space (bathroom) had created no problems. However, when the boy's room was used as a waiting room, access space, and hallway, his protest was loud and lusty. He began by leaving his clothes lying about, a sign of territorial possession. Humans, as well as animals, are known for their attempts to make their presence felt by littering. When family members began complaining that the clothes were a safety hazard and created an unpleasant sight, the boy began stealing toilet tissue from the bathroom. The severity of the problem came to light when the boy ran away from home, in a sense driven out by lack of privacy and lack of respect for his personal, private space.

The feeling of ownership that grows out of intimate and personal contact of family members with one another is often confused with license to intrude into the personal space of another. Under the guise of territorial rights, which parents mistakenly assume come with the territory of parenthood, adults snoop through children's mail, rearrange clothes in drawers, listen in on telephone conversations, and monitor conversations that occur anywhere in or near the family home. To a lesser degree, parents and adults do the same thing to one another, perhaps without realizing the dire consequences of uninvited intrusion into the territory, particularly the personal territory, of another.

Intrusion into the territory of others can be physical, as in the above example, or psychological and social. Perceived intrusion into one's psychological space often occurs with poorly defined territories where privacy is not possible, as well as in situations where family members lack the necessary skills to define and protect a personal territory. Lack of personal space in the home is often recognized, particularly for children, when the problem becomes a social one. Donald's story illustrates this.

**Example.** Donald was the youngest son and third youngest sibling of a seven-sibling, two-parent family of moderate to low economic means. The father was an auto mechanic, sporadically employed; the mother was a part-time clerk in a local supermarket. Donald came to my attention when he became a "management problem" in the local school system. At the time of our initial contact, Donald was a third-grader who was experiencing problems in the classroom, problems with his peer group, and problems at home. The nature of his "problem" was described to me variously as hostility, stubbornness, brain damage, emotional disturbance, acting out, and meanness. Donald appeared small, short for his age, slightly overweight, frightened, and anything but cooperative. With his family present, Donald sat in a corner of the room with his head down and his feet tucked under the chair. Encouraged to talk by both his parents, Donald remained silent and unresponsive. However, when Donald was separated from his parents, he became talkative and active. When he returned to the room where his parents were, the same behavior occurred: he was withdrawn, sullen, and unresponsive. This same behavior pattern was repeated whenever the parents were present. Similar patterns occurred when other members of the family were present, except with the youngest sibling, who resembled Donald somewhat.

During Donald's interaction with his younger sister, a pecking order was quickly observed, in which he was dominant. However, with all other family members and his peers, Donald was submissive. The submissiveness, however, quickly changed to active protest when Donald was pushed too far, either in the classroom or at home. Donald exhibited a need for territory of his own: personal space in which he could be dominant and assertive. The only territory that he had successfully dominated was his younger sister.

Donald's need—to me a very natural need—for expanded territory was accompanied by a lack of skills in what to do with the territory if it became available through school experience or peer group socialization. He therefore reacted with panic and self-protective maneuvers: hitting, spitting, and running away. I began by teaching Donald words to describe his environment and his need for greater control over that environment. Within a short time, Donald was able to describe his imaginary circle of personal space. It was larger than that of most other boys his age. As his social skills increased, however, his imaginary personal space became smaller. As his circle of peers grew, his time alone decreased. Because his daytime activity involved his gradual expansion into the social worlds of others, his sleep patterns changed. Initially, Donald slept in his bed, which was in the corner of a well-lighted room. During the night he moved around the bed but kept himself wrapped in a tight ball most of the time. As he became more adept at social skills, he slept more freely, was able to turn off the light, and moved his bed back to the center of the room. When Donald was able to return to regular classroom study, his mother removed him from therapy. As Donald gained his own sense of territory and expanded his skills in territorial assertiveness, he became a threat to his mother's rather fragile sense of territory, to her spatial and psychological dominance. As long as

Donald was submissive, he was her territory; however, when he became assertive, he became a threat to her sense of ownership and control. As so often happens in family therapy, when one member improves, another acts out the family problem. Although the family had refused therapy for themselves, they accepted it for Donald until he exceeded their expectations for autonomy. A similar pattern of behavior is now being manifested by the younger sister. Donald's future is uncertain.

It is difficult, if not impossible, to establish a sense of territoriality, that is, assertive ownership, without some tangible territory: room, house, or idea. Donald did not have a tangible territory, except for his younger sister; therefore, he lacked the opportunity to develop skills that are necessary to gain, protect, or defend one's own personal space. Without a space of his own, Donald developed a private sense of himself: combative, abusive, and uncooperative. His private sense of self became his territory, which he defended with a feeble, maladaptive pattern of responses.

According to Bakker and Bakker-Rabdau (1973), there are two essential components of territory: (1) it must be gained, and (2) it must be protected or defended. Skills must be developed in both realms: in expanding territory as well as in maintaining that which has been gained. Children who are raised in environments that tend to constrict their ability to expand the area of competence necessary to territorial management may grow up like Donald—wanting the territory but not knowing what to do with it when it is available. At the same time, children raised in environments that constrict movement but not skill building may produce children able to manage only small areas at a time. They have management skills, but the skills are limited to small, encompassed territory. Peter and Ann illustrate this.

**Example.** Peter and Ann were married for six years, with each year more problematic than the year before. One evening, in a "fit of rage," Peter hit Ann in the face; she packed up the children and left. Three weeks later they came for family therapy. Peter was the middle sibling of a two-parent, task-oriented family. Ann was the eldest sibling of a two-parent, emotionally close family. Peter was reared with the sense that "the task comes first." Ann was reared with the idea that "happiness is most important." Each set about gaining skills that would help them manage the territory in life that each considered most important: happiness in Ann's case and task completion in Peter's. As long as the expectation in marriage paralleled the skills each had, there was little tension. The expectation was consistent, in balance terms, with the abilities to fulfill the expectation. However, as each partner in the marriage began to expand an individual sense of territory—Ann into task projects (part-time job) and Peter into happiness projects (baby-sitting)—it became readily apparent that gaining the territory was much easier than learning the skills necessary to manage the territory. Both partners experienced increased frustration with their inabilities but were unable to accurately pinpoint the exact nature of the frustration. Although both partners wanted to expand a sense of individual territory, not only did they lack the skill to manage the new terrain, but each intruded into the competence area of the other. Unfortunately, although people raised in task-oriented families see the need for emotional involvement with others, the skill necessary for such involvement is not learned without a great deal of risk and self-disclosure. Conversely, people raised in happiness-oriented families see the need for task accomplishment in order to live but experience difficulty in appreciating the amount of time and effort that goes into building the skills to accomplish the task.

Essential to the ability to expand territory and at the same time gain some sense of mastery over the newly acquired territory (idea, location, or task) is the development of the self as a territory over which one has control in shaping one's destiny. Without a sense of self-control and self-destiny, merging one's formless territory with another is risky at best. The sense of self as a territory means looking at the self as worthy of protection and defense and entitled to expansion. The self is considered worthy of growth and entitled to a space of one's own. As a territory, the self is dynamic, expansive, and contingent on other territories. This idea of self begins or fails to begin to develop in the family setting. Where respect for others, protection of individual rights, provision of individual privacy, and encouragement of territory expansion and development of the skill to take care of the territory characterize group living that includes intimate involvement, personal interaction, and social interaction of family members, a strong sense of self has the opportunity to develop.

When people are treated as objects or as static territory that requires protection, defense, and constricted boundaries, the person has little opportunity for growth and little chance of doing much more than surviving. The quality of survival in such situations is, of course, questionable. If the individual has any strength at all, conflict is predictable. Bakker and Bakker-Rabdau point out, for example, that, although it may be possible to limit the territory expansion of children, when the children reach adolescence the ability to hold them within a constricted area is threatened. Territorial expansion and the acquisition of skills necessary to manage such territory are important components of every person's life. Such needs become more readily apparent during the adolescent years, when most familiar territory has been conquered and at least minimal skill has been acquired to get along in the spaces that one claims as one's own. However, it may be a mistake to assume that expansion of territory and acquisition of skill—physical, social, or psychological—stop at any particular age or at any one level of achievement.

Reaching out into new areas of endeavor is most probably a lifelong process. Children climb fences, ride bicycles, and learn new games. Adolescents engage in peer groups, begin dating, and think about college. Young adults develop careers, build houses, and establish ongoing relationships. Middle-aged adults expand careers, families, and hobbies; whereas older adults putter in their gardens, spend time with grandchildren, and travel. All seek ways to increase the amount of space that is familiar and to establish new skills to maintain the old and acquire new territory. Where such expansion does not continue, boredom and discontent are liable to become territories in and of themselves. Boredom may also result from not having enough confidence in the self to gain new territory or from a lack of recognition of one's ability to acquire new skills. Patterns of territorial expansion and management are learned in the family. Whereas Peter and Ann illustrate the influence of family patterns, the Halkins family illustrates family patterns and the result of trying to constrict the environmental searchings of family members.

**Example.** The Halkins family is a two-parent, five-sibling family of moderate income. According to the parents, the family atmosphere was pleasant and uneventful until the oldest child reached age 15, at which time discipline became a major problem. At the same time that the oldest boy was refusing to adhere to a curfew, other siblings were registering their protest by shoplifting, creating trouble in school, and arguing over minor details of household chores. The tighter the parents pulled on the reins, the more the entire sibling group rebelled. Although the parents maintained that the atmosphere was quiet and cooperative, the siblings all agreed that rules were rigid, that rule breaking was too severely punished, and that interests outside the family were all but impossible to pursue. Whereas the children were all expected to stay home except to go to school, both parents worked (had territory as well as skill) outside the home, and the father was going to school part-time (continuing to expand). While the parents were continuing to grow and were providing models for expansion, the children were expected to stay in the house and in the yard—both areas that the children had long exhausted in terms of new territory. When they sought out new areas of interest, however, each one got into trouble in some way or another, largely because the environment had been so tightly limited that learning any new skills in territory management was impossible. The desire to discover new territory took them out of the home and was so strong that all siblings were willing to risk severe punishment. However, their rovings about did not bring them into contact with any means for learning new social, economic, or psychological skills. Not until they became involved in family therapy did they have the opportunity for learning skills. When professional intervention occurred, it required great effort to persuade the parents that the children needed to explore more avenues and enhance their individual skills. The effort was minimally successful, and the siblings took turns running away from home.

The parents clung to the belief that children "belonged" to parents and that they should be "seen and not heard." The father was particularly adamant that his word was law and that anyone who broke his laws should be punished severely. The mother, who worked outside the home out of financial necessity, was considered by the father to be a rule breaker because she was not in the home where she "belonged." In his way of thinking, only the father, as head of the household, had any territory (house, car, children, wife) and any territorial rights (freedom of movement, freedom of inquiry, right to self-control).

Environments may be described as expansive or restrictive. Expansive environments allow for growth: gaining new ground and acquiring social and psychological skills to maintain that which is gained (idea, people, tasks). Within any given territory, individual privacy and personal space are as important as social interaction and family membership. In order to learn to appreciate the rights of others, one's own rights must be recognized and protected. Children, as well as adults, must be viewed as people who require room to develop—as individual people in their own right and as integral parts of family life. In expansive environments, such opportunities are more readily available than in restrictive environments.

Restrictive environments are characterized by lack of opportunity for acquiring new ideas, space, or friends or for learning skills necessary for successful involvement with others or effective management of tasks. Personal space and privacy are not usually recognized as essential; family membership is constrictive and possessive. Such families are described as clannish, closed to outsiders. People within restricted environments are treated as objects or territory and have little or no opportunity to learn skills of ownership or self-assertion. Self-assertive skills, independent of the family, are not encouraged and may even be punished. The need for independence and growth is so vital to individuals that conflict is frequent. The conflict, however, is not seen as a protest against restricted growth but is perceived by such families as open, unwarranted rebellion, as in the Halkins family.

## SUMMARY

Space and its influence on human behavior have been demonstrated by families to be an important component of family life. Although psychological and physical room to grow is essential, the acquisition of social and psychological skills to successfully maintain and effectively manage that which is gained is equally important. Individual space and privacy are essential for learning to spend time alone, just as social interaction within the family system is essential in learning to live cooperatively with others.

A sense of territory—a space of one's own—and a sense of personal ownership are vital to the acquisition of skills for expansion and management of space. Where territory of one's own is unavailable or the ability to manage territory is unlearned, territory and uniqueness of ownership will be obtained by other means: learning disorders, unique behavior patterns, multiple marriages. Other factors, such as stress and crowding, alter both the expansion of territory and the ability to manage the old and familiar. These factors will be discussed in more detail in later chapters.

Territory (space) and territoriality (ownership) are essential concepts in understanding behavior of people in general and of the family. Privacy, ownership, self-assertiveness, social and personal interaction, group identity, and family belonging are all components of the family's interactions with the environment—interactions that shape family relationships and influence individual destiny.

**STUDY QUESTIONS**

1. Describe Hall's concept of personal space. What is the relationship between space and interaction?
2. In what ways does a family's ability to acquire space relate to the family's ability to maintain space?
3. What is territoriality and how is it manifested within the family system?
4. Discuss privacy and its importance for individual development.
5. Discuss the concept of personal space for individual members and the family system. What is the relationship between personal space and territoriality?

**EXERCISES**

1. Keep an activity log for a week of where you go and what you do. How much time did you spend alone? How much time with others? Where do you spend the most time? What do you do there?
2. Do a home survey.
   a. In what areas is privacy most possible? Least possible?
   b. Where do people in your family spend the most time? Doing what?
   c. Who has the largest space in your home? The smallest space?
   d. How many things marked *yours, his, hers,* or *theirs* can you find in your home? How many marked *mine?*
3. Explore the imaginary space "bubbles" around you: intimate, personal, social, and public. What do you define as your personal space? How do you maintain your ownership of that space? How do you feel when others enter uninvited into your personal space? How do others react when you intrude into their personal spaces?
4. How many different kinds of language, in terms of space, can you identify in your daily discussions with others? Note how language differs in each of the

space zones (intimate language, personal language, social language, and public language).

5. How many space boundaries can you identify in your observations of others (for example, rules, sanctions, fences, walls, doors)? Diagram space boundaries of others: intimate, personal, social, and public. What differences in action and interaction do you observe within and between space "bubbles"?
6. What language do you use to indicate you feel crowded? How does that language differ from the language used by other family members? How is it similar?
7. What language do you use to indicate you have need for privacy? What is it like for you to spend time alone?*

*You may want to return to questions 5, 6, and 7 after the next chapter.

## BIBLIOGRAPHY


Aiello, J., and Aiello, T.: The development of personal space; proxemic behavior of children 6 thru 16," Hum. Ecol. **2**(3):177, 1974.

Bailey, K., Hartnett, J., and Glover, H.: Modeling and personal space behavior in children, J. Psychol. **85:**(1):143, 1973.

Bakker, C. B., and Bakker-Rabdau, M. K.: No trespassing! Explorations in human territoriality, San Francisco, 1973, Chandler and Sharp Publishers, Inc.

Beck, S., and Ollendick, T.: Personal space, sex of experimenter and locus of control in normal and delinquent adolescents, Psychol. Rep. **38**(2):383, 1976.

Blumenthal, D., and Reiss, S.: Do open space environments encourage children to seek immediate gratification, J. Sch. Psychol. **13**(2):91, 1975.

Brody, G., and Zimmerman, B.: The effects of modeling and classroom organization of the personal space of third and fourth grade children, Am. Educ. Res. J. **12**(2):157, 1975.

Ebert, E., and Lepper, M.: Individual consistency in the proxemic behavior of preschool children, J. Pers. Soc. Psychol. **32**(5):841, 1975.

Guardo, C.: Personal space, sex differences, and interpersonal attraction, J. Psychol. **92:**9, 1976.

Hall, E.: The Hidden Dimensions, New York, 1969, Anchor Books.

Kendall, P., Deardorff, P., Finch, A., and Graham, L.: Proxemics, locus of control, anxiety and type of movement in emotionally disturbed and normal boys, J. Abnorm. Child Psychol. **41**(1):9, 1976.

Lerner, R.: The development of personal space schemata toward body build, J. Psychol. **84:**229, 1973.

Lerner, R., Karabenick, S., and Meisels, M.: Effects of age and sex on the development of personal space schemata toward body build, J. Genet. Pscyhol. **127:**91, 1975.

Lomranz, J., Shapira, A., Choresh, N., and Gilat, Y.: Children's personal space as a function of age and sex, Dev. Psychol. **11**(5):541, 1975.

Maccoby, E., and Jacklin, C.: Stress a activity, and proximity seeking, sex differences in the year-old child, Child Dev. **44**(1):34, 1973.

McGren, P. L., and McGrew, W. C.: Changes in children's spacing behavior with nursery school experiences, Hum. Dev. **15**(6):359, 1972.

Pederson, D.: Developmental trends in personal space, J. Psychol. **83:**3, 1973.

Radl, L.: Childhood sleeping arrangements and later neurosis, Med. Insights **5**(2):16, 1973.

Somner, R.: Personal space; the behavioral basis of design, Englewood Cliffs, N.J., 1969, Prentice-Hall, Inc.

Valantin, S.: Problems raised by observations of children in various cultural environments, Early Child Dev. Care **2**(3):276, 1973.

Wilson, L.: Can an open space middle school meet the educational needs of minority youngsters? J. Negro Educ. **44**(3):368, 1975.

## Chapter 6

# FAMILY COMMUNICATION PROCESS

In viewing the family as a system, we have seen that the family is more than a collection of people. Family is also characterized by (1) relationships that begin in the past and are imbued with historical remnants, such as the unfinished task; (2) connectedness and psychological bonding, which bind people together in deep and influential ways, for example, in emotional honesty and unconditional acceptance; and (3) territorial expansion and management, that is, reaching out for new experiences and developing social and psychological skills for coping with those new experiences. Family is also characterized by a unique and complex communication process.

### DEFINITION

Communication is the exchange of information, a process whereby meaning is exchanged between people through the use of commonly understood symbols. *Family communication* can be defined as the organization and use of words, gestures, expressions, sounds, and actions to create expectations, portray images, describe feelings, and share meaning.

The organization and use of the tools of communication refers to the ways in which family members seek to communicate with one another. Such organization may be loose and non-goal-related, as in informal discussions, or quite structured and goal-directed, as in providing direction or teaching value orientations. In loose, unstructured communication, the flow of information may be lateral (from one person to the next), vertical (up the ladder of family power and influence), or episodic (bounce from person to person). Where communication is unstructured, the situation will determine the organization of the actual process. The more severe or intense the situation, the more structured communication will become. If Johnny, a two-year-old, falls and scrapes his knee, he may communicate his need to his older sister, mother, or grandmother, depending on who is available. However, if Johnny breaks his leg, usually a parent first, and then a medical person, will be the focus of his need communication.

Structured communication may be hierarchical (bottom to top), wheel-shaped (person with most influence at the hub), star-shaped (multiple lines of communication), or of some other structure, depending on the lines of communication in any particular family. Where the structure is hierarchical, the person with the most power and influence is at the top, for example, the head of the household. The person with the least influence is at the bottom, as in the case of a very young child. Lines of communication in such families closely parallel the chain of command that characterizes family interactions. The "head" of the family gives orders, grants permission, and applies corrective measures when orders are not followed. Such families are characterized by the rather traditional, authoritarian structure in which the man is the head of the household and women and children are to be "seen and not heard."

Where the structure of communication is wheel-shaped, the person with the most influence and power is at the hub of the wheel, equally accessible to each of the other family members. Whereas all have equal opportunity for input, final decisions are made by the person, or persons, at the hub of the wheel. However, the person at the hub of the wheel is dependent on the persons at the rim to provide information; the nature of the decisions made will reflect the nature of the information provided by those outside the hub. Major responsibility for effective decisions rests with the person at the hub of the wheel. This form of communication is represented by many contemporary families in which both parents assume decision-making responsibility but include the children or less influential others in gathering information necessary for adequate and effective decision making.

Communication that can be described as star-shaped or circular has no main leaders or decision makers. The flow of information does not follow any particular chain of influence or power in the family, and there is no one particular mechanism for decision making or decision implementation and no means of evaluating the adequacy of communication and interaction. Such communication structures are represented in families in which all family members are considered equal, with no leaders or ultimate decision maker. In such families, no adult takes adult responsibility for parenting and decision making, and children generally assume the responsibility for raising themselves. Structure alone will not assure effective communication, adequate decision making, or egalitarian information sharing.

## PURPOSE

Words, gestures, expressions, sounds, and actions are social and psychological tools that family members use for various purposes: teaching, informing, influencing, and understanding. The ultimate goal of family communication is to initiate and maintain interaction, one member with another. Where family communication has, as its basis, understanding of and interaction with other family members, the final outcomes will differ significantly from those of communication that is designed to control or influence, regardless of the need for understanding or the kind of interaction that develops in the process.

Arnold was a junior in high school when his worried father brought him to my office complaining that Arnold had been kicked out of school for the third time in one month. What, his father wanted to know was wrong with Arnold? When asked what he thought was wrong with Arnold, the father expounded his opinion for the next 30 minutes, ending with, "I can't control him anymore."

Where control is the issue, understanding is difficult to attain. As it turned out in Arnold's family (father, mother, a half brother, two sisters, and one grandchild), each knew very little about the other. The reason they ended up getting to know each other better was that Arnold's actions made it impossible *not* to get to know each other better. What was "wrong" with Arnold was that Arnold's family did not talk or listen to, confide in, or understand one another. Arnold's actions were a signal that all was not well within his family system. In that sense, Arnold's behavior was a message—to his family about their lack of involvement with each other; to his father about his lack of concern for as opposed to control of family members; to the school about its apparent disregard for Arnold as a person and his needs for understanding; and to the world at large that he was doing the best he could to get help for a troubled family, even if it meant getting in trouble himself.

Arnold used the means available to him to get his message across to other people: school officials, his father, the therapist. Arnold's message was communicated by his downcast eyes, his slumped shoulders, his disobedient nature, and finally by his open rebellion. As in other families, the messages communicated in Arnold's family came by various routes: behavior, gesture, and word. And as in other families, the least significant were words. The old adage, "Actions speak louder than words," applies in families just as it does elsewhere.

## CHANNELS OF COMMUNICATION

Mehrabian estimates that approximately 7 percent of a message is conveyed by words, with the majority of information actually conveyed by facial expression and physical posture, vocal modulation, and intonation. Closeness or distance, warmth or coldness, liking or disliking, and approval or disapproval can all be conveyed by one family member to another without a word being spoken.

Dismissal may be stressed by a flick of a wrist or a turn of the head. Uncertainty may be expressed by a shrug of a shoulder or a shake of the head. Confusion may be conveyed by a wrinkled brow, weariness by a sigh. Joy may be seen in a broad smile or twinkling eye, sorrow in a teardrop. Failure may be expressed by a slumped shoulder, downcast eyes, or a turning away of the entire body. Hurt may be caused by a sharp tone, regardless of the words used. Communication can occur with or without the use of words. In fact, the most authentic communication may come from the face and body posture. Toby is an example of nonverbal conveying as much as verbal communication.

A seven-year-old, Toby was referred to my office for psychological assessment. For the first three visits, Toby sat in a chair in the corner of the family therapy room. He began each visit by saying, "I'm not going to talk to you." During the first visit, he sat with his arms folded across his chest, one leg slung over the arm of the chair, with a big scowl on his face. During the second visit, he sat in the overstuffed chair, with both legs slung over the arms of the chair, and played with the buttons on the cushions. He occasionally looked to see what I was doing (working at my desk). Near the end of the second session, he asked if he could go to the play room, which he did. On the third visit, Toby marched into my office and announced that he wasn't going to talk to me anymore. He then turned around, marched into the play room, and began playing (my associate, a clinical nurse specialist, was waiting for him there). In the middle of the play session, Toby marched back into the family therapy room, stretched out on the couch, and went to sleep.

With the use of very few words, Toby registered his fear and mistrust of me (silence and distance), his need for self-protection (arms folded across his chest), his dissatisfaction with having to be there (scowl), and, at the same time, an overall casualness about the whole affair (leg slung over the arm of the chair). As the sessions progressed, Toby registered curiosity (watching me work, picking at the buttons on the chair, venturing into the play room) and increased trust and openness (both legs slung over the chair, moving around the office, sleeping on the couch) and demonstrated uncertainty as to where he wanted to be (in the family therapy room with me or in the play therapy room with the play therapist). He recognized authority in the territory by one question: "May I go to the play room?" He attempted to establish his own sense of authority and self-control: "I'm not going to talk." When he learned that no one wanted to take away his sense of self-control, he demonstrated the ability to cooperate and to be curious and the need to be physically close, but not too close.

Two general observations about Toby stand out: (1) his uncertainty about where and how he wanted to be and (2) his wavering trust in adults and the environment in which he found himself. The two observations are very much interrelated. Toby registered his uncertainty by refusing to talk but making no efforts to leave the situation; by being timid and shy one session and bold and loud on other occasions; and by wavering back and forth between the play therapy area and the family therapy room, the play therapist and myself. During the initial sessions, Toby was able to register his feelings with a minimum of words. Only later did we learn that Toby's parents were divorced and that Toby was an abused child. Like most children of divorce, he did not know where he wanted to be or whom he wanted to be with; like many abused children, Toby had little or no insight into what he did that triggered abusive behavior in adults. In many ways, Toby's behavior in therapy was an accurate replication of his real life experiences, which he revealed to us through actions, gesture, and physical movement. His lack of insight and the unpredictable nature of his mother's response led Toby to doubt his own abilities and lack trust in adults and the environment. Any behavior could bring on separation and abuse, and any adult was a potential abuser. Toby lived in a very uncertain world; he registered his uncertainty everywhere he went: at home, in school, and during therapy. Like Arnold, it was Toby who, through his actions, brought his entire family to a position where they were forced to deal with each other.

For many families, including Arnold's and Toby's, learning to communicate is not any easy task. Whereas certain factors act as barriers to communication, other factors facilitate the process.

## Barriers to communication

Several factors make communication more difficult: individual inability (emotional or physical), faulty assumptions and unreasonable expectations among family members, power struggles between family members, emotional dishonesty and lack of authenticity, and inconsistent or contradictory messages.

Individual differences in physical, emotional, or intellectual ability may retard or enhance the family communication process. Most children, for example, are able to learn the basics of communication particular to any family by the age of six. Mental retardation, excessive physical activity, or physical disability may alter individual ability to acquire and use the tools of communication that characterize family and cultural patterns. The greater the difference between the individual and the family, the greater the potential for problems in family communication. Outside help may be necessary in learning to cope with the differences as well as in learning how to communicate along different lines or using different modalities.

Faulty assumptions and unreasonable expectations hinder each member's ability to use his or her own talents and develop skills without fear of not meeting the expectation or of falling short of some unnamed family goal. Faulty assumptions occur regarding the roles one is expected to assume, the behaviors one is expected to exhibit, the beliefs one is supposed to hold, and the values to which one is supposed to subscribe. Expectations may concern individual performance, family commitment, or group loyalty. Assumptions and expectations come from family experience (past and present), sociocultural norms, individual aspiration, or religious beliefs. Where there is conflict among the various sources of expectations, there is potential for family conflict in trying to integrate the assumptions and expectations into family life.

Power struggles and faulty assumptions often go hand in hand. Faulty assumptions about how people are supposed to act or think or feel based on their sex, family position (parent or child), or age, regardless of talent or predisposition, often lead to power struggles for various leadership or decision-making functions. The mythical belief, for example, that men must be strong and women weak leads to conflict in the situation where a couple might exhibit the reverse abilities. Hal and Elaine exemplify this situation.

Hal is a tender-hearted and easy-going fellow. His wife, Elaine, is decisive and goal directed. Because of his belief that men are supposed to be strong and independent, Hal finds himself struggling for a leadership function that he doesn't even want. Elaine finds herself struggling to make Hal the leader, regardless of the fact that she demonstrates better ability. Each blames the other for what seems to be a trap. Actually, Hal is trying to force himself into something he's not; Elaine is trying to be something she's not and fights with Hal to be someone he's not. Their power struggle stems from an inability to accept personal behavior and ability that do not fit a social norm.

Power struggles emerge out of a need for excessive control, the belief that certain people are supposed to do certain things, unclear expectations for family members, or a structure of family communication in which one member controls the source of information as well as the means for decision making. The more structured the communication process and the less the opportunity for democratic participation in family communication, the greater the potential for power struggles. As was discussed in Chapter 5, most individuals exhibit the need to grow—to expand territory and to acquire more skills. When those basic needs are thwarted or constrained, out of mythical belief about relationships or family responsibilities or for whatever reason, struggle against power figures can be expected. A power struggle can emerge between husband and wife, mother and child, or child and child; however, it more often occurs between a child and one or both parents. The Halkins family in Chapter 5 is an example. Unable to exercise individual autonomy and self-control, each person began by struggling against the parents, particularly the father, and ended up by running away. Had emotional honesty been possible, the need for power struggles might not have been so great.

Emotional dishonesty, lack of authenticity, and contradictory messages are all interrelated. Basically, contradictory messages occur where there is a discrepancy between what is seen, what is heard, and what is felt. As will be recalled, emotional honesty involves an open and accurate description of how one feels and what one is thinking. Authentic communication is sending messages in which the thoughts, feelings, verbal statements, and physical actions and body movements are consistent with one another, the sender of the message can be trusted to be as open and honest as possible, and the receiver of the message, in responding, can be confident that the response will be accepted in light of the message sent.

However, where there is a contradiction between what is said and what is done, the receiver of the message cannot be sure whether to respond to the words or to the actions. Either response may cause conflict, because the sender of unauthentic messages is not always aware of the true nature of the message or the need underlying the communication. For example, a mother who wrinkles her face in disgust as she picks up her child is sending a mixed and contradictory message: pulling close and expressing distance. A frustrated husband who stands in the middle of the room with raised fist and reddened face and screams, "Don't leave me!" to his wife registers anger and the need for distance with his body and cries out for closeness with his words. Neither he nor his wife can be sure of the "real" message being sent without some knowledge of the entire context in which the communication occurs.

The entire context involves not only the events that precede the interaction and the physical setting in which the interaction occurs but the components of the actual message—gesture, tone, words, physical movement, and facial expression—as well. Facial expression and body posture may be more accurate indicators of underlying feeling than are words. However, families also develop habits of relying on one form of communication (words) more than another (actions), rather than using an integrated system of words, feelings, and actions. In addition, families have members who develop (or are assigned) differential ability in using words, employing body movement, or both.

Children, for example, rely more heavily on body language and action to convey meaning. Adults usually rely on words. More often than not, women display a preference for verbal interaction; men attach more meaning to behavior. "He never says he loves me" and "I sent her flowers, what more does she want?" are not uncommon expressions of the lack of ability to understand or use more than one modality to express thought and feeling. There are, of course, children who are verbally articulate, and there are adults who are particularly adept at body language; there are verbally articulate men and body-oriented women. What is important to realize, however, is that families develop styles in communication, and many individuals within those families have differential ability to send and receive messages in more than one communication modality. Where individual differences are great and where the styles involve contradictions, there will be potential problems in family communication. The same barrier can be an asset if family members are able to learn from and use the multiple modalities available for sending and receiving messages. Within the same families where barriers to communication exist, aids to communication can also be found.

### Aids to communication

Several factors serve to enhance or facilitate the communication process: (1) respect for alternate modalities of personal expression, (2) opportunity for optional responses to communication, (3) empathy for one another, (4) mechanisms for making decisions and resolving conflict, (5) shared experience and common goals, (6) the existence of an information network, and (7) patterns and identifiable styles of communication. Respect for others and respect for self lead one to be more accepting of differences between oneself and other family members. Self-respect is nourished in family interaction where warmth, caring, and acceptance prevail. Confidence in oneself as worthwhile, important, and integral to family interaction grows in family communication that is characterized by listening, questioning, and understanding. Such an atmosphere is conducive to communication.

## STYLES OF COMMUNICATION

Opportunity for thinking, feeling, and acting in various ways provides family members with a broad set of skills in sending, receiving, interpreting, and returning messages in a variety of settings, social situations, and family networks. Such opportunities are made available through freedom, within limits, to feel, think, and act experimentally. Where experimentation with learning is prohibited, communication skills will be limited. Experimentation through trial and error within the family setting is essential to survival in situations outside the family setting, where individual experimentation is less tolerated. For example, a small child, prevented from learning to eat with a knife may yell angry words at his mother. Within the family he may come to learn that such feelings are transitory and may depend on the immediate situation. Feelings that can be expressed without fear of retaliation may lead to enhanced understanding—of his own feelings, of his mother's feelings for him, and of the nature of the relationship between the two. Such opportunities are rarely available outside the family setting except in other intimate relationships, which only come later in life.

Empathy, or the ability to put oneself into the shoes (acts, thoughts, or feelings) of another, enhances the communication process. Being able to sense another's feelings, to speculate on another's thoughts, or predict another's actions expands skills in interpreting and being sensitive to the feelings and actions of others. Sensitivity to and familiarity with others enhance the ability to understand, accept, and be tolerant of individual ability in communication and interaction. Of all family members, children seem to be the most sensitive and responsive to the feelings and needs of others. Adults who remember what it was like to be young, naive, and volatile are also sensitive, empathetic family communicators. Aged family members, caught up in remembering and reassessing the past, are often more empathetic and sensitive to the young than are their parents, who are caught up in working for and maintaining family goals and ambitions.

Shared experience and the commonly held goals that characterize family life enhance the communication that family members have with one another. Shared experience provides a framework of familiarity; common goals provide a sense of direction for family members. The ability to move in certain directions and use those shared experiences depends on the nature of the communication network that exists for decision making, conflict resolution, information sharing, and making satisfactions and dissatisfactions known.

Communication styles in families can be characterized generally by networks that are autocratic (hierarchical structures), democratic (wheel-shaped structure), or egalitarian (star-shaped structure). The more versatility in networks, the more effective and satisfying the outcomes. In decision making, for example, autocratic style involves one person as the ultimate leader or decision maker. In case of family crises or uncertainty, autocratic decision making is probably the most effective. Democratic decision making requires information from all involved, but ultimate responsibility for decision making rests with one or two people—usually the adults or parents. While children are young and inexperienced, this form of decision making seems to be the most appropriate. Egalitarian decision making involves each individual as an equal partner in gathering information and sharing the decision making. As young children become young adults, this form of family decision making seems most useful. Group participation provides young adults and growing children the opportunity to experience decision making in a setting where help and consultation are available for learning and experimentation.

Families that primarily employ only one style of communication, for example, autocratic methods, will be less flexible and less adaptable to changing situations than families who are able to employ one, two, or a combination of styles depending on need and ability at any given time. Conflict resolution, making satisfactions and dissatisfactions known, and sharing information will differ according to the communication pattern in any particular family. Communication networks can be used to enhance overall communication if the network is known to all family members. Where one member uses one style, for example, a democratic style, and another member employs another style, for example, an autocratic style, lack of communication with the potential for conflict, may occur. However, when all family members know and are able to participate at a level provided by any particular network, communication will be productive and feelings of satisfaction may occur.

## FACTORS SHAPING COMMUNICATION STYLE

The use of any particular network of communication, with its resultant style, is influenced by a number of additional factors: (1) physical setting in which the communication occurs, (2) perceived intent of the communication by those involved, (3) social setting, (4) cultural background of participants, and (5) family context.

### Physical setting

The physical context in which communication occurs influences the interactions that take place there. According to Hall, specific expectations exist based on the nature of the interaction or the distance indicated by the communication (intimate, personal, social, or public). Hugging and kissing, for example, would be expected in an intimate zone, or location. However, the same behavior might raise eyebrows at a social gathering or public meeing. The physical distance that separates members of a group from one another sets up social and psychological expectations for the interactions that will occur.

Depending on the physical distance between family members, eye contact can mean anything from seduction to a mild warning. Sitting with one's arm over the back of a chair can mean anything from relaxation, if the chair is empty, to protection and possession, if the chair is occupied. Depending on whose space is involved, for example, mother's kitchen, father's chair, or sibling's room, occupation of that space by another can mean anything from companionship to intrusion. The size or shape of the physical setting, the sounds and activities characteristic of it will also influence the kind of interaction that occurs there. A big room, a dark closet, a bathroom, a hallway, concrete walls, and high, beamed ceilings all influence the type of interaction that will take place. Whether or not privacy is possible in a particular location may determine how intimate the conversation becomes. Color, noise, and freedom of movement within a physical setting may determine how freely family members interact or how constrained conversation and social interaction become.

Physical barriers, such as walls, winding staircases, and long, narrow halls, may either provide privacy or block family members' attempts to get closer together. Rooms designed for individual privacy, for example, bedrooms, father's den, and mother's office or sewing room, may at the same time foster family distance by limiting the space available for larger gatherings. Face-to-face contact is necessary for personal, intimate interactions. Physical space must be available if face-to-face contact is to occur. One couple frequently came to our office simply to be able to have the time and space to talk personally with one another—time and space that they could not find in a small, two-bedroom house with five children. The physical location, the meaning attached to that location and its size, shape, color and sounds, and the number of people who occupy or own a specific location all influence the kind of interactions that are possible. The intent or purpose behind an interaction also influences communication style.

### Attribution of intent

A father drives the car into the garage and waves a greeting to his young son who is playing in the front yard. He shouts hello over the roar of the engine and pulls the car into the garage. The young boy leaps from the flower bed in which he is sitting and runs to hide in his room. The father's intended greeting, extended arm and raised voice, was interpreted by the boy to be a warning. The *purpose* of the gesture, greeting by the father, and the *ascribed intent* of the gesture, warning or discipline as perceived by the boy, were widely discrepant. Each participant in the interaction was operating in the psychological context, or framework, of the immediate experience. The father was glad to be home from work; the young boy was feeling guilty because he thought he had been caught in the flower bed.

According to Heider, the attribution of intent, what others think a message is all about, is as important in shaping the outcome of the interaction as is the actual purpose underlying the message. That is, what another person (observer-boy) *thinks* is the reason behind another individual's (actor-father) actions has as much or more influence in shaping reactions as does the actual purpose behind the action. The father intended to greet the boy; however, the boy attributed to the actions the intent to discipline.

Had the boy not been in the flower bed, his father's greeting may have been just that. Attribution of intent is influenced by (1) familiarity with the other person, (2) experience with similar situations, (3) ability to decipher physical and verbal messages, (4) patterns of interaction established in the past, and (5) the nature of the immediate situation.

A parent who sets a ten o'clock curfew generally does so with the safety and welfare of others in mind; the average teenager interprets the gesture to be a direct attack on personal freedom and social movement. The simple question about destination, "Where are you going?" has as its purpose information seeking. The intent is to obtain an answer. The answer, however, will differ depending on the context and the perceived intent or purpose. An unsure young teenager out on the first date, responds with anger and anxiety: "Now where do you think I'm going?" A despondent widow, in the process of selling her home, responds despairingly: "I wish I knew." The young child, with other things on his mind, responds flippantly: "To Larry's." And the college student, leaving home for the first time, answers: "Out into the big, cruel world." Defense, despair, indifference, and anxiety are all revealed by an answer to the same basic question, but each individual is in a different psychosocial climate. Each person responded out of (1) the perceived intent of the inquirer (nosiness, concern, fact finding, or challenge), (2) the nature of the immediate situation, and (3) the extent of familiarity with similar situations.

Familiarity with the other person or with the situation may facilitate the interaction in that words, gestures, and actions have come to have a shared meaning among family members. Familiarity can also hamper communication in the sense that too much can be taken for granted where little is actually known. Although family members are familiar with one another and know about family habits (favorite words, unique gestures), they may not know or understand the meaning that a particular family member is attributing to the immediate situation. They may also be wrong about the particular need that the family member is trying to fulfill through a specific communication at any given time. Familiarity and shared life experience are essential to understanding one another; however, caution must be exercised lest partial familiarity lead family members to take family interaction for granted.

### Social context

Power, status, and proximity of others influence the intent that we ascribe to the actions of others and the nature of interactions. By nature of the family experience, family members have different status within the family, experience various levels of power, and are subject to physically close, psychologically intense encounters. Parents are generally perceived as having more power and more status than children. Exceptions may be found in families where there is an exceptional child, a member with a chronic illness, or a live-in grandparent. In each instance, the power relations and the status of various family members are altered. A chronically ill member, for example, may require special clothing, special handling, and expensive health care. The family budget, family interactions, family social life, and future plans may all have to revolve around the chronically ill or exceptional family member. In those instances, the individual actually exhibits a great deal of power, through control over and dependence on the entire family system.

Proximity of members, that is, closeness in terms of age, belief, sex, or interest, will influence the nature of communication. Research studies indicate, for example, that people who live closest together generally know more about one another and become more involved with each other. Neighbors will be closer physically and know more about one another than will people who live two or three blocks apart. Marriages are more apt to occur within communities than between neighboring towns. People who share similar beliefs, such as religious beliefs, will spend more time with one another than those with differing beliefs. Physical closeness in itself will increase the opportunity for communication, of a social as well as of a personal nature. We know more about and talk more with the people with whom we spend the most time. For that reason, people who spend a great deal of time in the work setting are often more comfortable talking and being with their fellow workers than they are with their own families. This is largely because of the increased amount of time together and hence contact and communication that workers often have. In many cases, the amount of time and the intensity of contact in the family setting and in family social activities is less than in work settings.

In addition to the physical setting, the psychological context, and the social setting is the cultural or ethnic context in which the family is embedded; this context is a subtle yet powerful component of family communication.

### Cultural context

The cultural context and the social setting in which family interaction occurs largely determine the rules for communication and the boundaries within which members are supposed to act (think, feel, and behave). Although the boundaries that separate differing minority, ethnic, and social groups are increasingly fluid, there are nonetheless strong expectations regarding behavior and interaction that are based on perceived cultural norms and social expectation.

The expectation regarding various cultural groups may or may not coincide with the contribution that unique cultural backgrounds actually make to the life style and interaction patterns of any one family or family group. There is no doubt that cultural history and ethnic embeddedness influence family interaction and individual belief. There is no doubt that cultural differences account for some variation in family behavior patterns: belief, action, and attitude. A review of contemporary literature reveals the subtle, yet thorough impact of cultural embeddedness. Also revealed is the result of the misunderstandings on the part of people about the cultural, ethnic, and religious uniqueness of others. More often than not, misunderstandings grow out of expectations based on myth rather than knowledge and experience.

Cultural, ethnic, and religious heritages supply families with rich, meaningful experience that shapes interaction with one another and influences members' relationships with others outside the family boundaries. Angelou, Potok, Kitano, and others provide in-depth accounts of growing up Black, Jewish, Japanese, and as members of other unique cultures. The experiences recounted are joyfully, beautifully, and painfully similar: rich history and widespread misunderstanding and discrimination based on stereotypical concepts.

One must exercise caution in attributing to culture that which is cultural influence and to myth that which is mythical. There is increasing evidence to suggest, for example, that poverty may be a subculture in this country, as influential in shaping attitudes and habits as identification with any other particular culture or ethnic group. Polansky's account of Appalachian mothers points out by examples the significant and desperate situation created by mountain poverty. Being different, in financial, social, religious, or cultural characteristics, can be an asset as well as a liability for the family system; either way, the influence must be considered in assessing family interaction and communication.

Knowing about one's own ethnic and religious background is essential to understanding the uniqueness created by such experiences. Becoming familiar with the cultural and ethnic backgrounds of others (through reading, experiencing, and observing) is similarly an important component of learning about the communication and interaction patterns of family systems.

Cultural and social settings influence behavior through norm setting, explication of expectation, language shaping, attitude development, and value orientation. The sociocultural context sets the stage, provides a framework for meaning, and marks the outer boundaries of acceptable interaction. A more intimate and intense context is provided by the family system itself.

**Family context**

The family system itself (constellation, size, individual ability and interest, financial status, and association with nonfamily groups) plays a part in shaping the communication pattern and interaction process within the family. Family constellation (that is, one parent, two children; two parents, three children; two unrelated adults and their respective children; grandparents, parents, and children) will influence both the style of communication and the nature of interaction. The only child, for example, will receive more frequent adult-to-child communications than will the child who is a member of a three-sibling, two-parent family. One-parent families will have fewer adult-to-adult communications than will a family system where both parents are present.

Family systems that include children of the same sex will have different life experiences (social, physical and psychological) than families where there is a mix of boy and girl children. Life experiences will provide family members with a different set of skills, according to the makeup of the family system. Families who have no live-in grandparents will have little opportunity for developing skills of communicating with older people. Families where there is no physical illness may feel totally incapable of coping with sudden illness or death. A woman who grows up with no brothers may lack the social skills of companionship with her husband. A man with no sisters lacks developmental experience with members of the opposite sex and may be at a disadvantage in knowing how to interpret what he sees and hears.

Styles of communication learned in the family system will be carried over into nonfamily group experiences and the formation of future family systems. These styles will influence and be shaped by family history, psychological bonding, availability and use of space, and opportunities for learning and experiencing alternative modalities for expression of thought, feeling, and action. The effectiveness of communication within the family in reaching, teaching, touching, and sharing will largely determine whether family members are effective as actors, communicators, receivers, and individuals in the current family system and family systems in later life.

## SUMMARY

Whereas communication has many purposes within families, namely, to convey meaning, to share impressions, to impart knowledge, to influence and shape opinion, the ultimate goal is to establish meaningful and sustained interaction with significant others. The final outcome is influenced by many factors: physical location, social setting, cultural background, and family context. Factors exist that serve both to enhance and to inhibit the communication process. Communication and interaction are integrally related processes that shape and are shaped by family life style and individual ability.

**STUDY QUESTIONS**

1. Define family communication and discuss the relationship between words, gestures, actions, and body movement.
2. What is attribution of intent, and what is its relation to interpreting messages sent and received?
3. Describe three ways in which communication can be organized, and discuss the relative usefulness of each pattern.
4. Describe three barriers and three aids to effective communication. In what ways can barriers be used as aids?
5. What is the relationship between physical environment and communication?
6. What is a contradictory message, and what is its effect on psychological development and family interaction?

**EXERCISES**

1. Of the three major components of the communication process—words, body movements, and actions—identify two of each that are unique to your family system and two of each that your family system shares with other families.
2. Communication is for various reasons. Find examples in your family system where communication is used to:

| | *Words* | *Gestures* | *Combination* |
|---|---|---|---|
| a. Provide direction | | | |
| b. Seek clarification | | | |
| c. Reveal dissatisfaction | | | |
| d. Convey approval | | | |
| e. Express feeling | | | |
| f. Provide tension release | | | |
| g. Add confusion | | | |
| h. Protect another | | | |

3. What evidence do you find in your family of contradictory communication, that is, someone saying one thing and doing another? What is the effect of such contradictory messages? (Example: "Come sit on my lap," his mother said, frowning.)
4. Describe the contexts in which you were reared: physical, psychological, social, cultural, and familial. Which seems, in your experience, to have had the greatest impact on your communication style? How does your experience compare with that of one or more of your classmates?
5. Select for reading one of the following and compare and contrast with your own family experience: *My Name is Asher Lev,* C. Potok; *I Know Why the Caged Bird Sings,* M. Angelou; *Hard Living on Clay Steet,* J. Howell; *Black Elk Speaks,* J. Neihardt.
6. Observe a ten-minute interaction of your family in a natural setting. Include at least three people. Note their positions, the direction of their comments, and the frequency of their comments. Who speaks to whom? Who sits closest and

farthest away? Where is the center of activity? What is the overall mood of the interaction? (We will return to this exercise in later chapters.)

7. How would you describe the communication network in your family: autocratic, democratic, or egalitarian? Give examples of situations in which one, two, or all styles were used. What effects did you note (effects that were similar or different depending on the particular style)?

**BIBLIOGRAPHY**

Angelou, M.: I know why the caged bird sings, New York, 1970, Random House.

Birdwhistel, R. L.: Kinesics and context; essays on body motion communication, Philadelphia, 1970, University of Pennsylvania Press.

Daniels, R., and Kitano, H.: American racism; exploration of the nature of prejudice, Englewood Cliffs, N.J., 1970 Prentice-Hall, Inc.

Fast, J.: Body language, New York, 1971, Pocket Books.

Hall, E.: The hidden dimension, New York, 1966, Anchor Books.

Heider, F.: The psychology of interpersonal relations, New York, 1958, John Wiley and Sons, Inc.

Howell, J.: Hard living on Clay Street; portraits of blue collar families, New York, 1973, Anchor Press.

Kitano, H.: Japanese Americans; the evolution of a subculture, Englewood Cliffs, N. J., 1976, Prentice-Hall, Inc.

Mehrabian, A.: Interpersonal communication. In Hampton, D., Summer, C., and Webber, R., editors: Organizational behavior and the practice of management, Glenview, Ill., 1973, Scott, Foresman and Co., p. 70.

Neihardt, J.: Black Elk speaks, New York, 1975, Simon Schuster, Inc.

Polansky, N., Borgman, R., and De Saix, C.: Roots of futility, San Francisco, 1972, Jossey-Bass, Inc., Publishers.

Potok, C.: My name is Asher Lev, Greenwich, Conn. 1972, Fawcett Publishers.

Wiener, M., and others: Non-verbal behavior and non-verbal communication, Psychol. Rev. **79:**185, 1972.

## Chapter 7

# FAMILY MENTAL HEALTH

Family systems are characterized by (1) historical connectedness with other family units and family members, (2) emotional connectedness within those units and between family members, and (3) a unique physical and social connectedness through shared space and a common communication process. Family mental health is a reflection of the nature of that connectedness expressed generally in interpersonal effectiveness. Family mental health reflects the family's ability to function effectively as a system whose purpose is to prepare its members for participation in larger and more complex social systems. Thus mental health is a multifaceted, multidetermined entity, the evaluation of which does not single out any one aspect of family life as more important than another but considers a wide range of abilities and activities. Activities and behaviors most important to effective system functioning and thus to mental health are: information processing, decision making and implementation, emotional development and expresssion, conflict management, and productivity and change. Family mental health is actually an inference made from a family's ability to engage in essential activities under varying conditions.

Judgments regarding the effectiveness of any one family system must take into consideration not only the inner workings of the family itself, but the cultural, social, and geographical contexts in which the particular family system exists. What may be characteristic in one part of the country may not be typical in another part; what may be important for one family may be less important for another. Each family must be judged, therefore, not only in terms of system effectiveness and individual differences but in terms of the environmental, social, and psychological demands and influences on that family.

Individual mental health, or effectiveness, can be considered within the perspective of family membership and family mental health. That is, individual mental health will be a reflection of the nature of the relationships that characterize the particular family from which the individual originates. One can infer much about an individual's family by observing how that individual moves, behaves, thinks, and feels. Similarly, observing family interactions and activities makes it possible to infer how individuals from those families will interact with others. In families where the nature of connectedness results in ineffectiveness of the family system, individual behavior will largely reflect that ineffectiveness. Where the nature of connectedness results in effective functioning and positive, productive interactions, individual behavior will be similarly effective. The point should be made that in the case where individuals originate from family systems that are less than effective, the individual can, through training, education, and therapy, alter the current and future nature of connectedness with others. Although past family connectedness cannot be changed, an individual's understanding of and reaction toward that past can be altered, with particular emphasis on how those relationships affect the present and future. An unexamined past may dominate the present and shape the future: misunderstanding generates misunderstanding, abuse promotes abuse, coldness breeds distance. People tend to reproduce that with which they are familiar. Family relationships may be in many ways more powerful than the resources of any one individual family member.

Viewing mental health as a by-product of family relationships and as a measure of family effectiveness relieves any one family member of the blame or responsibility for ineffectiveness or dysfunction. Dysfunction is expressed in terms of levels of family effectiveness rather than pathology or dysfunction of any particular member or members. This does not remove from any one individual family member the responsibility for individual actions and reactions but emphasizes the aspects of that individual which are related to family membership and the family's overall system effectiveness. Thus, individual mental health is a reflection of family mental health; family mental health is a measure of the family's overall system effectiveness, particularly in terms of information processing, decision making and implementation, emotional tenor, conflict management, and productivity and change. That individual mental health is a reflection of overall family functioning can be illustrated by the following example, in which a child was erroneously labeled by her parents as the "patient." However, the "patient" was really the entire family system.

## EXAMPLE: ALLISON'S FAMILY

Allison was a three-year-old child, the elder sibling of a two-sibling, two-parent family unit. She was referred for evaluation and consultation because of sleep disturbances—sleepwalking, crying out in the night, and restless napping—all followed by little or no recollection of the events when later awakened. There were no apparent medical reasons for Allison's behavior; developmentally, Allison was average or above average in language, social skills, and motor performance. There were no motor, social, physical, or intellectual deficits that might have explained Allison's behavior.

Allison's parents were young, bright, energetic, and socially and financially successful. Each spouse's parents were living and well and close geographically. The grandparents maintained a close association with Allison's family unit. Each spouse was reportedly close to respective family of origin; however, Allison's mother seemed to have a better working relationship with her family than her father did with his. On the surface, Allison's parents seemed to have a good relationship (close, warm, honest, and supportive) with another. This relationship, however, turned out to be cold, manipulative, and filled with contradictory messages.

Verbal expressions of support were accompanied by body language and gestures that were nonsupportive and contradictory. Social status and material gain were more important than mutual understanding, personal growth, and expression of feeling. Actual time together as a family was limited to mealtimes, in which grievances were aired and unresolved arguments occurred. Expression of feeling varied from slamming doors to clamming up, from yelling to crying, from confrontation to withdrawal. There was rarely a time, however, when feeling expressed was feeling felt: fear became anger, distrust became fault finding, need became demand. Overall communication lacked both honesty and authenticity.

The lack of authenticity and the presence of contradictory messages in the communication process within the family contributed in direct ways to Allison's sleep disturbance. During the day and early evening hours, Allison absorbed the confusion, unarticulated conflict, and unexpressed fear; at night she worked out her responses to that confusion in age-appropriate ways: sleep disturbances. As conflict became more open and emotional expression more authentic, Allison's sleep patterns became less disturbed; when conflict escalated, Allison's sleep problems returned. The child's behavior was a means of expressing her feelings and confusion regarding the nature of interaction between her parents and between her parents and herself. On a subliminal level, she was aware of and terrified by sights, sounds, and feelings that she could not understand or control. By altering modalities of expression between her parents, it was possible to observe their impact on Allison and on her behavioral responses to their interactions. Allison's responses were a direct result of her membership in a less than effective family, rather than a result of any developmental stage, physical problem, or psychomotor deficit experienced by Allison. Her disturbed sleep was the smaller of a larger situation.

Another characteristic of Allison's membership in the family that contributed to her responses to family interactions was her ordinal position. "Ordinal position" refers to birth order of individuals—first, second, third, fourth, fifth, and so on—within the family. Birth order influences the nature of interaction within the family system. Allison, for example, was the firstborn child. Firstborn children, particularly of immature parents, experience the uncertainty with which the parents interact with not only the child but each other. Thus, firstborn children are highly vulnerable to experiences that not only fail to support the child's needs but undermine the child's attempts to fully trust and depend on others. If the child is also the first grandchild on one or both sides of the family, there is the added pressure of high expectation for performance, development, and of filling the "child position" in a family of adults. As in Allison's case, the expectation for perfection in such instances is also great. Expectations of firstborn children are high for carrying out unfinished tasks and for carrying on family heritage and tradition.

Firstborn children are often treated like miniature adults, with expectations for early use of language, physical ability, and self-sufficiency. However, firstborn children may be expected to act like babies or children when parents feel like being parents. The firstborn may become a parent or spouse surrogate, taking the position of the other adult and offering comfort, approval, and acceptance for one or both parents or parent figures. As additional children are born, the firstborn may be given additional responsibility for child care, home supervision, and self-sufficiency. The assigned responsibilities may far exceed the child's ability, thus leading the child to feelings of failure, powerlessness, or helplessness. However, where assigned responsibility results in successful management of others, for example, of younger siblings or peers, the firstborn child may grow up with an inordinate sense of power and control as well as a need to please those in a position of authority. In either case, the ability to accurately perceive one's place in the family will be limited, and a lack of balance between ability and responsibility may occur, much of which can be related to ordinal position in the family of origin. Because of their habitual interaction with adults, many firstborns lack relationship skills with peers and younger children, except in an authoritative or managerial role. Allison was clearly assigned more emotional responsibility than was appropriate to her age and life experience. She vacillated between feelings of total control over the family and feelings of total helplessness.

Second- and third-born children, however, are more peer oriented, less approval motivated toward adults in their activities, and less cautious in relationships with each other and others outside the family. Allison's younger brother was less demanding of the mother's time, more content to play alone or with others, and was generally more settled in his activities. He was seemingly less affected by the family turmoil, with some effect, however, showing up in blunted affect and a heightened lack of trust in others, including the grandparents. His path was less difficult, largely because of Allison's having gone before. For example, there was less concern with his diet, less attention paid to his ability to pass developmental marks on time, and more time given him to experience his own world without adult supervision and intervention. All in all there was less pressure on him from parents, who were becoming more experienced, and grandparents to perform, to develop according to given norms, or to fill emotional needs of the adults.

Birth order of parents or partners in marriage, as well as the birth order of their own children, will influence their relationships with one another, particularly where there may have been conflicts between birth order positions in the family of origin. Allison's mother, for example, was the second-born child of a two-sibling family, whereas Allison's father, John, was the firstborn of a three-sibling family. There was a great deal of conflict within John's family between John and the second-born sibling, his younger brother. At the same time that John was assigned responsibility for his younger brother, he felt robbed of his child position by the birth of still another younger brother. Developmentally, John was never able to get his share of being taken care of or of having his parents all to himself, even for a short period. At the same time that he was experiencing emotional deprivation, he was being assigned care-taking responsibilities for the very person with whom he shared what emotional resources existed within the family. The sense of competition and stretching of emotional resources that he experienced with his siblings was regenerated when he found himself having to share his wife and extend his caretaking responsibilities beyond her to include his own children. Unresolved conflict in previous relationships frequently reappears in later relationships, particularly if that conflict occurred in family or close relationships. Unless tools are gained to resolve conflict, patterns of uncertainty, confusion, and discontent will tend to be repeated in each ensuing generation.

Emotional involvement and the ability to resolve conflict were lacking in Allison's family. As a member of the family, Allison was directly affected by that lack. Later, in the process of therapy, other family members disclosed symptoms indicative of being affected: stomach pains, headaches, backaches, and sleep disturbances. Family members absorb, often at a nonverbal level, tension and conflict that exist within the family system. The impact of that emotional absorption is more intense where the conflict is intense and, at the same time, unexpressed or ignored. When participants experience lack of agreement or more intense conflict but deny its existence, messages are sent to others that are confused and contradictory. Disagreement is manifested through action, gesture, and other forms of silent language: wordless communications whose underlying message is characterized by a confused meaning or conflicted feeling.

The tension created in Allison's family by misunderstandings, contradictory messages, unresolved emotional deprivation, and unexplored feelings was released through family members' restlessness, sleep disturbance, and general irritability. Whereas Allison's nightmares were perhaps a safety valve for the expression of tension and release of withheld feelings within the family, particularly between parents, the impact on her as an individual and as a child was detrimental and psychologically costly—both for her and for the entire family.

The psychological cost to Allison and other individuals who are identified by their families as "the one" having problems stems from the fact that the individual is often blamed, singled out, or otherwise labeled as the "patient." Where one individual is labeled as the patient, there is a failure on the part of the family to recognize that the individual is part of a larger process and that the individual's behavior (thoughts, feelings, and actions) is a reflection of that process. As the identified patient, the individual must not only act out the problem but resolve it as well. The individual is unable to share with other family members the task of improving the situation, for the family mistakenly assumes they have no part in generating or maintaining the problem. As an identified patient, the individual has a difficult time knowing what aspects of behavior are self-owned, for which the individual is responsible, and what parts of interaction are family-owned and thus the responsibility of others. Blame by others often becomes self-blame. Energy that might otherwise be spent for developmental and emotional growth instead becomes invested in establishing ownership of actions, sorting out contradictory messages, and struggling with the blame for the family's overall ineffectiveness.

The psychological cost to the family of identifying or silently electing one member to work out conflict or express family feeling is that such activity precludes the opportunity to work things out more directly and transfers the responsibility for actions and interactions from the family itself to individual members or to outsiders. Thus, the family loses the opportunity to gain skill, enhance their abilities in problem solving and conflict management, and deepen their emotional involvement. In a large sense, the adults in Allison's family (parents and grandparents) were the source of and had responsibility for the feelings, thoughts, and disagreements; however, relationships were founded on contradictions, deceptions, and lack of honesty—within the family and between family units. Rather than confront the inconsistencies, deceptions, and emotional dishonesty, Allison's parents attempted unsuccessfully to ignore the contradictions, to pretend that they did not exist. However, the tension created soon manifested itself, first in Allison and finally in all family members. Allison's problems initially became the focus of attention for a period and diverted the parents' energies from dealing more directly with one another, with the marriage relationship, and with the interactions that grew out of that relationship. However, as the cost of their avoidance began to mount, namely, sleeplessness, irritability, general distractibility, and family disorder, they were forced to seek outside help. Although the problem was clearly a "family problem," Allison was elected (unintentionally) to represent the family as the identified patient.

Making one family member carry the blame or responsibility for family effectiveness decreases individual growth potential, diminishes the family's opportunity to share in the family growth process, and robs the family of the opportunity to develop and use the resources within the family system, resources that aid the family in fulfilling obligations and participating in activities that facilitate effective outcomes and contribute to fuller family relationships.

Participation in activities that facilitate effective functioning can be observed and evaluated in terms of overall family mental health. Such evaluations are based on observations of the family's ability to engage in activities essential to group functioning, family interaction, and individual development within family systems. These activities represent both parameters of family effectiveness as a system and areas of assessment in terms of overall family strength and weakness. Although these criteria will be discussed separately and in detail, it must be remembered that it is the overall pattern or organization of all activities and abilities within the family system that is most indicative of the family's overall system capabilities. The abilities themselves reflect and are influenced by past situations, family history, individual asset and liability, geographical location, cultural embeddedness, and social setting—many of the same factors that shape the family communication process. Final judgments involve an assessment of patterns of actions and interactions manifested in different situations, as well as an evaluation of the contextual factors that influence a family's ability to fully engage in activities essential to overall functioning.

The following discussion focuses on activities that are necessary strengths for a family system in order to interact meaningfully, grow productively, and manage its affairs. The patterns that evolve from such activities can be used as criteria to assess basic system effectiveness, with particular reference to systems that are historically connected, emotionally bonded, and human centered. Basic characteristics that any system must possess to remain operative are information exchange, productivity, the ability to create an atmosphere conducive to growth and expansion, and a mechanism whereby disagreements can be aired and resolved. These characteristics, in terms of family systems, are: information processing, decision making, emotional atmosphere, conflict management, and productivity and change.

## FAMILY SYSTEM

### Information processing

Information processing is the gathering and use of information in order to make the best decisions possible. How any family goes about making decisions—in childrearing, problem solving, setting priorities, and so forth—will be in many ways reflective of the nature of information sought and the quality of the resources utilized.

Information sought by families generally falls into two categories: information that supports what is already known and information that challenges what is being considered. Families who characteristically seek only information supportive of what is already known (from friends, family members, or ministers) are selective about where they get their information and often make limited use of resources that will challenge or question the options the family has chosen. Territorial behavior may be restrictive in such families; communication styles are autocratic. Often, the family or someone in the family has already made the decision and merely goes through the motions of gathering data. Information sought is supportive and the resources used are limited, often known to the family, and ones on which the family may be highly dependent. Information gathering and resource utilization of this nature are narrow and reflect a lack of flexibility and openness on the part of the family system. Such family systems may be seen by outsiders as clannish, fanatical, old-fashioned, or loners. However, many families use such forms of information seeking and resource dependence without being actively aware that they do.

Conversely, families who tend to seek a variety of information, both supportive and that which may challenge or suggest alternative outcomes, also tend to use a wide range of resources: friends, stangers, clinicians, educators, journals, ministers, and so forth. Territorial behavior is expansive, and communication patterns are democratic or situationally flexible. Such families seek advice, education, counsel, and information from resources external to their own system, weigh the merits of such information, and consider those aspects that are helpful to productive outcomes. Information is not accepted simply because it supports or rejects or because it does not support any one position that the family may be considering. Flexibility is also shown by a self-awareness of the family's abilities and limitations, with outside assistance being sought not only for information but for actual help and guidance where needed. These families can be contrasted with families who rarely use outside sources because of failure to recognize their own limitations or needs for assistance or because they engage in absolute dependence on one outside resource for all information, assistance, clarification, suggestion, and so on.

Families who characteristically seek and use a wide range of resources are described by others as having a sense of openness and curiosity about the world around them. The security of their emotional bonds permits expansive boundaries and social receptivity to others. Community relations are good, and there is openness to others. Outsiders are welcomed and the boundaries of the family are permeable, in marked contrast to closed families, in which outsiders are seen as unwelcome intruders and potential threats. Many people become involved with family systems only to find themselves unwelcomed outsiders for the duration of the relationship.

Although most families fall somewhere between the two extremes of information gathering and resource utilization, families develop patterns that reflect a preference for either selective information seeking and narrowed range of resources or divergent information seeking and a wider range of resources. Occasionally, a family will appear to use a wide range of resources but in most cases seek information of a limited nature, chiefly of a convergent or supportive nature. Communication networks, territorial behavior, and information seeking within the family system are all interrelated.

Questions regarding the information-using ability of families are: To whom does the family turn for information? To what extent is information supportive of what is already known? To what extent does information sought represent a challenge or raise further questions? What is the chain of information seeking (one main person or all participate) within the family? What kinds of resources are sought, for what purposes? What kind of help is the family willing to seek and accept? Is the family an active seeker of information or a passive recipient? Does the family appear self-reliant or totally dependent on others? Does the family seek help that dominates or assists their attempts at independence and growth? The information network can be described with regard to internal characteristics of the family as well as external with regard to community involvement and social interdependence.

The nature of the family system's information seeking and pattern of communication will be reflected in the quality of decisions derived through the decision-making process.

## Decision making and implementation

Decision making is the process whereby a family gathers data, mobilizes resources, and obtains opinions of and participation by family members on a particular issue or action. The decision-making process involves a technique of information gathering, a style of communication, social receptivity, and territorial expansiveness. Essential components of effective decision making are full participation by members, decision reached by consensus, and culmination in an activity that serves to carry out the decision made. Families make daily decisions in problem solving, allotment of time, and use of leisure, as well as decisions carried out over longer periods of time, as in childrearing, education and spiritualization of members, financial investments, and design and use of family space and resources. In making daily and long-term decisions, the family system develops patterns of making and carrying out decisions. The methods used to make decisions will affect and be influenced by the emotional atmosphere and productivity of the family system.

Decision making that leads to effective outcomes and satisfaction among members is generally characterized by patterns that are organized and flexible, seek input from all involved, are people centered as well as task oriented, exhibit strong but fair leadership, have support and active followers, and include a plan for carrying out the decision. Although leadership does exist within the process, different family members may assume the responsibility for leadership depending on the nature of the decision to be made. Regardless of who assumes leadership responsibility, an effective decision-making process requires support among family members for the person in that position. The roles assumed by family members in their information-seeking activities are similar to those assumed in decision making. Other activities and responsibilities are assumed by family members based on family need, individual and situational demand, and ability or talent. Whereas all members, for example, may gather information, offer input, and make suggestions, it is generally the responsibility of adults or more experienced members to see that the final decision made is helpful and considerate of all involved. Although a consensus is sought from members with regard to the final decision, members with greater experience and ability generally carry more influence and assume more responsibility for the overall process and final outcome. As members gain in experience and ability, influence increases and more responsibility can be assumed. Full participation generally depends on ability, willingness, knowledge about the issue at hand, age, and experience. Age and experience particularly add to member influence in the family system in which the decision-making process culminates in effective actions and high member satisfaction. Cooperation and compromise are the rule rather than the exception; overall style is democratic and inclusive. Decisions by consensus rather than majority rule are characteristically more effective.

Conversely, decision-making processes that lead to less than effective outcomes or fail to result in any constructive action tend to be characterized by fixed rather than flexible patterns, involve passive rather than active participation by members, demonstrate lack of balance between task-oriented and people-centered concerns, include little or no input from outside resources, reflect limited input from family members with one or two members controlling overall process, and generally fail to develop a plan for carrying out decisions. Member satisfaction with process and outcomes in such families is generally low. Stylistically, such processes either are marked by rigid patterns of control by a few or lack organization altogether. Members of such families are generally locked into traditional sex- or role-defined positions: for example, children should be seen, not heard; only men are heads of households; and women are followers, not leaders. The entire family may be dependent on one or two members who assume an information-filtering role and maintain rather tight control over the actual decision-making process. Final outcomes are the autocratic decision of one or two members, with other members often unaware that a final decision has been made. For example, a major purchase may be made, rules developed, curfews set, and priorities established, all without the participation and input of other family members. Lack of awareness and participation by those affected also decreases the probability that members will support or successfully carry out decisions. More attention may be paid to task completion, with less concern for people's feelings. Consensus within the family system is less important than getting the job done. There is a sense that one or two members somehow know what is best for others; these members often act without informing others. Community relations are generally weak, and utilization of outside resources is often lacking.

Decisions made do not always culminate in decisions carried out. Failure to take action following decision making can be attributed to a variety of causes in addition to those mentioned above; the most frequent is the lack of a plan to carry out the decision made. For example, many families decide to spend more time together, spend less money, watch less television, raise children, have a good marriage, communicate more, or be more open, without developing a concrete plan for carrying out the decisions. Lack of resources, whether physical or financial; limited skill or ability; failure to establish a timetable; inability to delegate specific assignments within the family; lack of priority setting; failure to establish an alternative plan; or failure to recognize family limitations may result in failure to develop plans for implementing decisions that the family makes. All contribute to the failure to carry out decisions made. Making decisions, an important part of the total decision-making process, may be negated by the family's inability to develop a plan for implementation.

### Emotional tenor

Another important ingredient in decision making and implementation is the emotional atmosphere of the family system in which the decision is made. The ability to create an emotional tenor that is warm, accepting, and honest is an extremely important strength for a family system to have.

"Emotional tenor" refers to the emotional environment or psychological atmosphere present in and created by the family system. It will reflect the nature of the bonding between family members—cold or warm, close or distant, honest or dishonest, authentic or manipulative—as well as the emotional climate—other- or self-centered, conditional or unconditional, contradictory or congruent, one of expressed or unexpressed messages. The ability to establish a positive emotional environment is essential to effective family interaction. Ingredients of a positive emotional environment include warmth, tenderness, and openness; consistency within communications; and overall emotional honesty.

Emotional honesty involves an earnest attempt to relate to others what one is feeling and thinking and how one feels in response to others. Because of the risks involved in disclosing oneself to others, there must be an atmosphere within the family of acceptance and trust—an emotional tone that flows out of the bonding within the family system. Conveying messages that are congruent and noncontradictory is also important.

Contradictory messages involve feeling one way and acting another or saying one thing and doing another. The atmosphere created is confusing and potentially harmful in terms of the emotional development of those involved. Congruency comes, not necessarily from doing or being the same day in and day out, but from the fact that what one says is supported by what one does, that what one feels is revealed in what one says and does. Congruency stems from actions that substantiate verbal messages, from verbal messages that support or are supported by facial expression and body posture. The image that others perceive is balanced and orderly, with harmony between parts (words, actions, and feelings) of the message.

Where the emotional environment is characterized by emotional dishonesty and contradictory messages, the emotional tenor will be uncertain and nonsupportive. Family interaction will reflect that lack of support, and individuals within the family unit will be unsure of their worth as family members. Relationships may tend to be cautious, partially honest, tenuous, or manipulative as members attempt unsuccessfully to make their needs and feelings known to others. Self doubt and lack of trust in others are fostered by such emotional environments.

Supportive emotional tenor involves not only emotional honesty and consistency in messages, but also the physical expression of support. Families who use physical touch, comfort, and verbal statements of intimacy—sexual and nonsexual—provide concrete evidence of family support for one another. These families can be contrasted with noncontact families, in which members, because of a lack of evidence, are never really certain of their worth; their contribution to the family is never fully clear.

A supportive emotional tenor allows for emotional expression and involvement that are appropriate to age and experience. Children give love to parents as children to adults. Parents give love to one another as adult to adult, parent to parent. Children also give love to and receive love from one another. Children are not expected to give adult love to parents, as is often the case in families where abuse occurs; nor is one adult expected to provide childlike love for another adult. A supportive emotional tenor is not only supportive of psychological and social needs for growth but protective against excessive demands that might be placed on any one member, whose age or experience may be insufficient.

Where the emotional tenor is supportive, affection is not withheld or used as a means of getting others to do things, as in the carrot and donkey syndrome described in an earlier chapter, nor is love used as a lever to form alliances within the family system, such as those that form the basis of attachments between members of many divorced families. Understanding is more important than control; actualization of human qualities is more important than goal attainment or material gain; mistakes by others are not taken as personal failures by parents or older siblings; and differences as well as similarities are valued and encouraged among family members.

Individuation, or the process whereby the individual develops as a person separate from, yet a part of, the family system, is encouraged by the family system that strives for mental health and sociopsychological effectiveness. The emotional tenor encourages separateness as well as togetherness. The effective family system is not threatened by individual efforts to establish uniqueness and does not consider itself a failure if all members do not think alike and act alike. Differences in opinion, attitude, and action are encouraged.

Support and encouragement of individual members by the family unit are essential in order that differences as well as similarities may be revealed. Similarities are often revealed through closeness and shared intimacy; differences are revealed through disagreements and conflicts: both are essential to family growth and individual development. Allowing disagreements and supporting conflict probably constitute one of the more difficult tasks confronting the family system. Ability to discuss and incorporate those differences is another essential characteristic of the effective family.

**Conflict management**

The recognition of areas of difference and disagreement and problem solving in those areas constitute conflict management. An emotional climate that provides for emotional honesty and consistent communication will also permit and encourage the expression of individual differences in opinion, belief, feeling, and action. Essential to expression of differences are the ability and willingness to negotiate compromise and to resolve conflicts that may grow out of such differences between subsystems within the family system.

In settings where honesty and openness in communication are possible and encouraged, a natural outcome will be that not everyone will think, act, or feel the same. As differences emerge, the family system must consider how those differences are to be incorporated into family life, that is, what compromises will be necessary in order that individuation can be encouraged and family integrity maintained at the same time.

The difficulty that most families have in incorporating differences and negotiating compromise stems from the belief that conflict is bad, that differences are indicative of family failure. Disagreements and arguments, which are natural by-products of individuality, are therefore discouraged, ignored, or actively suppressed. Such families believe that total agreement and harmony are the characteristics of a "healthy" or "good" family. Lack of total agreement and the appearances of differences within the family system are taken by many families as a sign of personal failure and family inadequacy. Although differences undoubtedly exist in such families, the lack of toleration prevents the expression of disagreements in ways conducive to their resolution. Inability to allow for differences makes it necessary for individuals within such families to either conform, compromise, or leave the family setting altogether. The increasing trend toward divorce and incidence of runaways may be indicative of lack of toleration in relationships and family systems for individual differences. Where self-survival and individual expression are issues, individuals may choose to leave family systems rather than compromise in ways that often lead to physical illness, emotional liability, or psychological harm.

Where differences are encouraged and disagreements tolerated, family interaction is generally rich and individual participation is high. Mechanisms are developed by such families (discussion, family conferences) by which members can make opinions known and differences felt. Although conflict may be predictably evident with regard to issues such as sex, politics, and religion, differences of opinion are not taken as signs of failure or indicative of family disintegration. Harmony, in the sense of total agreement, is not as essential as the ability to listen to and perceive the divergent ideas, feelings, and opinions of various family members. Harmony *is* important in the sense that consistency exists between what is said and what is done, between what is felt and what is expressed, and between what is heard and what is perceived. Harmony between family members or within the family system in terms of attitudes, opinions, or actions is not equivalent to stability, nor is conflict a sign of dysfunction. Families who are able to let conflict emerge, who seek to understand rather than persuade or control, and who attempt to settle differences openly tend to be more effective and to make more satisfactory decisions in the long run. Compromise, negotiation, and flexibility within the family system are necessary not only for resolving differences but for coping with change as well.

Skills in conflict management go hand in hand with flexibility in providing for individual differences; mechanisms for emotional support and expression go hand in hand with mechanisms for expression of disagreement and dissatisfaction; emotional support and expressed differences contribute to more effective use of internal and external resources and thus more satisfactory decision making. Effective decision making is an essential component of a family's productivity and ability to cope with social, cultural, and familial change. Productivity and coping with change are activities essential to effective family functioning.

**Productivity and change**

"Productivity" refers to the ability to set goals, establish priorities, and carry out family tasks. "Change" is the concomitant ability to alter plans, reorder priorities, and reestablish goals with regard to personal need and situational demand. The adaptability of the family system is reflected in its productivity—financial, social, and emotional—and its ability to change when faced with circumstances that demand alteration in family interaction, productivity, emotional states, or social organization. The ability to give up old ways and try new ones requires flexibility. The ability to assess a situation as being harmful or a goal as being unattainable requires objectivity and the ability to compromise. The ability to recognize that priorities may need to be reordered requires not only flexibility but self-examination as well. Negotiation is an essential process in a family's productivity, and ability to change is vital to survival and adaptability.

Areas of productivity in which family system must demonstrate skill include childrearing, job acquistion and advancement, economic security, social status, education of members, individual growth and development, and religious education. To be socially and psychologically effective, the family system must be able to assess the resources necessary to achieve goals and alter priorities in line with resources. Goals set should reflect the resources available and the priorities established. Reasonableness of goals, timetables for achieving goals, and strengths and weaknesses in relation to goals must also be assessed.

The ability to flow with changing times—adapting behavior, reassessing goals and priorities, examining beliefs and values with regard to current developments, and altering those priorities in light of family growth, individual development, and situational demand—is similarly important for effective families. A family that lacks flexibility and adaptability runs the risk of extinguishing itself or perpetuating its own rigidity. Members are often silently rebellious, consciously waiting for the opportunity to show their rebellion or to leave the situation.

Change and adaptability are particularly necessary for families in which the expectation within the family is at odds with the social and cultural expectation outside the family, with which family members come into frequent contact. Religious and ethnic groups whose family members come into daily contact with outsiders must somehow come to grips with the discrepancies that exist between beliefs, values, and life styles within the family and outside the family. Where there is lack of adaptability or inability to negotiate compromises, family members either will be defensive with outsiders or will be forced to choose between discrepant ways of life. Failure to recognize and somehow cope with differences on the part of the family system will force individuals within that system to make decisions, cope with changes, and adapt to differences on their own.

When there are growth spurts among family members either in age, education, or experience, the family will need to incorporate those changes into the overall scheme of family life. Where there is an overall inability or lack of willingness on the part of the family system to adopt changes or incorporate individual differences, the likelihood that family structure will alter in response to personal need or situational demand will be high. Family structure is generally a response to personal need and is subject to change when those personal needs change. Similarly, where family structure is a result of situational pressures, the structure may alter when the situation changes. Structure in itself cannot be taken as a determinant of family mental health but is one factor among other factors that influence family interaction and individual development, as was illustrated in Allison's family. Therefore, family structure is subject to change just as other organizational and system structures are subject to change as needs and demands change. Divorce, separation, single parenthood, coupling without children, and communal families are all alternate family structures whose effectiveness will largely reflect the same abilities and activities as in the traditional family structure. Essential to any family group, regardless of structure, is the need to process information, make decisions, balance task demands and personal concerns, express emotion, support conflict, and be productive and cope with change. Flexibility, compromise, and adaptability are qualities the effective family must have in order to engage in activities essential to family growth and development.

The following outline can be used to synthesize data gathered regarding a family system's ability to (1) seek and process information; (2) make and implement decisions; (3)develop a positive, supportive emotional tenor; (4)

recognize and support individuation, differences, and conflict; and (5) be productive with regard to family goals and flexible in light of personal need and situational demand. It is important to keep in mind that it is the *pattern* of these activities and overall ability of the family that will reflect the mental health of the family system and personal effectiveness of any one member. Weakness in one area or inordinate strength in another cannot be used alone as a measure of the family's effectiveness. Other areas that must be considered include: individual deficits and strengths, particularly with regard to physical or developmental weaknesses; ordinal position of family members; people-centered or task orientation of family unit; social and cultural context; and geographical and environmental conditions.

**Family mental health checklist**

*General*

Individual deficits: social, motor, intellectual, physical, or developmental
Family constellation: ordinal position (sibling order)
Sociocultural context: norms, practices, and beliefs specific to cultural, ethnic, or religious group
Environmental conditions: home, neighborhood, and community

| | |
|---|---|
| *Information seeking* | |
| ☐ Extensive resources | ☐ Limited resources |
| ☐ Divergent information | ☐ Convergent information |
| ☐ Independent | ☐ Dependent |
| ☐ Flexible | ☐ Inflexible |
| ☐ Family, friends, professionals | ☐ Family only |
| *Decision making* | |
| ☐ Full participation | ☐ Limited participation |
| ☐ Organized | ☐ Chaotic |
| ☐ Flexible | ☐ Inflexible |
| ☐ People centered task | ☐ Task *or* people |
| ☐ Shared leadership | ☐ Autocratic or no leadership |
| ☐ Consensus of opinion | ☐ Persuasion or demand |
| ☐ Follow through | ☐ No plan of action |
| ☐ High member satisfaction | ☐ Low satisfaction |
| ☐ Resources evaluated | ☐ Little evaluation |
| *Emotional tenor* | |
| ☐ Warm, close | ☐ Cold, distant |
| ☐ Authentic | ☐ Manipulative |
| ☐ Honest | ☐ Dishonest |
| ☐ Other-focused | ☐ Self-centered |
| ☐ Unconditional | ☐ Conditional |
| ☐ Congruent | ☐ Contradictory |
| ☐ Supportive | ☐ Nonsupportive |
| ☐ Physical expression | ☐ Unexpressed feeling |
| ☐ Age/experience appropriate | ☐ Misuse and abuse |
| ☐ Understanding | ☐ Control |
| ☐ Individuation encouraged | ☐ Individuation a threat |
| ☐ Differences encouraged | ☐ Similarity pushed |
| ☐ Conflict supported | ☐ Conflict suppressed |

*Conflict management*

| | |
|---|---|
| □ Individuation supported | □ Individuation unsupported |
| □ Balance (individual and family goal) | □ Imbalance |
| □ Conflict as positive | □ Conflict as negative |
| □ Disagreements allowed | □ Disagreements suppressed |
| □ Cooperation-compromise | □ Cooption-control |
| □ Negotiation | □ Persuasion |
| □ Family conference | □ Closed-door discussion |
| □ Flexibility | □ Inflexibility |
| □ Productive | □ Nonproductive |

*Productivity and change*

| | |
|---|---|
| □ Set goals | □ Goals unclear |
| □ Establish priorities | □ Priorities unidentified |
| □ Family tasks | □ Individual pleasure |
| □ Resources adequate | □ Resources inadequate |
| □ Personal needs considered | □ Lack of consideration |
| □ Situation demands included | □ Lack of assessment |
| □ Adaptability | □ Rigidity |
| □ Periodic reevaluation | □ Little or no evaluation |
| □ Positive actions | □ Emotional reactions |
| □ Alter goals | □ Goals firm—achievable or not |
| □ Reestablish priorities | □ Rigid priorities |

## SUMMARY

Family mental health is a judgment made about a family's ability to participate in activities essential to individuation and integration of family members within the family system and to individuation and integration of the family as a system within a larger world of systems (family, community, religious, and societal). Just as the individual is, in Drazin's words, the stem through which history flows, the individual family system is the conduit through which and by which not only family heritage is perpetuated but also social, cultural, and ethnic values and beliefs. As an active, living conduit, the family must be capable of receiving, translating, and passing on its historical responsibilities; receiving and fulfilling contemporary responsibilities; and planning for an emotionally secure future—for itself and for its individual members. Therefore, the family must be capable of selectively using information, making decisions, setting priorities, humanizing and spiritualizing members, and of coping with change. The more capable the family is in these essential activities, the more effective the family system and the more useful its members will be (as products of a viable system).

Judgments made regarding the overall mental health, or effectiveness, of a family system must also involve consideration not only of those factors (social, cultural, and environmental) that influence the family's ability to fully utilize resources and develop internal capabilities but also of strengths and weaknesses of individual members (developmental, intellectual, and physical). The overall profile that the family presents, under varying conditions, will be most indicative of family effectiveness. Individual effectiveness will in many ways reflect the nature of the family system from which the individual originates: what affects the individual affects the system, and what alters the system will have impact on individual members.

The entry point through which an outsider (therapist, counselor, or nurse) gains access to the system may influence the judgments and evaluations which that outsider makes about the mental health of the system and individuals within the system. Unless care is exercised, one may select, or the family may have selected, an individual as the identified patient instead of taking the broader view of the family as identified patient. Viewing the family as a system means seeing that, although each individual member contributes to family make-up, it is the family's overall activities and abilities that in the final analysis must be evaluated in terms of effectiveness. Lack of effectiveness is expressed in altered family ability rather than in individual pathological state. Taking a composite family profile, as described in later chapters, is essential not only in accurately describing family as a system, but as a preliminary step in assessing and evaluating family mental health as well.

**STUDY QUESTIONS**

1. Define family effectiveness, and describe the five indices that can be used to assess effectiveness.
2. Describe patterns of behavior that would characterize an effective and an ineffective family. In what ways are the families alike, and in what ways are they different?
3. Describe information processing and its relationship to decision making.
4. Discuss ordinal position and family expectation regarding individual performance.
5. Discuss ways in which conflict can be used to enhance family effectiveness.
6. Discuss the concept of individuation and its relationship to family productivity and change.
7. Discuss the relationship between emotional tenor and family effectiveness.

**EXERCISES**

**Recall family profile**

In these exercises you will function as a passive observer who relies heavily on recall as well as observation. This will set the stage for comparison with your role, in situations of lesser familiarity, as a participant observer whose goals are clearer and whose appraisal is more systematic. Without interviewing or active participation of family members, complete the following:

1. Describe the community (environment) in which your family resides. For example, is it rural or urban, large or small? What kind of government does it use (mayor or city manager)? What is the nature of business (industrial, commercial, or agricultural)? How accessible is the community by various modes of

transportation (bus, train, plane, or trucking)? What is the ethnic, religious, and cultural make-up of the community? What boundary lines can you find between groups (streets, railroad tracks, buildings, and so forth)? What health facilities or professionals are present in the community (clinics, hospitals, or private practitioners)?
2. Describe the nature of resources utilized by your family (own, extended family, other relatives, friends, neighbors, clergy, or health professionals). This can be initiated by recalling how the family celebrates its good times (birthday, birth, or promotion) and copes with its bad times (illness, injury, death, or disappointments).
3. Describe the nature of decision making in your family. *Hint:* You will generally find that the *kind* of decision to be made (financial, personal, educational, or religious) will influence the nature of the decision-making process. Traditional families, for example, leave financial or economic decisions to heads of households, generally men; decisions regarding children, home, and caretaking are left to mothers and daughters. The less traditional family generally shares more of the responsibility. Note participation in terms of age, sex, and experience.
4. Describe the emotional tenor of your family. Note congruency, emotional honesty, supportive nature, and opportunity for individuation. In what ways are emotions expressed?
5. Describe the nature of disagreements and differences within your family. How are they tolerated? Around what issues is conflict or disagreement most likely to occur?
6. Describe your family at five-year intervals: five years ago, five years from now. How is the family similar to or different from other families you know (socially, financially, materially, educationally, and spiritually)? What would you change in your family if you could? What goals has your family set for itself? Which were reached? Which were not reached? What change has your family undergone in the last five to ten years (birth of children, job change, residence change, death of close friend or relative)?
7. Using the profile categories (checklist) provided at the conclusion of the chapter, describe your family.

## BIBLIOGRAPHY

Barry, M.: Feedback concepts in family therapy, Perspect. Psychiatr. Care **10**(4):183, 1972.

Kelly, J.: Make conflict work for you, Harvard Business Rev., July-August 1970, p. 103.

Laing, R. D.: The politics of the family, New York, 1972, Vintage Books, Inc.

Lange, J.: Families in turmoil, Menninger Perspect. **4**(1):14, 1973.

Maddison, D.: Crises in the family—the family in crises, Ment. Health Australia **5**(1):4, 1972.

Murrell, S. A., and Stachowiak, J. G.: Consistency, rigidity and power in the interaction patterns of clinic and non-clinic families, J. Abnorm. Psychol. **72:**265, 1967.

Nagaraya, J.: Family dynamics and mental health of a child, Child Psychiatry Q. **3**(4):7, 1970.

Sedgwick, R.: The family as a system; a network of relationships, J. Psychiatr. Nurs., March-April 1974, p. 17.

Sedgwick, R.: *Family mental health; a social psychological approach.* In Kneisl, C. R., and Wilson, S. H., editors: Perspectives in psychiatric nursing; issues and trends, vol. 1, St. Louis, 1976, The C. V. Mosby Co.

Toman, W.: Family constellation; its effects on personality and social behavior, New York, 1969, Springer Publishing Co., Inc.

Chapter 8

# THE INDIVIDUAL AND FAMILY MENTAL HEALTH

## ROLE OF THE INDIVIDUAL

Whereas the nature of the contribution that individuals make to family relationships is influenced by factors such as age, sex, and physical attributes, there are essentially six ways in which individuals make their presence known and their participation felt in the family system. These six avenues of individual subsystem expression are in the capacity of (1) link, (2) translator-interpreter, (3) source-resource, (4) agent, (5) victim, and (6) index.

### Link

The individual may serve as a link in a chain—connecting past with future, present with past, family with other systems, and family with itself. It is through individuals that family bonding is established; linkages are formed between parent and parent, parent and child, adult and adult, child and child, and so forth. As an essential unit in bonding relationships, the individual is in a position to influence the nature of emotional connectedness within the family, as well as between generations. As described earlier, bonding relationships between Larry and his grandfather resulted in negative as well as positive outcomes for both Larry and his family. Larry was the link that brought the grandfather more actively into the family system and, finally, into other social systems as well.

Individuals are historical links that carry the past into the present. Genetically, the individual transmits physical and mental characteristics of the family. The outcomes can only be as good or bad as the source from which the characteristics are derived. In that sense, the qualities possessed by the individual as a link are reflections of qualities of the larger chain of people with whom the individual is connected. Genetic transmissions alone, however, do not fully describe a person's characteristics, for the individual is also a link between the family and the environment, between the family and social systems, between the family and its religious beliefs, and between the family and its values.

As a link having social, environmental, religious and psychological connectedness, individuals will influence and be influenced by those points of contact. Where there is poverty, environmental deprivation, social abuse, or religious fanaticism, for example, influences on the individual may be harmful. The burden on the individual of connecting disordered or deficit systems can result in individual stress and ultimate dysfunction. There are instances in which social systems use individuals as tools for financial or political gain. Small children, handicapped individuals, and the elderly, in particular are targets of such abuse.

Where the contacts are strong and positive, the interactional outcomes will reflect this. Individuals with such connectedness will have strong sense of their importance as bridges between systems. Where the worth of individuals as bridges between systems is recognized and valued, individuals will be more apt to continue to function in that capacity long after the original family linkages are gone. However, where individuals are not particularly valued as significant links—social, physical, or emotional—individuals will be less likely to establish themselves as positive connections between or within systems. Children of divorce, for example, may view themselves as inadequate linkages in the family and may hesitate to reestablish that function following divorce of parents or in future relationships outside the family system. Broken linkages leave vulnerable individuals wondering whether the fault is within the linkage or within themselves. Although the entire family system can generally be held responsible for broken linkages, children and naive individuals often assume the responsibility for the break to be entirely their own. Self-blame leaves such individuals doubting their ability to function as links in future systems.

Individuals serve as links between present systems and future family groups. The responsiveness of the system to new links, or members, and the individual's responsiveness to the family system have a bearing on the interactions and relationships. The individual is an essential unit in the communication process. Where the individual is a responsive link in that process, the flow of communication will be smoother and more productive than in the case where the individual is unwilling or unable to reciprocate. Recent studies indicate that some newborn infants are less responsive than others. Where the new parent is attempting to establish a linkage with an unresponsive newborn, frustration and disappointment may occur. In emotional bonding as well as in the communication process, there must be a willingness and an ability to engage in reciprocal interchanges. Essential to this reciprocity is the individual's ability to function as a translator and interpreter.

**Translator-interpreter**

Individuals as translators and interpreters bring to realization through performance the spoken and unspoken implied expectations and desires of the family. They convert nonverbal messages to verbal communication, verbal communication to action, and give meaning to the entire process.

Through individual activities of translation and interpretation, the family exchanges information through the use of commonly understood symbols. In a very general sense, sociocultural symbols must be translated from larger sociocultural systems by the family. Specifically, family messages (gestures, habit, words, and body posture) must be translated and interpreted by individuals within that system as well.

Through translation and interpretation, the family is able to establish a reservoir of meaning and shared knowledge from which to draw in the process of communicating with one another. Short-cuts in communication can be taken where such reservoirs exist. The gesture becomes known, the mood becomes predictable, the commonly used expression is well understood. Symbols used by the effective family are clear and well understood by the family system. Where symbols are used inconsistently or unpredictably, the communication system becomes chaotic and contradictory. Symbols used in the communication process are derived from the historical network of the family, from the sociocultural network in which the family is embedded, and from the contemporary network of the family. The more widely understood the symbols by the users, the better able family members are to make needs, opinions, and feelings known.

As translator-interpreters, individuals are influenced by internal needs,

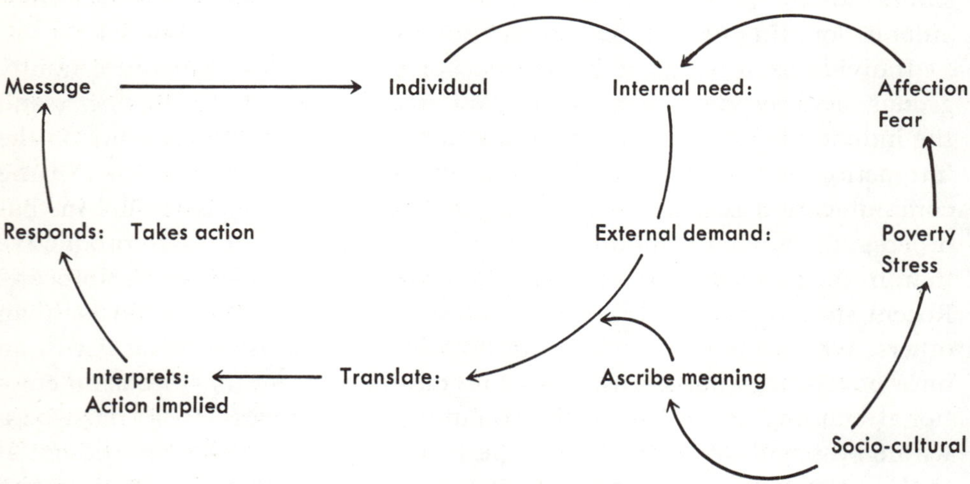


**Fig. 1.** Communication process: examples of individual as translator-interpreter.

external demands, and sociocultural context. The translator-interpreter activity is diagramed in Fig. 1.

Messages sent can be in the form of word, gesture, body posture, facial expression, or some combination of these. The source of messages in Fig. 1 is a family member or members. The individual receives the message through sensory channels: sight, sound, smell, and touch. The message will be filtered through and influenced by the internal state of the individual, physical as well as emotional. As the message is filtered through the person's internal state, external demands will be influencing the individual's reception as well as interpretation of the message. As will be seen in Chapter 9, in cases of heightened stress the information being processed by the family member will be diminished according to the severity of stress.

Meaning is ascribed to the message through the process of translation: the individual takes the words, gestures, and signals and, from experience and according to ability, applies *meaning*. The meaning that an individual attributes to the message is an extremely important component of the communication process. Raised fist may mean anger; furrowed brow may mean worry or concern; loud voice may mean fear. The meaning ascribed is a product of the internal state of the individual, the external demands of the moment, sociocultural context, and the historical meaning that the family generally attributes to such messages. As discussed in Chapter 6, attribution of intent, or what the person *expects* or thinks the message is about, has as much to do with individual interpretation as does the message intended by the sender. After meaning is ascribed, an action is implied. Raised fist—run; furrowed brow—show concern; loud voice—seek protection.

The final response made grows out of the interpretation and the action implied by the interpretation. That response by the individual then becomes a message in and of itself that is received and interpreted by other family members. As individuals send, receive, translate, modify, interpret, and respond to messages, each adds to the communication process. The greater the discrepancy between internal states of individuals within the same family, the greater the differences in the final interpretation and response.

Family members often operate under different external demands (school, work, marriage) as well, and these differences shape internal states and influence the overall communication process.

Where family members act contrary to their internal state, for example, feeling sad but acting happy or feeling anger and pretending indifference, contradictory and confusing messages are sent to other family members. Other members will tend to respond out of their own internal states and their perception of the external sets of demands, which include the internal states of others. Where misrepresentation by others occurs, appropriate responses are difficult to determine. As has been pointed out, individuals tend to respond to implied or nonverbal messages as strongly as to spoken messages. When verbal messages do not coincide with their nonverbal counterpart, contradictory and confusing information flows from person to person. Patterns of information exchange tend to be repeated in families as do patterns of emotional bonding and social interaction. Translator-interpreter activities within the family lie at the heart of the communication process and may serve to enhance or retard information exchange.

Another important activity of individuals within the family system is functioning as sources and resources, not only of information but of social, emotional, financial, and psychological inputs as well.

**Source-resource**

As a source of behavior, feeling, and action, individuals serve as models for one another. The individual as source can be a generative force: of energy, love, conflict, money, and information. Individuals may be stabilizers or disrupters, while teaching the same skills to others. As a resource, individuals may offer comfort, understanding, acceptance, support, and safety to other family members. With resources found among individuals within the family system, it is possible to create a full microcosm of society, in which individuals can successfully or unsuccessfully prepare for roles in larger social systems.

Much of what individuals do in larger systems is learned first in the family setting. Where skills are adequate, individuals will tend to think and act with a sense of competence and determination. Where the family is a source of inadequate skills of leadership, support, followership, financial management, and individual achievement, individual behavior in other systems will reflect that lack. When the family encourages and supports risk taking, self-analysis, group cohesion, and individuation and demonstrates the same through action and example, individuals coming from such families gain social and psychological skills for creativity, productivity, and self-acceptance. However, if the family's sources are lacking in example, individuals cannot be expected to demonstrate competence, self-confidence, or social commitments.

In the Halkins family, mentioned in an earlier chapter, the parents demonstrated by example territorial expansion: working outside the home, making new friends, and establishing religious and community ties. However, they expected territorial restrictions from their children. The parents were a source of conflicting messages, doing one thing and expecting another. There was one set of rules for parents and another set for children; however, the parents were unable to clearly differentiate by example the two sets of rules. The children imitated what they saw and paid little attention to what they heard.

The Halkins parents failed to provide an adequate source of modeling for their children. They were also unable to provide resources. There was little support, comfort, understanding, or acceptance on the part of the parents for each other and for their children. Their relationship to their children was similar to the relationships that each parent had had during childhood. Therefore, their own source of learning and their set of resources of emotional bonding were limited, leaving them little in the way of a reservoir to draw on in teaching and providing for their own children.

Children as well as adults can serve as sources and resources. Anyone who acts as a force that generates feeling, thought, energy, action, and information serves as a source within the family. In addition, anyone who responds to others with comfort, support, approval, and acceptance serves as a resource within the family. Resources can be social, emotional, financial, or physical. Where individuals with resources within the family are prohibited from using them, individuals develop skills that are limited. Children who have resources for loving and accepting but who are prevented from giving that love will soon learn to find other ways to make their presence felt and feelings known. Adults who have resources and cannot use them will seek other involvement and avenues of expression. Conflict may occur, lack of understanding may develop, and poor decisions may evolve because of underutilization of family resources.

How individuals develop as resources within the family will influence whether individuals become agents or victims of family systems in the long run. Where the process of individuation is positive, individuals will learn skills of an agent. Where the process of individuation is negative, individuals will learn skills of a victim—without which ineffective families cannot survive.

### Agent

Individuals as agents are people responsible for their acts. Agents are capable of and often take the initiative for producing an effect: for example, gaining territory, acquiring management skills, gathering information, initiating decision making, or making a change. Agents are able, willing, and responsive with regard to their impact on, relationship to, and interactions with other family members and the family system as a whole.

Individuals as agents are the result of a family system in which individual differences are supported and encouraged, where individuals are important to, yet separate from, the family system. Although the family system is totally dependent on the individual for its definition, it is recognized by such families that the individual is capable of survival and function outside the family system as well as within the system. Independence is encouraged; dependence is encouraged only where developmentally appropriate. Where interaction with others is concerned, interdependence rather than dependence is fostered by such a family system.

Where an individual within a family functions as an agent, as well as an interrelated family member, respect and privacy for individual endeavors are provided. The family territory has spaces that belong to individual family members and are not invaded by other members. Similarly, the individual is allowed to have thoughts, feelings, and opinions that may differ from and be in opposition to those of the larger family system and still be accepted. The private throughts and feelings of the family member are not intruded upon without invitation or forewarning.

Individuals acting as agents within the family are essentially advocates of the individual cause within the family stream of activity. Although a family goal might be to receive a college education, an individual agent might push for vocational education when appropriate or desired. The advocate for individuality and self-determination within the family system does not proceed at the the expense of the family system itself, however. Where the individual cause becomes more important than family survival, the individual may be acting as an "agent provocateur."

The agent provocateur is a family member who seems to sympathize with the family, identify with the family cause, act as though family membership is of value but then uses that membership to his or her own advantage. An aspiring executive, struggling medical student, or political aspirant who uses the family to demonstrate stability, gain support and security, or acquire a position and then dumps the family when success is on the horizon is an agent provocateur. A child who uses a parent to gain favors, attention, and privilege and then uses that parent against an estranged spouse is an agent provocateur. A mother who raises a child, only to use that child for financial support and social survival in later years, has acted as an agent provocateur.

A sense of the self as agent is an important outcome of positive relationships within the family system. Where one finds individuals acting in a self-determined, energetic, and responsible manner, family relationships are likely to be positive, warm, supportive, and honest, with individual development and expansion given as much encouragement as family-centered commitments. To be an agent means taking an active position with regard to one's actions and being responsible as the source of one's feelings and thoughts. Whereas an individual as agent recognizes that feelings, thoughts, and desires (internal needs) are influenced and shaped by other people's needs and social expectation (external demand), the final outcome is the choice of the individual. Individuals as agents *act* as if choice is an alternative consistently available to them as individuals as well as family members.

The opposite of being an agent in the family is being a victim. Victims take a passive stance, not only in response to actions within the family, but with regard to individual action taken outside the family as well. The victim acts as though life were directed by sources outside individuals as well as family or social groups; fate is the guide and chance determines the direction. There is little belief in choice, individual assertiveness, and little hope for change. Being an agent is a dominant force in the life of self-directed individuals; being a victim is the dominant force in the life of individuals who are shaped by their families to believe that their greatest contribution is to be a victim or scapegoat of the family system.

**Victim**

A family victim is an individual who is shaped to fill some need of the family. In the process of shaping, individuality and self-determination are sacrificed to the needs of the larger family system. In terms of family dynamics, the victim is a faceless member whose behavior is described not in terms of individual contribution and talent, but in terms of what others in the family feel toward and expect of that member. Victims are created by family systems who fear the process and potentiality of individuals who think and act for themselves. The family victim is frozen into the position of victim in order to maintain a certain situation within the family system.

The process of victimization of family members by the system can be so subtle that it escapes recognition by either the family or outsiders until an internal or external crisis precipitates the surfacing of a family victim. This most frequently occurs as attempts are made by that person to move from the role of victim to that of agent.

In the "only-child family," for example, the child may be set up as the recipient of adult and parental affection, attention, and expectation. Without the child, many families are unable to identify their family characteristics; without the presence of the child, the family, defined by child inclusion, is not a family. As long as the child acts like a child—dependent, passive, directed by adults and parents, and the center of adult attention—family interactions appear smooth and satisfactory: the definition of family is safe. However, when the child becomes an adolescent or young adult with individual thoughts, feelings, and experimental needs, family interaction may become conflictive and disordered. The child may be described as suddenly rebellious, hard to manage, or inconsiderate and may even be labeled "disturbed." What has actually happened is that the young person has begun to experience and strive for individuality, self-direction, and self-experimentation. The child-defined family, however, cannot survive without the child in the role of child, because it is too frightening for the adults to consider themselves in relationship to each other and to a changing and expanding family system.

A family system that sets up individuals to play out roles—father figure, baby, mommy, or helpless member—risks creating victims out of family members; individuals will depend on an unchanging role within the family to ensure identity. There are individuals whose strongest sense of identity is as family member in the family of origin. No other family system quite measures up; no other relationship is as fulfilling; no other social system is quite adequate. Such individuals are never able to see themselves as separate from their first families. They are victims of that system that cannot let them go. Men, women, and children can all become victims of the family process.

The widow who suddenly finds herself alone for the first time in her adult life and who cannot write checks, pay bills, settle debts, make decisions, and assert her individuality has probably been victimized by a relationship whose continuation and success were believed to be related to her dependence and his protection. In a sense, both the man and woman in such situations are victims of a process that made each think that family survival depended on faceless participation by members, regardless of individual need, desire, and ability. Goldberg's excellent book, *Hazards of Being Male* (1976), elucidates the risk that men run when their major contribution to family and society is role bound, disregarding personal preference and individual ability. Many research studies and books describe in some detail detrimental effects of the same process on women.

Perhaps the most cogent evidence of how women are victimized, not only by family but by social systems as well, is the research study by Broverman and associates (1970), in which subjects were asked to describe healthy men, healthy women, and healthy adults. Whereas the healthy man was described as independent, assertive, and decisive, the healthy woman was described as passive, dependent, and indecisive. The same qualities used by subjects to describe the healthy woman were the characteristics those subjects used to describe the unhealthy adult. They apparently believed that for a man to act with compassion, sensitivity, or passivity was to be "sick." Similarly, an independent, assertive, and decisive woman was "sick." Such studies show that men as well as women are victims of old-fashioned social notions of how people are *supposed* to act, regardless of individual ability, interest, and talent. Those same outmoded social expections pervade and influence many family systems, thus creating victims out of what could be productive, happy, emotionally honest family agents.

Adults who are led to believe that they must do certain things in order to fulfill a role and who are unwilling or unable to fulfill such obligations may victimize other family members (as in child abuse or a drinking spouse) or themselves (as in psychosomatic illnesses or emotional depression). Unable to be emotionally honest with themselves and unable to escape their own role as victims, such adults create a system of victims in which to hide and go unchallenged. However, in such families, sooner or later an individual comes along who challenges the role of the family victim, as Donald and Allison did. Such individuals then become representative of the larger problem in the family. As a representative of a "sick" family, such individuals may get labeled as the "patient." The individual is an index of, or signals, what is going on with the rest of the family. It is more accurate to view individual family members as family representatives or indices than to view them as "sick" or deviant.

In the healthy and in the unhealthy family, individual family members reflect, through action and attitude, characteristics of the larger family system. In this capacity, it can be said that individual family members serve as indices to the dynamics of the larger family system.

**Index**

Family members resemble one another—physically, socially, and emotionally. As a group of people bound by history, emotion, space, and common use of language, it may be expected that behavior patterns and social interaction will reflect not only individual qualities but family dynamics as well. Individual family members in their capacity of index reflect through action, gesture, word, body movement, and general communication the dynamics of the family system. The dynamics reflected by individuals will be those which occur and have occurred historically in the family—between members and between family units. Where family dynamics are rigid, contradictory, or exploitative, individual behavior will tend to be closed and manipulative. Where family dynamics are warm, accepting, and consistent, individual behavior will tend to be more open and honest. In the former system, individuals will tend to act like victims; in the latter, individuals will tend to act like agents.

As a guide to family dynamics, the individual can be a good source of information about the family's history as well as the family's present situation. The "old-fashioned" individual, for example, may reflect a historically dependent family that is still being run by a matriarch or patriarch who has been dead for years. In such families, individuals are dominated by the family legacy—social, economic, and emotional. To assert individual wishes or needs is to risk being cut off from the legacy. Such individuals often appear not only old-fashioned but rigid and fearful as well. As a positive index of the past, individuals may take pride in naming, in completing the unfinished task, or in maintaining the family sense of place and direction. Connectedness with the past is maintained through naming or similar goals or professions without the past being dominant, however.

Individual family members exhibit through their sense of emotional connectedness to others the nature of emotional bonding in the contemporary family unit. Where the family attachment is superficial and exploitative, individuals will display lack of trust and inability to establish deep, meaningful relationships with others. The ability to tolerate frustration, disappointment, or failure and the ability to cope with success are generally learned in the family setting.

Two primary examples of individual action and interaction reflecting emotional bonding in the family system are suicide and emotional or physical abuse. The suicide victim often reflects the larger family system's inability to approve, accept, and care for its members. Perhaps because of limited resources, particularly emotional resources, the family system must kill parts of itself in order for the resources to go around. A member is selected who can accomplish the task. In a sense, most cases of suicide are actually family homicides acted out by individual members. Similarly, in emotional and physical abuse of a family member, adult or child, emotional attachment lacks meaning and capability of filling family need. Meaning is found, in a rather twisted sense, through the abuse of one another. In Erikson's words, "To be bad is better than to be nothing at all." The abusive family system will be described in detail in a later chapter. It is worth noting, however, that an individual's fear of closeness, rejection, failure, or success indicates a family system that has not dealt altogether fairly with its members.

Individual intrusiveness or lack of respect for the time and space of others is reflective of the family's use of space. Individuals who do not respect the privacy of others probably did not have personal respect and privacy as members within the family. Where family members' rights are respected, individuals will carry that sense of respect to other systems. Where families encourage territorial maintenance as well as territorial acquisition, individuals will have a sense of caring for persons and property as well as a desire to expand that territory. Family respect of members contributes to self-respect; family consideration of individual time and space encourages respect for the time and space of others. Similarly, if the family internal social and psychological space has been characterized by closeness and intimacy, the interpersonal ability of individual family members will be enhanced. However, where family interaction has been typified by relationships that are public and social, based, for example, on what people will think, individual concern and orientation will reflect this.

Like the emotional network, the communication network of the family will be reflected by individual ability and performance. Individual activity in decoding and coding messages outside the system, for example, in school, will reflect translation and interpretation activities in the family system. The ability to act spontaneously and with enthusiasm is correlated with clear, efficient coding abilities on the part of the individual. Children with perceptual and learning problems at school can generally be found in home situations where messages are decoded, or translated, in confusing and contradictory fashion. Internal needs of the individual and external demands of the situation are difficult and often impossible for the individual with coding problems to distinguish. Just as individual behavior is reflective of family interaction in terms of history, bonding, and territory, individual behavior reflects the family's contemporary concerns and orientations. The family's contemporary concerns can be classified as either person-centered or task-oriented. Person-centered family systems focus on emotional needs, character development, personal expression, and individual development of family members. These concerns will be reflected in emotional bonding, management of intimacy and toleration, and support for individuation within the family system. Task orientation refers to the family's concern for achieving goals, acquiring material possessions and social status, and finding solutions to problems. The first category of concerns focuses on interpersonal needs, whereas the latter category focuses more on acquisitions, achievements, and problems. The latter concerns will be reflected in the family's productivity, concern for work and job, information gathering, and decision making.

Where the family orientation is balanced between performance and people, individuals will tend to be able to balance goals and personal needs. However, when the family's orientation is not balanced, individuals will tend to evaluate themselves in terms of either the job accomplished or the person-centered need filled. Some families are so oriented toward tasks that they measure themselves by materials acquired, goals achieved, or status gained. Character development and other person-centered needs are considered by such families as secondary or unimportant. Conversely, some families are so oriented toward character building and person-centered needs that they measure themselves by emotional expression, experiential encounters, and personal involvement. Personal involvement is given preference over goals and accomplishment. Either extreme is not particularly effective as a well-rounded approach to either getting the job done or developing the character of individuals.

## SUMMARY

Family members' contributions as individuals to the mental health of the family can be described variously by individual function: (1) link that has historical, genetic, social, emotional, and environmental connectedness; (2) translator-interpreter of belief, value, judgment, meaning, and verbal and nonverbal messages and essential link in the communication process; (3) source-resource of behavior, feeling, action, comfort, understanding, acceptance, support, and safety; (4) agent capable of initiating and taking responsibility for acts, with a firm sense of self-worth, competence, and self-determination, interrelated with yet separate from the overall family system; (5) victim frozen into a position, role, or situation in which individuality is sacrificed for family gain or protection; and (6) index who reflects through action, word, gesture, attitude, general behavior, and social interaction the larger system. Family history, emotional bonding, communication patterns, territorial acquisition and management, and contemporary orientation of the family are manifested in individual performance, feeling, and involvement with others.

It should be emphasized that family members may be involved simultaneously in any or all of the above modes of expression and participation in the family system. What generally happens, however, is that over a period of time each particular family system develops shortcuts for arriving at certain interactional outcomes and, in the process of those shortcuts, accustoms various members to participating in only one or two ways. Although such assignments may work in any one family, the individual who enters another family system with a different set of assignments may fail to fit in. A person who predominantly plays the role of translator in one family may be expected to function as agent or link in another family system. Family systems who encourage family members to take on various functions and activities aid those family members in making the transition to other systems, social as well as family, and at the same time enhance their own flexibility and productivity.

**STUDY QUESTIONS**

1. Discuss the importance of subsystem linkages from generation to generation.
2. Describe ways in which subsystems translate cultural heritage into family system expectations and norms.
3. What is the importance of the meaning that subsystems ascribe to messages? How do internal states contribute to meaning?
4. Discuss the importance of modeling within the family system. How does the source-resource ability of subsystems relate to agentry skills?
5. What are the most important ingredients in developing subsystems that are agents? Victims?
6. What is victimization? How does it come about? What are the long-range consequences?
7. In what ways is subsystem suicide an example of family ineffectiveness?

**EXERCISES**

1. Describe ways in which your family members contribute to the process of family through functions of link, translator-interpreter, source-resource, agent, victim, and index.

| | *Mother* | *Father* | *Sister* | *Brother* | *Other family members* |
|---|---|---|---|---|---|
| Link | | | | | |
| Translator-interpreter | | | | | |
| Source-resource | | | | | |
| Agent | | | | | |
| Victim | | | | | |
| Index | | | | | |

2. Describe the ways in which you function in the above named activities. Which functions are less developed than others? What aspects of your individual contribution would you change? (Less victim, more agent, for example.)
3. Are there individual contributions that are lacking in your family? If so, what are they?
4. Which family members' contributions would you alter? In what ways?
5. Which members seem to have the most varied contribution, that is, play the widest assortment of roles? In what ways do age and experience alter that contribution?

**BIBLIOGRAPHY**

Broverman, I., Broverman, D., Clarkson, F., Rosenkrantz, P., and Vogel, S.: Sex role stereotypes and clinical judgments of mental health, J. Consult. Clin. Psychol. **34**:1, 1970.

Caine, L.: Widow, New York, 1974, Morrow and Co.

Friday, N.: My mother, my self, New York, 1977, Delacorte Press.

Goldberg, H.: Hazards of being male, New York, 1976, Signet.

Kappelman, M.: Raising the only child, New York, 1975, E. P. Dutton & Co., Inc.

Sheehy, G.: Passages, New York, 1976, E. P. Dutton & Co., Inc.

Chapter 9

# SOCIETY AND FAMILY MENTAL HEALTH

There are many ways in which the larger set of social systems in which the family system is embedded influences and is influenced by the mental health of the family. Sociocultural influences, for example, aid in shaping the guidelines that the family uses in socializing individuals for their roles in society. Language, common uses of resources, religious preference, selection of schools, location of housing, and the family's choice of shopping centers are influenced by the social and cultural environments of which the family is a part.

## SOCIAL FORCES

### Technological developments

Changes that occur in the larger set of social systems most certainly influence family functioning. The rapidity of development of technically sophisticated devices, for the home and the office, has provided individuals with opportunities and conveniences unparalleled in history. With increased opportunity, there is increased sense of choice—of job or career, of marriage partner, of life style, of number and sex of children, of means of transportation, of kind of housing, of physical location, of mobility, of friends, and of sociocultural systems in which to work and live.

Change and its consequences are less predictable than ever before in the history of the family. As an open system, the family is particularly vulnerable to the influence and lack of predictability in the larger set of social systems. Many of the technological, industrial, and scientific advancements have been made without consideration of the interrelated system nature of society, environment, and family. The same techniques that work for social and industrial systems do not work when applied to the family system. Industry is concerned with output—quantity often at the expense of quality. The more cars sold, the higher the margin of profit; the more hospital beds filled, the lower the margin of loss; and the more refining plants in operation, the greater the production of oil. The same methods applied to the family system result in different effects: the higher the number of family members, the fewer the internal resources to meet individual need; the greater the emphasis on task, the less focus placed on character building and emotional development; and the greater the emphasis on social system performance, the fewer the opportunities for involvement with the family system and the lower the probability of skill building in interpersonal relationships. In the family system, the individual is a necessary and essential component; in larger systems, individuals are necessary but expendable subsystems.

In industrial and technological systems, the individual is dispensable, easily replaced with a lower-paid worker or a computer terminal. The techniques and opportunities that have been made available to industrial and social systems through rapid technological and scientific development, together with overpopulation and high rates of unemployment, culminate in individual replaceability. In industry, when a cheaper worker can be found, the individual may be quickly out of a job; in social systems, where a more willing worker can be found at less expense to the school, university, or hospital, the individual may be quickly removed from a slot; even in the family, if the emotional and social relationships are not suited to the partner's expectation, divorce is quickly and fairly easily obtainable. Choice, heightened individual opportunity, a sense of replaceability, and change without consequence, which predominate in industry, government, and the larger social systems, are reflected in the attitudes of some family systems toward individual family members and in individuals' attitudes toward the family as a psychological and social system.

Often, it has been said that we live in a throwaway world: if it doesn't fit, throw it out and buy a new one; if it is the wrong color, change the color or replace the object; if it is the wrong size, reduce or enlarge the size; when it gets old and worn out, throw it out or hide it from view; and, if it is defective, demand a replacement. Newness, perfection, replaceability, total satisfaction or your money back—all claims made by sellers, developers, and industrial conglomerates who are competing for the dollar, driving hard for the profit, sacrificing quality for the sake of speeded-up production. Similar attitudes prevail in the family toward the elderly (old and used), handicapped children (parts with flaws), obese individuals (trim is "in"), minorities (wrong colors), and spouses who don't agree or expect too much (demand a replacement).

Accompanying the easy replacement of the individual is the paradoxical "me-ism" and the resultant "I"-centered individual. During the last two decades, individual growth and actualization have been at the forefront of social consciousness. While social, industrial, and technological developments were proceeding at unprecedented rates, individual choice and pleasure, at the expense of group or family needs, were encouraged. The "you do your thing and I'll do mine" attitude has encouraged individuals to think of themselves as complete systems apart from family or social networks. One of the unfortunate but predictable outcomes of the "I"-centered social movement is the widespread sense of disconnectedness and lack of belonging on the part of individuals of all ages. The sense of alienation that the "I"-centered movement purported to alleviate has instead been intensified. The lack of emotional attachment within the family, between family and environment, and between individual and job is a mirror reflection of the lack of social commitment to and concern for system interrelatedness of industry and society, society and environment, and society and family system.

There is an overriding sense of individual replaceability that is accompanied by feelings of disconnectedness and lack of family worth and importance. The system relatedness between family and social systems and between social systems and environment has been neglected. Although there are many agencies and groups concerned with the preservation of the environment, with the maintenance of social structure, and with the continuation of the family as an integral social subsystem, there is yet a lack of united effort to achieve these goals.

Rapidly changing times and increasing uncertainty for the future create in individuals and families a sense of panic, despair, powerlessness, and futility. One of the more common complaints of family members is lack of control—over individual goals, group concerns, and family future. Although options certainly exist for the family member as well as for the group, personal inability to fully use such options, predict outcomes, and manage consequences only adds to the sense of frustration and lack of control. Too many options and too little knowledge of the consequences make it difficult for families to make appropriate choices with a sense of confidence in the result of those choices.

### Social developments

Fifty years ago, it was possible for a family to predict to a certain degree what the next day held for them. There were limited career opportunities, less opportunity for travel, and limited news and public media; more women worked in the home, and each family was more or less connected to a social network of extended family, community, and neighborhood. With enhanced career choices, heightened opportunities for travel, increased awareness through mass media, and fluidity in sex roles, the ability to predict the future for either oneself or one's family with any degree of certainty is severely limited. Few people live and die in the same community. Most people own or rent several houses in the span of 20 years.

Most children attend two or more schools every ten years. Many families drive a different car every three to five years. Fewer and fewer children pursue the career choices of their parents. Guidance, counseling, and directionality for families comes primarily from church, school, and mental health professionals outside the family system. Fewer and fewer people rely on common sense or experience to shape their lives, searching instead for the expert opinion and counsel. There is also a social expectation that each individual will maximize human potential and that each family will fully utilize a wide set of options, in school, at work, and during leisure or play hours.

Rapid change, lack of control and self-direction, a sense of social and physical mobility, lack of predictability in terms of career goals, and lack of confidence in oneself as source and resource, coupled with heightened social expectation for academic and professional achievement, place the individual within the family and the family system itself in a precarious and highly demanding position without, however, knowledge and skill to live up to expectations or meet personal and social demands.

## IMPACT OF CHANGE

Whereas modes of living have changed with the addition of modern convenience and technological sophistication, the social and personal skills of the family to cope with those changes have not always accompanied the changes. It is one thing to have a shortened workday; it is another for some people to know what to do with the increased amount of leisure time available. It is one thing to have day care centers and supports to relieve parents of parental responsibility; it is another to accept the fact that those agencies sometimes become family surrogates to parents and children who rely on their services. It is one thing to have social agencies available to assist the family with personal and financial needs; it is another thing for families to cope with officials within those agencies who establish rules for family living. It is one thing to make marriage and divorce equally desirable and another to cope with the feelings that accompany the dissolution of a marriage. It is one thing to view church and religion as tangential to life, and it is another to cope with the lack of spiritual meaning that accompanies the absence of some form of religious commitment.

Social and technological changes have increased the permeability of family boundaries without necessarily providing family with the skills to deal with the changes, including increased flow of information through mass media, increased sources of persuasion in television and advertising, a variety of opinions and ideas through books and magazines, exposure to different cultures and religions through social and physical mobility, physical travel and mental expansion, and simultaneous involvement of the individual family member with several social systems. The degree to which such rapid change represents an assault on the family system depends on the internal state of the family (sources, resources, emotional reserves) as well as the nature of the external demands that confront the family.

**Internal state of family**

The internal state of the family, particularly in terms of strategies for coping with change, is determined by a number of factors: family history of change, nature of emotional bonding, contemporary experience with change, and current stress load in the family. The internal state is reflected in family dynamics and individual barometric readings (physical illness or emotional actions and reactions).

**Family history.** The family's historical exposure to and experience with change provide contemporary members with experienced resources on which to draw for support as well as example. Where family in the past has successfully managed social and life events, coping with change is less frightening for those who have not yet experienced changes. Similarly, the loss of such important sources of experience, support, and leadership leaves the family with a void in the face of change. Having prior units, systems, or individuals who have successfully managed change such as physical mobility, social mobility (rise or fall), environmental hardships, loss of a child or other family member, or family fragmentation or social and political changes such as depression or war provides the contemporary family system with a sense of endurance and survivorship and the belief that adaptation is both necessary and desirable. With a sense of survivorship, that is, connectedness to a successful family system in the past, the contemporary unit can point to and imitate examples without which the family might be left to its own inadequate or underdeveloped resources. Increased physical and social mobility has created a gap between the contemporary family unit and its history, making comparison with and learning from other family systems more difficult. Contemporary family units turn more and more to professionals, social agencies, and government for the kinds of support, advice, and protection that were once expected from the extended family. In some ways, such heightened dependence on outside social systems reduces the possibility of family interdependence—physical, social, and emotional.

**Bonding.** Physical support and emotional bonding within the family affect the ever-evolving internal state of the family. Where bonding within the family system is supportive, productive, and warm, the family will have a greater tendency to function as a unit where change is concerned. The less supportive the bonding, the greater the probability that the family will function as a group of unrelated individuals when faced with pressure and change. The higher the group participation, the more supportive the family bonding. Families in which the connectedness is based on authoritarian control by one individual will be altered drastically when that member is ill or disabled. The family with authoritarian leadership may overnight become a leaderless group through the death or loss of one member. Where other members are ill equipped to handle daily concerns, the family system degenerates quickly into a group of individuals, each experiencing and coping in highly individualistic ways. Conversely, where emotional connectedness is reflected in democratic participation by all family members, change or stress is not so much a threat to the family system as a challenge with which it must learn to cope. The loss of one member, although a loss to the system, does not necessarily mean an end to all system functions, as might occur in an authoritarian structure of interaction. The emotional bonding of families, like the social structure and interaction patterns, has much of its origins in the past. Coping strategies, ways of supporting others, and styles of adapting to change (effective and ineffective) are learned from observation of and interaction with other family members. Although coping strategies are learned from other family systems and significant others, individual and family exposure to and experience with change test and hone the skills laid down in the family system. It is one thing to observe extended family units cope with change; it is quite another to be directly involved.

**Contemporary experience.** Exposure to and experience with change (physical, social, environmental, and emotional) can not only facilitate the honing of basic skills learned in the family but teach new ways of coping as well. With exposure to and successful management of change, individual members and family systems have the opportunity to experience themselves as competent and self-directed. Exposure comes through awareness of the potential of change, the observation of others' involvement with changing events, and education about the processes of individual change (biological and physical) and family change (new members, aging, and death) as well. Exposure alone can provide individuals and families with a sense of preparedness and a set of alternatives. For example, individuals who have some knowledge of biological changes can anticipate with some sense of confidence physical and maturational alterations in self and others. Couples exposed to parenting classes can anticipate the experience of a new member with some sense of what is going to happen. Families educated and sensitized to the loss or disability of a family member are better able to anticipate the grief and despair that accompany such loss. Loss or disability of distant members or close friends provides one with a sensitizing exposure to grief, without which the actual experience can be devastating as well as painful. Being exposed to family changes, death, divorce, or separation sensitizes one to the interrelated nature of the family network. Exposure to change is enhanced by experience with change—individual, social, and family.

Direct experience with change, for example, through physical illness, divorce, developmental maturation, birth of a child, or moving to a new residence, provides families with direct confrontation with events that test and, at the same time, build individual capabilities and group effectiveness. The nature of the experience and the ability to successfully incorporate, manage, or otherwise resolve the change are important determinants in the handling of similar and future situations. Each change successfully managed solidifies family connectedness, fosters self-confidence, and facilitates handling similar situations in the future. Whereas coping with change is generally thought of in terms of change that is detrimental, Holmes and Rahe (1967) believe that *any* change brings about alterations with which individuals and families must cope. Thus, change that is positive as well as change that is negative must be incorporated, resolved, or otherwise managed. The amount, frequency, duration, and cumulative nature of change to which the family is exposed are good indices of the current stress level in the family.

**Cumulative change.** The current management level of the family is determined not only by past methods of coping and experiences with change but by the cumulative nature of the change itself. Most families can tolerate a moderate amount of change: job changes, birth of a child, changes in residence, holidays, new purchases, developmental hurdles of individuals, and successful completion of goals. However, when a series of changes occur without sufficient time for resolution or management, change itself becomes a source of stress.

According to Holmes and Rahe, change can be charted and assigned a rank that corresponds to its ability to effect alterations in life style, physical health, and emotional stability. The higher the score, the greater the probability that physical illness or emotional instability will occur. Change, positive as well as negative, is capable of producing detrimental effects, particularly where the change is cumulative over a short period of time, as illustrated in Fig. 2.

Change of a limited nature in and of itself may not bring about alterations in the interactions and actions of the family. Where change is limited or successfully incorporated, tolerated, resolved, or otherwise managed, its effects are less detrimental. However, when change occurs with such rapidity or such intensity that management is not possible, effects on actions, interactions, and physical and mental health can be expected. Stress levels become evident: fatigue, irritability, and minor disorders occur.

As change continues to accumulate without some form of management,

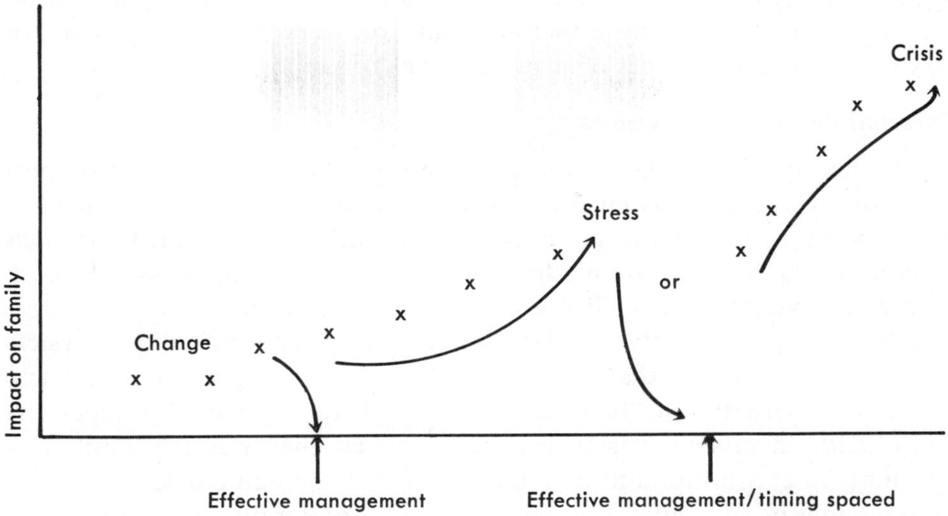


**Fig. 2**

the effect on the family and individual gradually increases—from minor change to major crisis. Change becomes stress, stress becomes crisis; crisis itself represents a major change in system function. Adequate management skills become inadequate; minor impact on the family becomes major. Where cumulative change reaches the crisis level, management skills that might be effective in situations of moderate change may be ineffective or inadequate. Life events, such as birth, death, remarriage, and maturational hurdles, that in themselves are generally possible to tolerate or manage may become totally unmanageable for even the most effective families. Timing and frequency are important variables. Recovery time is particularly important in coping with change.

The inability to tolerate large amounts of unmanaged change can be seen in changes in individual, as well as family, physical and mental health. Thus, the individual family member and the family system itself serve as indices, or barometers, of the adaptive levels in the family: the individual may complain of headache, backache, unexplained fatigue, or insomnia; family interaction displays unexplained changes, for example, irritability, indecisiveness, lack of productivity where productivity was evident, and alterations in the emotional atmosphere and psychological bonding.

Cumulative, unmanaged change due to an insufficient recovery period or inadequate management skills causes alterations in individual health as well as in the system functioning of family units.

The nature of the alterations is influenced primarily by the internal state of the family, as described above, and the nature of change. External demands and events may either facilitate recovery and management or serve as additional sources of stress and lack of support.

**External demands and events**

The family's embeddedness in social systems not only provides support but also places demands on the family as a unit for performance, involvement, personal and financial contributions, and commitment. Conditions external to the family system affect the family's ability to successfully cope with and manage change. For example, society's demands on individual members for productivity and extrafamily involvement affect the physical and emotional energy that individuals have left to engage in social and emotional interaction in the family system. Where the level of productivity and outside involvement is excessive, individual energy in the family system may be at a minimum; therefore, the family system has less resources in managing its own affairs. External demands on family members, particularly at work or in school, can add significantly to the level of stress that the individual brings home to the family system.

**Social and environmental change.** In addition to social expectation for performance and productivity, environmental conditions affect the family's ability to cope with change. Poverty; social and cultural deprivation; lack of opportunity for creative development and expression; urban renewal, which is accompanied by the removal of historical landmarks and elements of familiarity and connectedness with familial and social past; social change; political developments, with loss or change of familiar leaders and familiar patterns of performance; economic developments, with inflation; and increased governmental intrusion into the internal networks of individual and family life are only a few of the diverse sets of external demands with which families and individuals must contend. Positive acts of social and environmental change can have drastic negative effects on family functioning and individual behavior.

Urban renewal, for example, was intended to revitalize and update inner cities and central business districts in small towns. However, in the process of clearing old buildings and cleaning up cluttered vacant lots, people's lives were disrupted. Families lost homes; old people lost memories; communities lost their sense of individual identity and self-control; religious groups lost their churches; social groups lost their meeting places; children lost their playgrounds: society brutalized its connectedness to the past. New houses were built with thin walls and small rooms, in which there is little opportunity for individual privacy or a sense of territory in which one must be responsive and toward which one must exhibit some responsibility. New, big, concrete parking lots, devoid of social meaning, became the focus of teenage restlessness and a center for drug dealers looking for easy targets. Urban renewal brought more social ills than it cured and created more stress for families through its destruction of the past than relief through newness and contemporary facades. The sense of despair and the process of grieving that individuals and families have experienced because of the loss of familiar and trusted landmarks are only beginning to be recognized. The sense of individual replaceability is paralleled in impact by an overriding sense of replaceability and destructibility of individual homes, neighborhood stores, homesteads, farm lands, and small businesses. Not only has there been widespread experience with loss and destruction associated with social change, but with political change and economic development as well.

**Political and economic change.** During the last two decades, an alarming number of national leaders have been lost to society and the American family. In particular, the leaders who were associated with the presidency, as presidents and as candidates, were parent figures and representatives of an idealized family for many people. Individuals and entire family systems developed a sense of connectedness with those leaders and their families, a relationship that social scientists refer to as "parasocial." As an index of their feeling for presidential leaders and their families, for example, society referred to them as the "First Family," a revered and admired position. Their behaviors were imitated—fashions, dialects, hairstyles, childrearing practices, drinking habits, and social and religious practices. Political and social leaders as a group were admired, respected, and emulated.

It was probably inevitable that being placed at the pinnacle of social and political power would lead to eventual downfall. The altered status of political leaders, caused by assassination, misdeed, or poor judgment, has been accompanied by alienation in the social relationships between the nation's leading families and the families that emulated them. Trust turned to mistrust; admiration turned to disgust; respect turned to hatred of their success as well as of their mistakes. Disrespect for leaders eventually turned to lack of self-respect, largely due to feelings of having been deceived and taken advantage of. Supporting national leaders turned to blowing the horn on them. Closeness became distance; trust became suspicion and despair. Hope lies in the rebuilding of the connectedness by a new group of politicians aware not only of their own position of power, but of their position as examples for those who elect and watch them.

Economic developments such as rising prices, devaluation of the dollar, and increasing regulatory intervention by the government erode the family's sense of self-determination and control. With a decreased sense of control over destiny, the family has less incentive for system productivity and social involvement. Where money can be saved by delegating family responsibility to social and governmental agencies, the family will have less incentive for taking responsibility as a family unit. The welfare system, for example, rewards the one-parent family and punishes the working couple. Fragmentation of the family system is encouraged by economic and social policies that reward disorder through financial support and punish family unity through lack of insurance relief, educational benefits, and social recognition. Where a man is the head of the household, employed or unemployed, often less financial and social support is available than where a woman alone is the head of the household. Two elderly adults on fixed incomes can live together more cheaply unmarried than if they were to marry and risk losing Social Security benefits. Economic policies and practices are geared more and more to the task and less and less to the person. Tax incentives and loopholes work to the advantage of the wealthy and business conglomerates. Money rather than character, performance rather than personhood, and job rather than worker pervade not only the social and political arena but economic circles as well. Such attitudes necessarily have a tremendous shaping influence on the family and the family's attitude toward social, political, and economic development and change.

Where the person is considered to be and treated as unimportant and insignificant, individuals may have to go to great extremes to demonstrate to society that such attitudes are wrong and such practices unfair. Where the family as a unit is considered insignificant in policy making, social change, and environmental and economic development, the family system may, through a self-fulfilling prophecy, become as insignificant as it is socially, politically, and economically made out to be. If the family has in fact lost respect for its traditional importance to society, it may be because society first supplied the message through its political, social, and economic systems.

## FAMILY AS A BAROMETER OF SOCIAL SYSTEMS

Just as the individual within the family is an index of the dynamics of the family system, so the family system is a barometer of the dynamics occurring in the larger network of systems—social, political, and economic. The family is a tool with which the larger set of systems fulfills prophecies, completes unfinished tasks, establishes a sense of connectedness and perpetuality, communicates goals and ambitions, and creates a sense of space and territory. The family and individuals within the family are the tools with which systems compete with one another, in peace as well as in war.

The family functions in relation to larger systems much in the same way that individuals function within the family, each being a smaller component of the larger unit to which it belongs, individual to family and family to society. As discussed in Chapter 8, the ways in which individuals function in the family are as link, translator-interpreter, source-resource, victim, agent, and index. Family as a link is the connecting point between society's past and future, between ideas and practice, between fantasy and reality, between social preservation and extinction. Overlapping its link role is the family's role as translator-interpreter of social value, religious belief, and cultural practice. The family can only link and translate what is available to it. The quality of the linkage will be a reflection of that which is connected: family action and reaction can only be as good as the resources and sources available in the larger set of systems. Family is a source-resource of energy, idea, support, approval, and encouragement. Families, like individuals, can function as victims as well as agents. Where social systems are geared toward honesty as well as productivity, self-determination as well as group cohesion, norm flexibility as well as adherence to norm, and emotional development equal to task completion, subsystems will function more as agents than as victims. However, where the larger social systems regard the family as merely a tool with which to carry out their tasks and achieve their goals, the family will function more as a victim, used and abused for the sake of the larger system. Where family is victim, little consideration is given to unique needs and interests of the individual family unit; decisions are made for families rather than in conjunction with them; plans are carried out without consultation and referral; and productivity is considered in light of profit and gain, not individual system need and ability. As a barometer, or index, of social dynamics, family dynamics will reflect society's treatment of the family system as victim or agent. Attitudes that prevail and changes that occur in social systems will be reflected in family functioning and individual member health, both physical and emotional.

Although social change has a tremendous and often detrimental effect on the family system, the impact of change is mediated by the positive support that social networks can provide: resources to assist with change, competent and experienced others, opportunities for linking up with other families being similarly affected, and the possibility of the family's altering life style and patterns of behavior to accommodate change. The external demands that confront the family may either facilitate coping with change or act as a barrier to effective management. Although society places inordinate demands and unreasonable expectation on the family system, it offers wide and varied sources of opportunity, support, and choice—educationally, socially, and medically. Choice, as well as demand, carries with it the expectation for responsive performance. How the family confronts choice and demand involves an integration of the factors at work in the internal network of the family and the external demands of society and environment.

## CONSEQUENCES OF CHANGE

The consequences of change for the family system depend on the internal state of the family, the nature of change itself, and the external support available to and demands confronting the family. Internal changes in the family are both supports in times of change as well as the source of change itself. Adding new members, losing members, and illness or injury of members all affect the system functions of the family. Change in itself may or may not be detrimental, depending on management skills of the family system, availability of support and competent others, and the timing and severity of the change. The greater the change and the less recovery time between changes, the more severe the impact on the emotional and physical health of members and the more traumatic the impact on the social and psychological functioning of the family system.

Nowhere is the system nature of the family more evident than where the family must cope with change, internal as well as external. Adding another family member, young or old, upsets the familiar order and patterns within the family system. All elements of family life are touched: history is altered by new heirs and contributors; bonding is changed through new attachments and shifting in old alliances; territory must be expanded and allocated to accommodate the new member; and communication patterns, language and gestures, must be altered to meet the needs of the new member. Similarly, the loss of a member has a powerful impact on the family system. Attachments are broken; communication with that member is lost; territory is redefined; and the contemporary member suddenly becomes a part of family history. Changes in leadership, comfort, support, and approval all follow the loss or addition of members. Where the new member is markedly different—physically, emotionally, or intellectually—from others in the family, adjustment is often more difficult. Where addition and loss of members occur simultaneously, the impact of change can be very severe.

Where change is cumulative, with little opportunity for recovery or management, the family system will usually experience the following: (1) reduction in the family's ability to seek and use information; (2) decrease in the family's ability to make decisions and solve problems constructively; (3) lowered sense of family effectiveness and interpersonal competence; (4) heightened concern for physical health of members, with oversensitivity to everyday processes; (5) altered sense of community and social connectedness, with a gradual withdrawal from sources of support; (6) alteration in social and emotional interactions within the family; and (7) finally, where emotional and social resources within the family become depleted, a decrease in the overall productivity of family members at home, at work, and at school.

While the family system is experiencing the impact of change, individual family members may be exhibiting stress-related responses as well. Some of the more common stress-related reactions of individuals are (1) backache, (2) headache, (3) general irritability, (4) unexplained fatigue, (5) ulcers, (6) restlessness mixed with alternating lethargy and overactivity, and (7) depression for which no medical or physical reason can be found. Increasing evidence suggests that physical illnesses, injuries, and accidents are related to heightened levels of social and personal stress experienced by individuals and family systems.

## SUMMARY

The family system is affected by its embeddedness in a network of larger systems—political, social, economic, and environmental. The nature of that influence is both positive and negative. Social embeddedness provides the family with a set of supportive resources, availability of competent others, and protective services. Although society protects and supports the family network, demands are great and expectations for performance and productivity are high. Internal conditions in the family, the nature of changes themselves, and external events and conditions around the family influence the extent to which change represents a challenge that can be managed. Where change is cumulative and recovery time insufficient, family management skills may be insufficient for successfully coping with change, resulting in alterations in the physical and socioemotional health of family members as well as in the system functions of the family unit.

### STUDY QUESTIONS

1. What is the importance of the family system's historical exposure to and experience with change?
2. How does social system connectedness with the family affect the system's ability to change?
3. How does direct experience with change affect system productivity and adaptability?
4. According to Holmes and Rahe, what is the result of change—positive change as well as negative?
5. What is the effect of cumulative, unmanaged change?
6. In what ways does the suprasystem contribute to the family system's management skills?
7. In what ways is the family system a barometer of the suprasystem?

## EXERCISES

Refer to the sample chart that follows the exercises.

1. List at least two significant political, social, medical, and economic developments that have occurred in your lifetime. Examples are space travel, solar heat, and medical research leading to organ transplant. Which of those on your list has had the most observable impact on your family system?
2. Name and list critical life events that have occurred in your family in the last ten years; in your lifetime. Birth, death, divorce, moving, major surgery, legal problems, family quarrels, fires, injuries, and accidents are examples.
3. List illnesses, accidents, school problems, problems at work, and other major problems that individuals within your family system have experienced.
4. What correlations do you find between social events, major life events, and stress-related illnesses or accidents?
5. In what ways do your observations support the contention that change alone, unmanaged and in large amounts, can cause physical, emotional, and social problems for family and individuals?

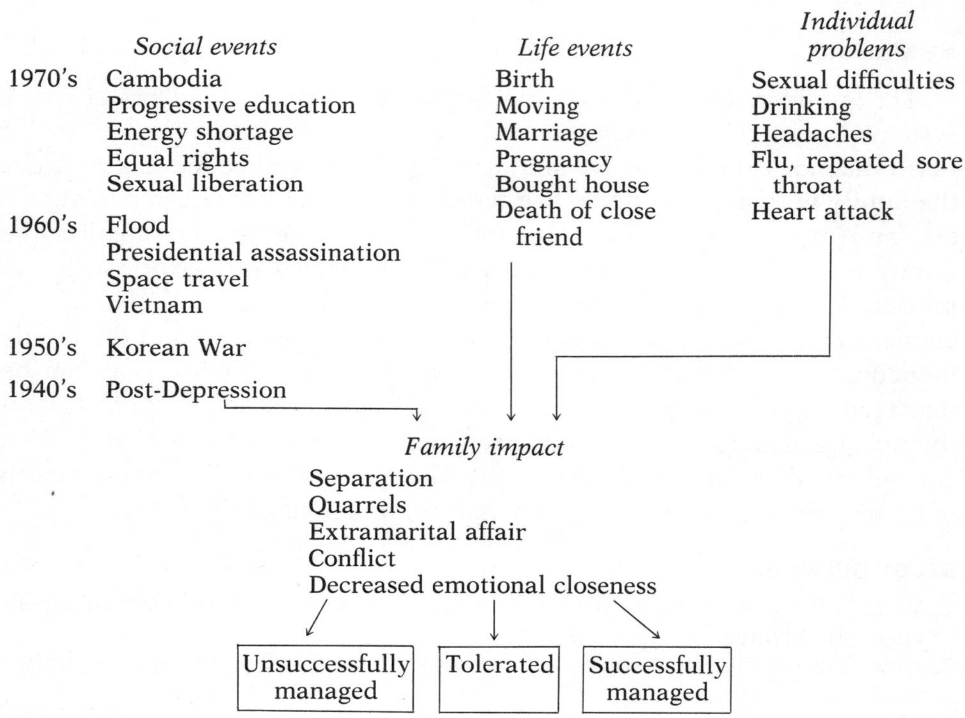


## BIBLIOGRAPHY

Hall, E.: Beyond culture, New York, 1977, Anchor Books.

Holmes, T., and Rahe, R.: The Social Readjustment Rating Scale, J. Psychosom. Res. **11**:213, 1967.

Laing, R.: The politics of experience, New York, 1967, Ballantine Books.

Polansky, N., Borgmen, R., and DeSaix, C.: Roots of futility, San Francisco, 1972, Jossey-Bass, Inc., Publishers.

Sedgwick, R.: Psychological response to stress, J. Psychiatr. Nurs. **13**(5):20, 1975.

Toffler, A.: Future shock, New York, 1971, Random House, Inc.

## Chapter 10

# THE CLINICAL STUDENT AND FAMILY MENTAL HEALTH

Students entering family systems to learn, to provide assistance, or merely to visit must be aware of their contribution to and impact on the family system. The greater the similarity between the student's family and the clinic family and the less knowledgeable and experienced the student is, the greater the potential for the student to fall into the trap of using the clinic family to resolve or work out relationships back home. The term *clinic family* is used in this book to refer to those families with whom the student comes in contact during the course of study; such families may or may not be actual clients in a clinic, health center, or medical complex. The more aware the student is of the dynamics at work in the student's own family, the greater the likelihood traps may be avoided, or, if not avoided, at least recognized. Relationships that students have with their own families are powerful and influential. It is reasonable to suggest that such relationships are at work in their everyday lives. It is unreasonable to assume that even the experienced student can always avoid overinvolvement with clinic families. Where relationships at home are warm and positive, the nature of the interaction with the clinic family can be productive. Where the relationship has been powerful and negative, remnants of unresolved feeling may be transposed to family systems having similar problems or who demonstrate similar dynamics.

This is not to suggest that students should not work with clinic families who are similar in makeup to their own families. Nor is there an intent to suggest that harm always comes to the clinic family through which students and clinicians work out their own relationships with significant others. However, students need to be aware of the impact their relationship with clinic families has not only on those families, but on themselves as well. Student impact is related to (1) the student's relationship to the original family system; (2) the attitudes, values, and beliefs of the original family; (3) the practices that characterize the student's family; (4) the clinic family's relationship with the health care system; and (5) the nature of the educational system in which students and professors are involved.

## THE STUDENT'S FAMILY SYSTEM

The student's origin is in a family system. As an essential and active component of that family system, the individual learns ways of acting and interacting. It is natural to carry around those habits and patterns, particularly those which reflect the most significant and powerful attachments the individual has experienced in the family. Where those relationships contain unfulfilled contracts or unresolved feelings, there is a tendency to seek their fulfillment or resolution in others. For example, a student who has experienced the loss of a parent or grandparent at a crucial phase of development may seek to complete that relationship with a parent, adult, or grandparent in a clinic family, particularly where even the vaguest physical or emotional semblance exists between the member of the clinic family and the member of the student's family. Similarly, feelings of abandonment, rejection, or lack of approval experienced by the student in family relationships may be attributed to the clinic family as problems and targets for intervention strategies. Just as the emotional bonding within the student's own family influences the nature of social and emotional attachments with others, the attitudes and beliefs held by the student's family of origin are also influential.

### Family attitude, value, and belief

Values, attitudes, and beliefs that students experience in their families of origin affect the nature of the relationships that students seek to establish with clinic families. Conflict, for example, is taken by many people to be a sign of family disorder and consequent failure. Realistically, conflict and disagreement are natural outcomes of human encounter. However, students from families in which conflict has been avoided may experience difficulty in working with highly conflictive families. Yelling, screaming, and throwing things (not people) are some families' ways of "letting off steam" or of "getting it out in the open." For many couples, such steam venting is followed by reconciliation and lovemaking. For other families, the more natural outcome is out-and-out battle. If a student comes from a battle-oriented family, conflict may be not only disturbing but frightening as well. Values and beliefs underlie the practices that families establish—toward themselves and others. Such practices shape individual family member action and interaction.

### Family practice

Practices that characterize the interactions of the student's family (for example, the handling of conflict and disagreement) shape the student's approach to similar issues. Although we live in an age of institutional egalitarianism, the practices of many individuals and families are characterized by prejudice and discrimination, based on sex, ethnic background, religion, place of origin, social status, political beliefs, physical appearance, and personal belief. Such practices reveal underlying beliefs that in turn color evaluations and judgments of other people, particularly with respect to the appropriateness and acceptability of their behavior.

Recent studies report, for example, that a high percentage of parents still prefer male to female children; that many still consider the assertive woman to be "maladjusted"; that men are still expected to be aggressive, strong, and dominant; that Blacks are still considered inferior; and, basically, that anyone who "deviates from the norm" is not to be trusted. That such discriminatory beliefs influence judgments about mental health has been widely documented. In a study mentioned earlier, Broverman and associates investigated the relationship between stereotypical sex-role expectations and clinical judgments of mental health. Clinical judgments about characteristics of healthy individuals differed depending on the sex of the person being judged. Adjustment was directly linked to the individual's ability to fulfill conventional role expectations. The expectations of conventional role fulfillment were, however, somewhat startling. Subjects were asked to describe the healthy adult, healthy man, and healthy woman. The healthy woman was considered to be less adventurous, more easily influenced, less aggressive, less competitive, more submissive, less independent, more emotional, more conceited about appearance, less objective, more excitable in crises, and less inclined to like math or science than her male counterpart, who was judged to be competitive, aggressive, independent, objective, decisive, and dominant. The adult standard of health, sex unspecified, paralleled expectations for conventional male behavior. Expectations regarding the unhealthy man, woman, and adult were even more revealing of discriminatory and differential attitudes. The characteristics of the *unhealthy* adult, sex unspecified, paralleled those behaviors believed by the clinicians to be characteristic of the conventional woman. Basically, what was considered to be healthy adult behavior—competent, adventurous, objective, aggressive, and decisive—was associated with behavior socially approved for and expected of healthy men. In addition, what was considered to be unhealthy adult behavior—submissive, indecisive, easily influenced, and excitable—was associated with characteristics believed to describe the typical, healthy woman. What was healthy for adults and men was believed to represent lack of adjustment and unhealth in women. Such judgments reflect what the authors of the study refer to as a "double standard of health," similar to the double standards that exist in social practices and beliefs. This study and studies by Rosenkrantz and co-workers (1968), Horner (1969), Sedgwick (1973),

Friedland, Crockett, and Laird, and others demonstrate basically that what is "masculine" is "healthy": dominance, adventure, independence, aggression, competition, and objectivity. However, when the same qualities are displayed by a woman, her behavior is judged by others and even by herself to be less socially acceptable; the adjustment of the individual is even questioned. Lynn (1959) points out, by way of explanation, that more social reinforcement and more cultural prestige are associated with maleness and the male role. Although such standards reflect society's views of individuals, those views are perpetuated and supported in the family system.

Such attitudes affect children as well as adults. Parents expect, from birth on, differing behaviors from their children, based not on interest and ability but on sex-role stereotypes. Girls are expected to play with dolls; boys are expected to play with trucks and guns. Girls are expected to be cooperative and helpful; boys are expected to be active and rambunctious. In our own clinical practice, a majority of boys who are referred for evaluation are referred because they are too quiet, reserved, whereas the majority of girls are referred because they are too aggressive or active. Reserved behavior on the part of boys is generally considered by parents to be "feminine," even in a six-year-old. However, girls who are aggressive, active, and athletic are viewed by many parents as "tomboys" and probably "headed for trouble," which generally means that no man in his right mind will want to marry an outgoing, athletic woman who thinks for herself. Parents of the so-called feminine boy are concerned that he will grow up to be socially unacceptable as a product of an effective family system.

Parents, through fear and avoidance, may create in the child a self-fulfilling prophecy. Perhaps the mistake lies in raising such children in terms of what they should not be rather than with regard to what they can become. Such children move through life avoiding what they should not do, rather than moving in a positive direction to fulfill their highest potential and make their most valuable contributions.

Sex-role stereotype is not the only standard by which families shape their members and judge others. Skin color, religious belief, social status, and ethnic background are all standards by which others are measured. To the extent that such standards are used by families without consideration of the effects of experience, social and cultural opportunity, environmental influences, and social shaping, judgments about others will tend to be prejudicial and discriminatory. Such practices affect not only the family system's view of and interaction with the larger world of people but will influence and shape the student's judgments, evaluations, and interactions with others, individuals as well as family systems. Lack of exposure to and experience with differing ethnic, religious, and social groups will limit the student's ability to appreciate the impact that such significant life experiences have on families and individuals. Where intense poverty exists, for example, students may be so shocked by the environmental disorder that considering the people as influenced by but separate from their deprived situation may be difficult at best. What students must never underestimate is the impact that their impressions, social evaluations, and clinical judgments have on families, rich as well as poor. Not only is the student a component of a family system, with its history, bonding, communication, and territoriality, but also a part of a larger social system (health related) with its history, connectedness, communication, and territoriality as well.

## EXPERIENCE WITH AND EXPOSURE TO THE HEALTH CARE SYSTEM

The health care system of which the student is a part is one of the largest social systems with which families and individuals come into contact during their lifetimes. From birth on, people are weighed, measured, tested, treated, evaluated, and judged by health professionals—at work, at school, in the community, and even in the home. The health care system is characterized not only by its size and diversity, but by its complexity as well. Nurses, physicians, dentists, pharmacists, psychologists, social workers, nutritionists, developmental specialists, physical therapists, occupational therapists, music therapists, art therapists, and physical and mental health technicians are only a few of the professionals who make up the health care industry, not to mention ancillary support services, business and insurance components, and the regulatory and evaluative components. For the individual, as well as for the family, such complexity may be overwhelming. The family may look to the student to help sort out and understand such complexities. Or, where the family has had negative experiences with some part of the health care system, the experience may cause fears and reservation about other components. Students may be viewed by families as advocates or adversaries, depending on the clinic family's experience with and expectations of the health care system in general and nursing in particular.

The student's own exposure to and experience with the health care system, either through personal or family experience, will influence expectations regarding one's own role, the role of other health professionals, and the role of the family as participant in and recipient of health care. If the student's family has had a productive, positive relationship with the health care system, particularly in its preventive aspects (for example, periodic dental examinations, physical health examinations, developmental screening and assessment, eye examinations, nutritional evaluations, or physical fitness screening), the student's feelings toward the health care system will be different from those of the student whose family has only had contact in emergencies and forced choice situations, such as coronaries, disability evaluations, retirement examinations, school physicals, abscessed teeth, reported physical abuse, or psychological examination required by courts in cases of divorce or suspected child abuse. Where the health care system is used as a source of remediation, treatment, or rehabilitation, the family's attitude is more that of a passive and externally controlled recipient than where the system is used actively as a source of education, information, and prevention. Where the contact chiefly has been in emergency or illness, the health care system will be seen only in relation to pathological processes and not in terms of its preventive potential as well.

## EDUCATIONAL SYSTEM: THEORY X, THEORY Y

Not only is the student a component of a family system and the health care system but of an educational system as well. The attitudes of the educational system toward students, for example, as active, self-directed, and trusted participants or as passive, in need of direction, and not to be trusted except where well supervised, will influence the students' valuation of and performance regarding opportunities, expectations, and clinical responsibilities. According to McGregor (1960), there are two major sets of assumptions that organizations hold regarding the motivation and performance of individuals within that system. The first set, which he refers to as Theory X, views the individual as having an inherent dislike for work; as needing to be coerced, controlled, and directed or threatened in order to maintain performance; and as liking to be controlled, directed, and told what to do in order to avoid taking responsibility for actions. This is basically a negative view of human behavior and is unfortunately prevalent in many organizations, including educational institutions. Therefore, it is necessary that the larger institutions have a rigid set of regulations and policies to direct, control, and otherwise supervise the human being, who in their minds is by nature evasive, irresponsible, and incapable of self-direction. The second set of assumptions, which McGregor refers to as Theory Y, views the individual as being as naturally directed to work as to play or rest; as self-controlled and self-directed, not necessarily in need of coercive control or threat of punishment in order to perform; under the proper conditions, as not only accepting but seeking responsibility; as capable of contributing to the solution of problems in creative and imaginative ways; and as having potential that, largely because of unfavorable conditions, is only partially utilized. In Theory X, the fault for inadequate performance is believed to lie with the individual. In Theory Y, performance is seen as the interactional outcome between management and those it seeks to manage.

Just as students and their peers are connected to family systems, so the students and their instructors are interrelated with a social system whose valuation of the individual as essential or nonessential will shape the nature of the interaction that students have, not only with their clinic families, but with their supervisors as well. If the supervisor or instructor is embedded in a system that embraces the Theory X set of assumptions regarding the nature of human beings, the student can expect more rules and policies and less active participation not only in making those policies but in carrying them out. The same is probably true for the instructors as well. Where institutions take a positive view of people, as being self-directed and responsible given the right conditions, the student can expect an emphasis on creating those conditions, under which optimal performance and experience can be attained. Where Theory Y is operative, not only the students but their instructors, too, will experience more freedom of thought, more opportunity for creative involvement, and a more active involvement in the educational process than where Theory X is operative. The nature of the relationship between the educational system and its components, of which students and professors are integral, will influence not only the students' educational experience, but also clinical experience. A heightened sensitivity on the students' part, not only to their own family system connectedness, but also to the social system embeddedness of their peers and professors, will facilitate a productive educational experience and a positive clinical involvement with families.

The assumptions that underlie the approaches the student elects to use with families, for example, those of McGregor's Theory X or Theory Y, will certainly influence the nature of relationships that are established and the clinical outcomes of the nurse-family relationship, in the same ways that outcomes that result from employing those assumptions in educational and organizational settings and relationships are shaped. It is my belief that the more active and involved the family can be in processes that shape their lives, including health care processes, the more responsive and responsible the family can become. In order for that participation to take place in the health care system, someone must teach families the skills necessary to maximize resources and create changes in situations that threaten or hamper the use of those resources. The responsibility for such teaching is a natural outgrowth of the relationship that the nurse has with the family, but only if the health professional chooses to initiate the teaching-learning process, with the family as consultee. With the health professional's assistance, family members can become agents of self-care instead of victims of the health care system. Clinical involvement between the student and clinic families is shaped by the attitudes and beliefs that the student has, not only about the role of the nurse as a health care provider, but about the family's role as health care recipient as well.

## CLINICAL INVOLVEMENT WITH FAMILIES

The student's clinical involvement with families can be broken down into three phases, the first of which is the preparatory phase. In the preparatory phase, the student acquires theoretical and academic knowledge of individual and group behavior; family dynamics; sociocultural and environmental influences on human performance and interactions; and the basic nature and characteristics of systems such as the family system, the health care system, and the educational system (systems in which the student is an integral and interrelated component). It is a time in which the student acquires clinical skills unique to the practice of nursing. Such academic preparation involves courses in psychology, sociology, speech communication and human relations, group dynamics, and clinical nursing. While students are acquiring academic knowledge regarding human behavior and its relationship to groups and the environment, students also actively study and research the family of origin: (1) membership, including distant and close members for at least three generations; (2) history, including unfinished task, naming, and centrality of place and purpose; (3) bonding, including the nature of emotional attachments that characterize the family; (4) territoriality and use of space, including use of psychological as well as social and physical space; (5) communication, including message patterns of verbal, nonverbal, gesture, and body movement; (6) the family's orientation—toward tasks, solutions, and problems or toward people, emotional development, and human relationships; (7) the role of individuals within the student's family, including the individual's ability to reflect family dynamics as agent or as victim; and (8) the nature of change—social, political, economic, physical, and emotional—and its impact on the family system. A vital part of the preparatory phase of clinical involvement is the student's own involvement with ongoing group experience.

The preparatory phase is influenced by the student's past history and family experience; values, attitudes, and beliefs and the practices that stem from those beliefs; experience with and knowledge of the health care system that the student represents as either advocate or adversary; the educational system and its set of assumptions regarding the basic nature of human beings; and the student's sense of self-worth as a connecting link between past and future, between education and practice, between family and social system, and between the self and the larger world of meaning.

The second phase of clinical involvement entails direct contact with families through interview, observation, and data collection. During this time the student begins to experience, personally and professionally, the meaning of system interrelatedness and the impact that an outsider's presence and participation have on the family system. The student's learning is directed outward, observing clinic families and testing principles of history, bonding, communication, territoriality, and orientation that characterize the dynamics of the clinic family to which the student is assigned. The student's role is largely that of participant observer, involved with, yet observing and learning from, the family unit. In participant observation, the student will use the process of interview to obtain valuable sociometric data such as age, sex, occupation, geographical origins, cultural and ethnic background, unique features, and significant events related to the family system. In participant observation, the student will also use the process of observation and associated techniques, such as psychograms and sociograms, to obtain information regarding patterns of bonding and communication within the family. The flow of historical events will be recorded in the family record; the flow of contemporary events will be recorded in the critical incident inventory of the family. Through participant observation, the student collects sociological and psychological data (historical and contemporary) that reveal the dynamics that characterize the particular clinic family with which the student is involved and from which the student seeks to learn. The kinds of data that are collected will depend on the questions that the student seeks to answer, for example, health status, emotional status, or use of leisure time.

Where questions are geared toward eventual problem solving and clinical intervention over a brief period, the nature and complexity of the data are more limited than where the question entails a rather detailed description of the interaction and communication patterns of the family system. Once the basic skills for interviewing and observing families are established, students may want to use abbreviated versions in order to expedite the identification of specific problems and possible solutions.

The third phase of clinical involvement with families is the intervention, evaluation, and termination phase of the clinical contract. The second and third phases of clinical involvement are overlapping largely because of the nature of the clinical process. Interviewing is, in and of itself, a form of intervention. Observation is a form of evaluation, as is data collection. The termination of the clinical involvement must be established at the outset of the contact. How long students are to be involved, the extent of the involvement, and the nature of expectations must be established in the early phases of clinical involvement. During the interview, the student becomes a part of the ongoing process of the family as a participant and as an observer. Participation and observation can, in and of themselves, constitute significant intervention in the lives of family members, depending on the family's previous experience with and current expectations of the health care system in general and the nursing student in particular. This is the phase of target identification, goal setting, identification of avenues of solutions, solutions, evaluations, and, finally, termination of the contract.

As will be discussed in later chapters, the basis or format of clinical involvement and participant observation with families is the contract, which represents a collaborative effort between the student and family and between the student and the educational system.

Although observation of and intervention with clinic families can certainly take place without the use of a contract, the use of a contract, written or informal, is based on a belief that health care strategies should be the collaborative effort of the client and the health care provider. As an active member of the interaction, the family or individual is considered to be a client who is responsible for and capable of self-direction and remediation. As a provider of health care skill and expertise, members of the health care team are considered as process consultants, whose primary aim is to facilitate changes in the situation that will enable clients to be better prepared to make decisions regarding their health care and to participate actively in the implementation of those decisions. At the same time that consultants are in a learning position, they are also in a teaching position in relationship to the family. The implications of and techniques for establishing contracts with the family as consultee and the professional as consultant will be discussed in detail in later chapters. At the outset of clinical involvement, however, the student must come to some decisions regarding the nature of involvement between the family and the health care system, particularly in terms of the attitudes and beliefs that will guide the student in establishing and carrying out clinical contact with families.

## SUMMARY

Clinical involvement with families, which can be broken down into the three phases of preparation, direct involvement, and clinical intervention, is influenced by such factors as the student's family history, particularly the emotional bonding; the values, beliefs, and attitudes, especially with regard to conflict and individual differences, of the student's family of origin; the practices that stemmed from those attitudes and beliefs, particularly in regard to judgments about the appropriateness and acceptability of the behavior of others; the nature of exposure to and experience with the health care system on the part of the clinic family and the student's family; the nature of the educational system in which the student is embedded, particularly with regard to the assumptions about and value placed on individuals by the system; and finally, the meaning that the student ascribes to the interaction between health care providers, namely, the nursing professional, and health care recipients, that is, individuals and families.

**STUDY QUESTIONS**

1. How is it possible for a clinician or student to "use" a clinic family to work out unresolved issues from their own family of origin?
2. What part do attitudes, beliefs, and practices in a student's own family play in the clinical relationship that the student seeks to establish with a clinic family?
3. Discuss Broverman and associates' findings (that what is "unhealthy" male behavior is associated with "healthy" female behavior) in terms of mental health of women.
4. What effect does a student's own exposure to and experience with the health care system have on clinical involvement with clients?
5. What is the relationship between McGregor's Theories X and Y, an educational institution's philosophy, and the clinical activities of students associated with that particular institution?

**BIBLIOGRAPHY**

Broverman, I., Broverman, D., Clarkson, F., Rosenkrantz, P., and Vogel, S.: Sex-role stereotypes and clinical judgments of mental health, J. Consult. Clin. Psychol. **34**:1, 1970.

Friedland, S., Crockett, W., and Laird, J.: The effect of role and sex on the perception of others (unpublished manuscript).

Horner, M.: Woman's will to fail, Psychology Today **3**:36, 1969.

Lynn, D. B.: A note on sex differences in the development of masculine and feminine identification, Psychol. Rev. **66**:126, 1959.

McGregor, D.: Theory X and theory Y. In The human side of enterprise, New York, 1960, McGraw-Hill Book Co. pp. 33-48.

Rosenkrantz, P., Vogel, S., Bee, H., Broverman, R., and Broverman, D.: Sex-role stereotype and self-concepts in college students, J. Consult. Clin. Psychol. **32**:287, 1968.

Sedgwick, R.: The contribution of sex and traditional vs. nontraditional role occupation on the perception of adjustment by others, Dissertation Abstracts International **33**(11):5499-B, 1973.

## SUMMARY SHEET: Chapters 1 through 10

1. Family members (who they were)
2. Family history: Unfinished tasks (what they did)
   Naming
   Centrality of place and purpose (where they came from, what they did)
3. Family bonding and significant attachments (what they believed, how they felt about one another): Conditional-unconditional
4. Use of space and territoriality: Intimate
   Personal
   Social
   Public
   Acquisition—maintenance
   Expansive—restrictive
5. Patterns of communication (dominant gestures, body movements, unique features): Honest-dishonest
   Congruent-contradictory
   Aids
   Barriers
   Styles (autocratic, democratic, mixed)
6. Individual contribution: Diverse
   Limited
   Predominant
   Use of individual as victim or agent
7. Critical incident, events, situations, and changes
8. Impressions regarding strengths and weakness in:
   Information processing
   Decision making
   Conflict management
   Individual differences
   Emotional atmosphere
   Productivity and flexibility
9. Impressions regarding basic mental health of family
10. Major pitfalls to avoid in clinical families

PART II

# Clinical concepts and clinical process

## Chapter 11

# PERSONAL GROWTH AND PROFESSIONAL PREPARATION OF THE CLINICIAN

A vital part of the student's clinical preparation is involvement with and experience of an ongoing group. As a member of a family, the student has already experienced the emotional attachment and social embeddedness that characterize the family system and make the family a unique psychosocial system. The sense of history, emotional connectedness, and social embeddedness that the student experiences in the family of origin shape not only the student's beliefs and attitudes about families but ways in which the individual establishes interpersonal relationships with peers as well as clients. To fully appreciate the nature of human relationships and their impact on consequent interactions, including the clinical process, the student must be able to examine and evaluate as well as experience the formation, growth, and consequences of the dynamics that underlie those relationships. Because of the intensity of the attachments and the student's personal involvement with the family system, objective examination and evaluation can be a difficult and complex task. An ongoing group experience is a vehicle whereby the student is able to experience and, at the same time, examine not only the development of a social system but the formation of emotional and social bonds as well.

At the same time that the group itself is an object of study, members of an ongoing group can offer support and understanding as well as challenge and stimulation to one another. Availability of competent others, sharing with peers, and self-study facilitate among group members a sense of social bonding. Students can experience firsthand the formation of a social network; they can experience the opportunity to try out new ideas, share observations, clarify perceptions, engage in the formation and development of human relationships vital for human growth, participate in active planned change, and explore new techniques and tools of observation, assessment, and intervention.

## DEFINITIONS

The following definitions, ideas, and suggestions are offered to assist students in learning about group dynamics and human relationships in light of their participation in an ongoing group of peers and colleagues. References are provided at the end of the chapter for students who wish to pursue further the study of small-group dynamics.

### Group process

"Group process" refers to the dynamics that occur as a result of individual action and group interaction in a group setting. Group process essentially differs from family process in that group dynamics are more characteristic of a social system, the goals of which are generally outcome oriented, in terms of tasks and productivity. Thus, the primary activities center around information processing, decision making, and productivity, with less emphasis on emotional atmosphere and promoting a sense of psychological connectedness. Some family systems function primarily as social systems, just as some social systems undoubtedly function primarily as psychological entities. Basically, however, family is both a social and a psychological system, whereas the group is primarily a social system with secondary emotional characteristics and benefits. Group process, in the clinical sense, is a tool, to be observed, manipulated, or used for the purposes of learning.

As a focus of observation, the group process can be examined in a variety of dimensions: for example, stages in growth, phases in development, styles of communication, patterns of interaction, orientation toward task completion and people-centered needs, individual contribution to group dynamics, use of space and territoriality, impact of change, methods of problem solving, issues of power and influence, impact of conflict and disagreement, and evidence of stress and tension.

### An ongoing group experience

"Ongoing group experience" implies the coming together of specific persons for a designated period of time. Small groups generally limit their members to seven or eight people who meet two to three hours per week, in order to provide for optimal interaction and maximum participation by all members. Although membership may be left open—that is, those who wish to participate may and those who do not may feel free not to attend—for beginning groups it is generally a better idea for a given group to meet for a specified number of weeks, usually a semester or throughout a clinical rotation. Membership may be determined in several ways: random assignment, drawing lots, alphabetical order, or by student choice. *How* membership occurs should be observed across the various groups formed from one class in order to observe any effect that membership assignment has on consequent group interaction.

At the same time that the effect of membership selection is observed, individual group members can sensitize themselves to the various ways in which members establish a sense of belonging or lack of belonging in the ongoing group. There may be those in the group who never actually establish a sense of membership but choose instead to remain on the periphery of group process. Their contribution to the ongoing group process will differ from that of the member who seeks and works at establishing not only a sense of belonging but a sense of social and personal connectedness as well.

**Stages of growth**

Observable changes in group dynamics as the group progresses from an unrelated, loosely connected set of individuals to an interrelated, mutually interdependent, functioning social system reflect stages of growth. Observable changes can be identified in communication, interaction, and overall participation. As a social system evolves from the loosely connected individuals, the group will develop rules, and ways of behaving that are associated with that particular group. The development of such parameters constitutes the formation of system boundaries, just as the development of interdependence constitutes the evolution of the social system itself. Basic group rules are that each member attend all meetings; that meetings last for a designated period of time, for example, two to three hours on a weekly basis for a semester or for the period of a clinical rotation; and that members draw up and agree on a set of guidelines that the members can use in group participation. Guidelines might describe goals to be achieved, the kind of emotional atmosphere that is expected (open, honest, supportive), dress codes (informal), meeting times (weekly), focus of meeting (group dynamics), and use of media (videotape or recorders). Each group may choose to establish a set of guidelines that best suits the needs of members and serves to facilitate particular goals set by members or instructors. Where no particular guidelines are supplied, the members can agree on meeting times, duration of group experience, the basic nature of the group process (task, problem solving, discussion, personal disclosure and growth), and any tools or techniques that the group may expect to encounter (role playing, use of videotapes). Goals established for the group or by the group will tend to shape group outcomes and therefore should be chosen with care. Stages of growth may be observed in a variety of dimensions as may the phases of development that the group will experience. Generally, stages of growth and phases of development will be closely parallel, depending on the particular model or framework that one selects to use in the examination of group process.

## Phases of development

"Phases of development" refers to the emotional, social, and interpersonal maturation of the group. Whereas stages of growth are reflected in observable changes in communication, interaction, individual participation, and sharing and the emergence of rules and guidelines, phases of development are reflected in the group's progressive emotional and social involvement and understanding. Phases of development can be described in terms of Hall's (1969) territorial dimensions: public, social, personal, and intimate, as illustrated in Fig. 3.

The student's peer and colleague group will generally begin in the *public phase* unless members of the group have become known to one another through clinical experience or academic projects that have required students to function together as a group. In the public phase, discussion and interaction focus on very general non-group-related matters that occur outside and apart from the group dynamics. Members themselves could be replaced and the topics of conversation would not change appreciably. There is no particular feeling of closeness, or group membership; individuals do not feel a commitment to either one another or the group that would exceed that felt toward any other group of strangers or individuals. The dynamics of the group parallel those of any public gathering whose predominant interactions are shaped by the environment, outside authority, or forces external to and separate from the group itself. Group mem-

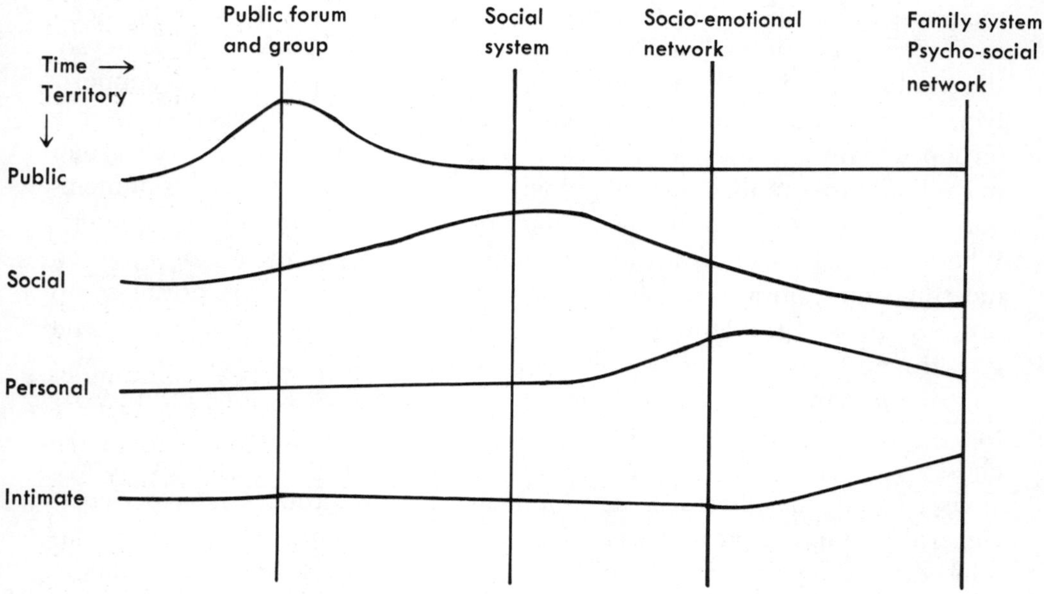


**Fig. 3.** Phases of group development.

bers usually participate at the level of observer, or onlooker, rarely experiencing direct involvement.

In the *social phase* of group development, members begin to develop a vague sense of social connectedness and a sense of network identified with group membership. Members begin to address each other as members of a particular group; however, discussion centers primarily on social system functions such as establishing goals, seeking and clarifying information, making decisions, implementing plans, and maintaining productivity. Concern for personal connectedness, belonging, or emotional development is low during this phase of group development. As a social system, the group can effectively function at this level and achieve goals, implement plans, and terminate group interaction. Members participate in an associative fashion that requires a greater involvement than does the public phase and a certain amount of interdependence in order to be effective. However, little is actually known about each other as unique individuals; there is minimal self-disclosure, and any commitment felt is for the group as a social setting. The personal and emotional distance that is maintained in this phase is bridged in the next phase; the "personal" phase.

The *personal phase* of development is entered when the group begins to recognize members as unique individuals with personal concerns, needs, expectations, and ambitions. Conversation will focus not only on getting the job done, as occurs in the social phase, but on who can best do the job in terms of ability and interest. Individual group members will gain individual identities as well as group identity. Members become less replaceable and their loss is particularly noted by the group. In this phase, members will develop feelings toward one another and toward the group as an entity. Trust, confidence, conflict, and other personal concerns will emerge and continue to grow as the group passes into the "intimate" phase of maturation.

During the *intimate phase,* the group achieves closeness, a sense of interpersonal connectedness and a feeling, of responsibility toward emotional development and support as well as toward social performance. In this phase of development, the group as an emotional entity has its greatest potential; group as a form of relating is viewed as legitimate and important. Issues of emotional honesty, personal authenticity, communication congruency, and self-disclosure are paramount. Members work at developing a deep sense of trust; express hidden fears; explore confusions and conflicts; and investigate beliefs, attitudes, and expectations that until now may have been hidden or undisclosed.

The intimate phase of development is one in which members take the greatest personal risk, that of revealing the "inner self." Where the group is emotionally mature, the risks are taken within a framework of support and acceptance. Goals established within this phase grow out of emotional needs and the desire on the part of the group to meet the individual needs of members. This phase of development is more characteristic of family systems than of social systems; in a peer or colleague group it may rarely be reached, except for isolated instances between individual members.

The various phases of group development may occur simultaneously or in an overlapping fashion; however, group generally progresses from a public phase of interaction through a social phase and on into a personal or intimate phase in a rather sequential fashion. Where development exceeds growth, the level of maturation is not likely to be maintained by the group as a whole. Where the group is a peer or colleague group, development will generally proceed from public to social and stop. Individual members may establish personal or intimate relationships, but it is unlikely that such experiences will be shared by the group as a whole, because of time constraints and the overall learning orientation of the group itself. The purpose of the group, the ability of members, and the external constraints with which a group must cope all influence maturational levels of groups, as revealed in styles of communication and patterns of interaction. The communication process, just as patterns of interaction, can be studied in conjunction with or apart from the group's stages of growth and phases of development.

**Communication process**

The communication process involves the exchange of information between members within the group. Information exchange in a social system, as in the family system, employs verbal and nonverbal forms of expression, including words, gestures, actions, and body movements. As in family communication, these forms are used to create impressions; to respond to actions, impressions, and expectations of others; to make feelings, thoughts, and opinions known to others; and to initiate, maintain, or alter the dynamics that occur between people. Communication may be used for control, understanding, exploitation, or teaching; it can be directive, structured, and purposeful or nondirective, confusing, and distracting.

**Styles of communication**

Styles of communication are ways in which communications are organized to achieve certain ends; for example, understanding, control, or learning. Styles of communication can be observed, recorded, and evaluated. The observation and recording of styles of communication involves observing who says what, to whom, for what purpose, and with the consequence and then depicting by use of a diagram the origin, flow, frequency, duration, and consequence of communication. Such a diagram is generally referred to as a sociogram and can be used to identify styles of communication (democratic, autocratic) as well as barriers and aids to the communication process. As will be seen there is a close relationship between the communication process and the patterns of interaction that evolve in the group.

### Patterns of interaction

Patterns of interaction are ways in which group members establish territory (physical, social, or emotional); create boundaries (rules, sanctions, innuendos); initiate network functions of social bonding; and progress toward the development of a social system. The use of the space, the initiation of social bonding or networking, and the development of rules and behavioral sanctions can be observed and examined by individual members as well as by the group as a whole. The use of the self as a legitimate subject of observation and learning is one of the more productive and useful aspects of an ongoing group experience. As will be seen, both patterns of interaction and styles of communication will reflect and be shaped by the orientation that the group takes toward itself: as primarily a problem-centered, task-oriented group; a people-centered, personal-growth-oriented group; or a group that balances work demands with people needs.

### Orientation

The concerns around which the group organizes its efforts and focuses its energies define its orientation. Task-oriented groups are primarily concerned with task accomplishment, problem solving, and goal achievement. Competition, conflict, power struggles, priority setting, and goal identification are primary concerns of such a group. People-centered groups, however, are primarily concerned with character development, personal growth, and emotional expression. Understanding, experience, intimacy, honesty, and openness are issues of primary concern in such a group. Too heavy an emphasis in either direction, however, leads to the development of only parts of the human relationship and to group control by a group member with a particular orientation. Some group members will believe that getting the job done is most important and that any thing else is a waste of time, just as others will believe that self-disclosure and personal growth are more important than the job at hand. The group as a social system seeks to join and organize such interests and abilities into a unified whole. Individual uniqueness, in ability as well as in orientation, is a vital contribution that each member makes to the group.

### Individual contribution to the group process

The part each member plays in the ongoing dynamics of the group is that individual's contribution to the group process. Individual contribution can be made in terms of unique interest and abilities; particular cultural or ethnic background; specific attitudes, values, or expectations; individual family background; or the kinds of responses that individuals are able to draw from others. Individual contribution may be observed in differential abilities in listening and caring, organizing and directing, sharing and cooperating, confronting and clarifying, and in verbal and nonverbal expression. Each individual has something of value to contribute to the group process. A mature group draws on, encourages, and incorporates individual uniqueness, providing space and support for individual members to explore their individuality as well as their group identity.

**Group identity**

Group identity is the sense of group membership that grows out of participation in the formation of the social system. The sense of belonging to or being an essential component of the larger network of a social system may not carry with it the emotional intensity of membership within a family system but does provide the student with an opportunity to experience being a system within a system: connected to yet separate from; dependent on yet independent from other group members; cooperating with yet confronting; supporting and receiving support while expecting clarification and emotional honesty; holding onto old ideas but examining and trying out new values and attitudes as well; and working toward unified goals and maintaining individual identity and integrity. As a member of a social system whose main purpose is learning, the student is afforded the opportunity to practice not only skills related to system functioning—information seeking, decision making, productivity, and management of individual differences—but also skills necessary for initiating, establishing, and maintaining clinical relationships.

**Skills in relationships**

Skills in relationships include the basic tools necessary for initiating and maintaining interaction: listening, reflecting, observing and clarifying observations, caring and sharing that concern with others, and being able to confront and express one's own feelings and beliefs. Building a relationship requires as much work and involves as much responsibility as does the creation of any other living entity. A relationship becomes a link between those involved within its parameters. The quality of the linkage is very much dependent on the efforts, abilities, and commitments of those involved.

*Listening* implies a willingness to hear ideas, attitudes, and beliefs that may be contrary to one's own. Listening means having to sort out how much of what is being expressed (verbal, nonverbal) belongs to, or is owned by, the person doing the expressing and how much is owned by others, including the self. Fears, angers, doubts, or joys may be feelings that belong solely to others and are merely expressed to the willing listener. One of the ways to establish ownership of feelings is to check out one's impressions through the process of reflection and clarification.

*Reflecting* is the process of taking one's impressons, checking them against one's own internal barometer of the situation, and checking it against impressions made by others. Where what one hears, sees, or senses is in direct opposition to what one is being told, either one's senses are in error or the situation is not being honestly represented. This may happen when another individual says one thing and means another or expresses one feeling (anger) but acts out another (indifference) or when what one is hearing is so painful, frightening, or contradictory to one's experience that one is hearing one's own internal message instead of the actual message being sent. In order to sort out the difficulty, the process of clarifying one's own observations and perceptions with others is essential.

*Clarifying* means comparing one's own impressions, perceptions, and sensations with those of others: the person sending out the signals as well as others who may be directly involved in the process. This is an invaluable asset that the group offers its members, that of being able to compare with others who are sharing a similar and simultaneous experience. With seven group members, it is often possible to have seven different impressions, all of which are partially correct. Difference in emotional background, social experience, and group expectation add to differences in perceptions that group members have. It is particularly important to clarify signals with the sender of the signal, in terms of intent, impact, and need. One perceives another's need, not only based on request but on internal dynamics created with the receiver.

*Caring and sharing* mean being open with others in terms of one's own feelings, ideas, and needs and sensitive to the feelings, ideas, and needs of others. Part of caring and sharing is the mutual working out of the parameters of the relationship. In the clinical relationship, as is discussed in the following chapter, the contract is the vechicle by which clinician and client work out the parameters of the clinical relationship. Caring and sharing mean taking risks in terms of being rejected, unaccepted, or not needed. With clients, it often means being with someone who resents needing someone; sharing with someone who has never learned to share; or being emotionally honest with someone who has never learned to be honest with the self, let alone with others. In some cases, it means teaching another how to share and setting an example for others when one is at a point in life when sharing and caring are in the developing stages. It often means practicing acceptance, and pretending that one accepts others unconditionally. With enough practice, caring becomes second nature. When caring becomes second nature, the student has opened the gates to personal growth.

**Personal growth**

Personal growth is the experience of oneself as an expanding social, physical, and psychological system. It is the discovery not only of oneself as a dynamic entity, but of one's connectedness to a larger world of people. Personal growth is the unfolding of oneself and the discovery inherent in that unfolding of experiences, ideas, hopes, and fears that come not only from within but from encounters with others as well. Personal growth entails learning to feel for and care about others: to experience another's failure with a private sense of remorse; to feel another's loss as a diminishing of one's social territory; to sense another's fears with a recognition that many share the same fears. It is to share another's pain and to grope for understanding. It is to reach out and touch another, to allow differences and support change. Personal growth begins with the recognition that one is connected: to history, to society, to family, to a human network. The process of personal unfolding only begins with such a discovery; it is a process that continues throughout one's lifetime. A group experience in which one can begin the unfolding of self, if only in small stages, is essential to any professional whose life goals include helping others with their own unfolding processes.

## GUIDELINES

There are some basic "do's" and "don'ts" associated with an ongoing group experience that will facilitate both group process and the personal growth experience of individual members. They can be summarized as follows.

*Do:*

1. Establish a set of goals that will guide the group and individual members through the unfolding process. Examples of such goals are: (a) to strive for emotional honesty—to say what one feels, and to feel what one says; (b) to work toward congruity in messages, trying to make words, actions, and gestures carry the same clear message; (c) to aim toward a revealing of self; (d) to concentrate on gaining a heightened sensitivity through feeling, empathy, and listening; (e) to concentrate on heightened awareness in perceiving, reflecting, and absorbing; (f) to observe and learn about forces within the group such as common needs that pull the group together and conflicts that push the group apart; (g) to strive for communication styles that are democratic, open, and honest; (h) to establish interaction patterns that include a variety of individual actions—passive and onlooking, parallel, associative, agentry; (i) to observe and learn about how structure (guidelines, rules, organization) affects group interaction and individual participation; and (j) to identify and explore issues that

come up in the group, such as conflict versus harmony, "I" versus "we," and task versus atmosphere.

2. Explore alternatives and expand options in thinking, feeling, and acting.
3. Explore and examine beliefs and attitudes.
4. Expand "hunches" and develop a strong intuition about group dynamics, individual messages, and self-needs.
5. Practice sensitivity and constructive communication.
6. Practice authenticity.
7. Explore the meaning of social networks and the impact of the physical environment on the functioning of the network. Notice the effect of closed spaces, wide ranges in temperature, and placement of tables, chairs, and windows.

*Avoid:*

1. Ruling by majority just to accomplish a task.
2. Ignoring individual differences.
3. Ignoring feelings out of fear.
4. Letting outside issues push the group process and the ongoing events in the group out of discussions and interactions.
5. Pushing for the "ideal"; rather, strive to be real.

The group will contain within its boundaries an unlimited set of sources and resources. Each member will be competent in something, just as every member will lack some skill. Together the group can grow, learn, challenge, stimulate, comfort, confront, and expand alternative choices. The group experience can provide a forum for ideas and an arena in which members can try out new techniques and practice old skills. The relationships and interactions that are established within the group can be used as a basis for study and exploration. The basis for personal growth stems from the kind of relationships that one is able to initiate, establish, and maintain. The relationships that one is able to establish, personally and professionally, have a direct bearing on the success or failure of the clinical process of which the clinical student is a significant member.

The foundation of the clinical process is the relationship that is established between partners in the process. Because of the importance of the bond that forms between members of the clinical team, including family members, care must be taken to assure that the bond is based on sensitivity, trust, mutual respect, and confidence. The formation of such a bond is a slow, painstaking process that requires not only sensitivity but skill. An ongoing group experience, shared with other developing clinicians, provides students the opportunity to develop sensitivity and test interactional skills. The use of a contract, as discussed in Chapter 12, assures that the members of the clinical team are aware of and agree to expectations and goals. Mutual responsibility must be exercised by all members to assure the fulfillment of the contract and to assure that relationships formed will be beneficial, productive, and growth inducing for everyone involved. The group experience provides a foundation on which group members can continue to build throughout their clinical experiences.

## SUMMARY

An ongoing group experience composed of seven to nine peers who meet on a weekly basis for a period of 12 to 16 weeks provides the clinical student an opportunity to experience and participate in the formation of a social system; to participate in and observe emotional and social bonding; to share in the process of individual self-disclosure; to observe patterns of interaction and communication; to try out new ideas; and to practice clinical skills of listening, caring, reflecting, clarifying, and supporting. Through participant observation, students are active participants as well as objective onlookers. An ongoing group of peers and colleagues is one of the best places to hone ideas, establish system intervention strategies, clarify observations, and test interpersonal abilities. There is probably no better way to practice skills of listening, reflecting, supporting, and confronting than with a group of peers who are involved in the same educational struggle and through that shared experience are able to identify with one another's fears, hopes, confusions, and ambitions. And there is probably no greater challenge than to make oneself, one's membership in a group, and the group interaction itself the object of study and evaluation. It is a challenge, however, well worth undertaking.

### STUDY QUESTIONS

1. Although differences between a group experience and the family system may appear subtle, such differences can be found. Discuss the origin and effect of such differences.
2. Which phase of group development most closely approximates family experience? What is the significance of personal disclosure during this phase?
3. What part does group orientation play in the styles of communication that are used by a group?
4. Name five basic tools necessary for human interaction. Discuss ways in which basic lack of tools contributes to ineffective group functioning.
5. In what ways can group development be compared and contrasted with territorial behavior in the family?

### EXERCISES

1. *Decision making:* Of the following ten qualities, decide individually and as a group which are the four least important and the four most important. (Reach individual decision before discussion as a group.)

| | |
|---|---|
| Social recognition | Sense of accomplishment |
| Pleasure | Inner harmony |
| Family security | Health |
| Self-respect | Freedom |
| Happiness | Equality |

2. *Information seeking:* As a group, discuss how decisions were reached in Exercise 1, noting contributions that various individuals have made to the group process.
3. *Risk taking:* Rank members of group in terms of (a) height, (b) weight, and (c) value. How did responses of group differ with each task? How honest were *you* in judging the value of another person? How did you decide on what *value* to use as a criterion?
4. *Conflict:* Select three topics from the following list and discuss pros and cons: (a) capital punishment, (b) abortion, (c) living wills, (d) organ transplants, (e) mandatory institutionalization for emotionally disturbed, (f) birth control information for teenagers without parental consent, and (g) euthanasia, particularly in the case of terminally ill patients.
5. *Self-disclosure and intimacy:* Discuss with the group your: (a) greatest fear, (b) worst mistake, (c) strongest ambition, (d) favorite group members, and (e) least favorite group member. Treat this exercise with care: observe carefully the impact both on yourself and others.
6. Select an area of your life you would like to examine, for example, emotions: (a) your inability to direct anger; (b) your relationship with your mother-in-law, relatives and/or others; or (c) your inability to be "up front" with others, that is, to say what is on your mind. Describe the situation to the group; direct members in acting out parts in the situation; get impressions from group members regarding the situation, including your alternatives and options. Try out the alternatives on a group member, with other members observing. What did you learn?
7. Take time in the group to try out new behaviors: being assertive, being cooperative, being argumentative, taking leadership, assuming followership, being close and friendly, or being distant and shy. In trying out new behaviors, note and share with the group your feelings. Observe carefully not only your internal reaction but the group's response to you as well.
8. Use the group to practice clinical skills: interviewing, observing, assessing, and goal planning. How well do you use feedback and assistance from others; how readily do you assist others in learning new skills? How well can you include as well as exclude, appreciate as well as criticize, examine new ideas as well as hold old values? In what ways do you make a contribution to the group and the group to you?
9. Chart the group's stages of growth and phases of development as well as your own individual progress. Do your growth and development exceed, parallel, or come after the group's?

| *Week* | *Public* | *Social* | *Personal* | *Intimate* |
|---|---|---|---|---|
| 1 | | | | |
| 2 | | | | |
| 3 | | | | |
| 4 | | | | |
| etc. | | | | |

## BIBLIOGRAPHY

Burton, A.: Encounter; theory and practice of encounter groups, San Francisco, 1969, Jossey-Bass, Inc., Publishers.

Egan, G.: Encounter; group processes for interpersonal growth, Belmont, Calif., 1970, Brooks Cole Publishing Co.

Frankl, V.: Man's search for meaning, New York, 1969, Washington Square Press.

Hall, E.: Hidden dimensions, New York, 1969, Anchor Books.

Hall, J.: Decisions, decisions, decisions, Psychology Today **5**:51, 1971.

Jacobs, A., and Spradlin, W.: The group as agent of change, New York, 1974, Behavioral Publications.

Jourard, S.: The transparent self; self-disclosure and well-being, New York, 1964, D. Van Nostrand Co.

Kelly, J.: Make conflict work for you, Harvard Business Rev. July-August 1970, pp. 103-113.

Laing, R. D.: The politics of experience, New York, 1967, Ballantine Books.

Mayeroff, M.: On caring, New York, 1971, Harper & Row, Publishers.

Pfeiffer, J., and Jones, J.: A handbook of structured experience for human relations training, Iowa City, 1969, University Associates Press.

Racy, J.: How does a group grow? Am. J. Nurs. **69**:2396-2400, November 1969.

Smith, P., editor: Group processes, Baltimore, 1970, Penguin Books.

Thibaut, J., and Kelly, H.: The social psychology of groups, New York, 1961, John Wiley and Sons, Inc.

Chapter 12

# CONTRACTUAL AGREEMENT BETWEEN CLIENT AND CLINICIAN

The process that clinical nursing students undertake in studying and working with families is basically that which the more experienced clinician uses in working with individuals or groups. Interviewing, observing, assessing, goal setting, intervention strategies, and evaluation procedures are all essential components of the clinical nursing process, whether that process is applied to the single individual, the individual in groups, or the family as a system.

The essence of the clinical process, particularly with family systems, lies in the relationship that is established between the clinician and the client or patient. The relationship is the basis on which the entire clinical process is founded. The student comes to the family as a budding clinician, a representative of the health care system, a representative of the educational process and as a person with needs, attitudes, and beliefs. The family comes to the student with expectations, needs, concerns, and complexities. There may be discrepancies between what the student expects and what the family is able to offer in information, disclosure, and inclusion into the family process. However, the outcomes will depend not so much on the contradictions and discrepancies as on how the relationship between the clinician and family is handled.

## PARTICIPANT OBSERVATION

As participant, the student becomes part of the process that is being observed and studied. As observer, the student maintains a clinical distance that permits clearer judgments and a more objective evaluation of the process. As a participant with the family, the student will be privy to information not available to outsiders. The family will be asked to share intimate details of their life together—health, medical, social, sexual, economic, and emotional. Where the relationship is based on mutual respect and trust between the clinical student and the family, the nature of the information revealed may be quite personal or intimate.

To build a clinical relationship founded on trust and mutual respect is a delicate and painstaking process. As much as the clinical student becomes a part of the process that involves and centers around the family system, because of the clinical role and responsibility, the study must maintain a posture of observer of the family system as well.

To be a part of the process is not synonymous with taking out membership in the family system. Family membership is a privilege and responsibility of those who share common history, who engage in intimate and intense emotional attachments, and who make a time commitment to one another that exceeds the commitment that one would make to social or professional groups. Although the student may "feel" that a family considers the student "one of the family," the student will be wise to remember that family membership is emotionally and historically different from membership in social systems, requires ongoing work, and entails a personal commitment to the family system itself. The student's commitment is to the clinical nursing process in which the family is a client—to be observed, assessed, evaluated, and, where possible, assisted.

In a very real sense, the clinical student is an observer with a task. The nature of the task sets the student apart from the family system, whose task it is to be self-centered and self-involved. The student's task is to be clinically involved, not personally committed to any particular family. The emphasis on clinical distance and objectivity is made primarily because it is one of the most crucial yet one of the most difficult aspects of the clinical process. Becoming overinvolved with a client is not a problem peculiar to the clinical student but is shared by many clinicians in the field of mental health. Overinvolvement with clients and overextension of the professional self into the personal self of others are based on a characteristic common among people in the helping professions (such as nursing, psychology, social work, and ministry), that is, the need to rescue people from themselves. This need may be described as "rescue fantasies."

## RESCUERS AND VICTIMS

To want to rescue a person or persons from their situation, whether that situation be poverty, emotional abuse, or social ignorance, is a feeling that clinicians often experience. However, many people do not want to be rescued or removed. They prefer to take responsibility for their own lives, including the decision to change or not change. The rescuer intent on delivery of people from their fate generally becomes the one needing rescue. The rescuer becomes victim rather than agent in the process of human change. Rescue fantasies, or the need to salvage or drag people from their current predicaments, are often based on McGregor's (1960) Theory X of human behavior. As discussed in an earlier chapter, Theory X holds a rather passive view of human beings, in which the person must be directed, controlled, and managed by one who knows more about people than people know about themselves. This attitude underlies the notion of people as "patients," that is, passive recipients of the health care system, and of professionals as "experts" who "deliver" predetermined services.

Another view of people in relation to the health care system is as "clients." The notion of the health care recipient as "client" entails taking the Theory Y view of people, which is basically to see them as active, self-directed, and responsible. In this view, clients do not need to be rescued as much as educated. Clients do not need direction and control as much as guidance and understanding. The professional is not an "expert" who provides a predetermined service but a resource on which the client draws in order to gain clearer understanding, to determine a viable set of alternatives, to identify consequences of given alternatives, and to ultimately gain a sense of self-direction and self-confidence.

The basis of the client-clinician relationship is the contract. Underlying the concept of clients as self-directed, responsible individuals is the need to provide a means whereby clients can become equal partners in the health care process. Such a means is provided through the use of a contract that is collaboratively derived by client and clinician.

## CONTRACT

The contract is basically an understanding and agreement between consenting parties, in this case the clinical student and the client family system. The contract may be written or verbal, informal or formal, but must be a conscious and collaborative effort between those involved. In many cases, the contract may simply involve the need on the part of the student to learn more about family dynamics and the family's agreement to serve as the target of examination and investigation, generally for a specified period. The student clearly understands that the primary reason for the family's presence in the situation is to provide the student with information, observational data, and other data that aid the student in learning. Similarly, the family understands that any direct provision of service will be a secondary component of the learning process, unless the student is clearly able to provide some service and so states at the outset as an element of the contract. Both parties then discuss expectation and understanding regarding the nature of the relationship to be established and the time for which the relationship will be operational.

As the clinical student progresses in skill and sophistication, the elements of the contract may be expanded to include agreed-on services to be provided: for example, health screening, behavioral assessment, goal planning, health education, or provision of nursing care. Where the educational opportunities include a nursing clinic as a clinical practicum site, it is often possible to exchange services with clients. For example, in a nursing clinic that I directed, it was possible to contract a ten week learning experience in exchange for health screening and blood pressure monitoring for family members. The family agreed to be interviewed and observed for ten weeks by community mental health students in exchange for a health assessment of each member provided by a staff member or nursing student in the clinic.

The nature of the contract will vary depending on the need of the parties involved, the level of ability of each party at the time the contract is agreed on, and the nature of the constraints that characterize the particular situation. The use of a contract, in and of itself, implies (1) a belief that all members of the contract have rights and responsibilities and (2) an expectation that each member will exercise rights and perform responsibilities according to the best of his or her ability at any given time. The contract is an ethical and professional agreement as binding as any social or legal document.

### General elements

The general elements of the contract involve a discussion of who is to be involved, what may be generally expected to occur, and over what period of time the contract is to be carried out. More specific stages of the contract can be discussed as elements or phases that must be carried out jointly between the clinical student and the clinic family system, in the belief that outcomes of the clinical process are a joint responsibility shared by all participants in the process. The client is seen as an active, responsive, thinking, and self-directed system who can be guided, assisted, and educated to a better way of life. The clinical student is an educated resource whose skill and expertise are used to facilitate the clinical process.

### Specific process components

Specific phases of the contract include (1) entry, (2) setting up the components of the contract, (3) agreeing on the focus of effort, (4) discussing methods of data collection, (5) understanding how the data will be handled or analyzed, (6) possible outcomes, including any interventions, and, finally, (7) decisions regarding evaluation and termination of the clinical process.

**Entry.** Gaining entry means obtaining access to the client system and establishing legitimacy for involvement. The way in which one enters another system significantly influences the nature of the relationships that are established in later parts of the contract. A family that *volunteers* to be a client for the purpose of learning and understanding actively invites the student, clinician, or researcher into the process of family life. The clinical student, then, is welcomed by the family. Where a family is referred by another professional, agency, or system, the relationship that the student is able to establish will be partially determined by the relationship that the family had with the referral source. The clinical sudent generally gains access to the family system through the health care system—community health agency, mental health clinic, or nursing clinic. Thus, the clinical student's legitimacy in the family is either by virtue of the family's previous contract with a health agency or through the student's initiated contact. The contact is generally either through the health agency or via a telephone call that the student makes to the family. In many situations, it may be up to the student to establish a point of entry. How a student enters the family system—for example, through a family member, a health agency, a medical service, an educational institution, or a self-initiated process—influences the focus of the contract and whose agent the student appears to be. If possible, it is best for the clinical student to gain entry through either educational or health-related systems; thus, the student and the family are better able to keep the focus of the contract more clearly on learning and health-related activities of education, assessment, and evaluation.

**Establishing the components of the contract.** This refers to what is to be included in the relationship being established. In establishing the components of the contract, principles of collaboration, negotiation, and clarification are employed. The family and the clinical student explore together expectations, time commitment, and scope of activities that might be included. A simple statement that conveys the clinical student's need to learn more about family dynamics and the family's willingness to assist in that process may be sufficient in the beginning phases of clinical involvement. As the student gains skills and becomes more clinically sophisticated, it will be possible to discuss a broader range of activities, such as goals to be worked on, intervention strategies to be included, services that can be provided in exchange for the family's participation, and elements to be negotiated should either party wish to withdraw from the contracted agreement. The scope of the contract may be narrowly defined—data collection and observations of the communication process in the family system for a ten-week period, using specifically named techniques and tools—or more broadly defined—ten-week interview and observation period of family dynamics with the benefits of the family being in the information that is gleaned during that ten-week period. Once the general scope of the contract is established, specific concerns, activities, and needs may be discussed. Specifically agreed-on elements of the contract become the focus of the contract for the time specified in the agreement.

**Focus of the contract.** The focus is the specific direction that efforts will take during the period the clinician is actively involved with the client. In the case of clinical students who must work within a time constraint determined by academic and course schedules, the focus might be quite narrow: for example, interviewing the family for the purpose of determining family membership; taking a family history to identify patterns of communication according to principles of democratic leadership; or assessing the family's strengths and weaknesses as a family system. Where the clinical student or clinician is interested in learning about the dynamics of family interaction in order to assess family effectiveness, the focus of the clinical contract may be quite broad and detailed, and including, for example, interviews to complete the family record, observations of family interaction and communication, assessment of family's ability to establish an emotional atmosphere that allows for maximum individuation, evaluation of family decision-making abilities, and a determination of the overall level of productivity. The outcome of such a detailed clinical process evolves quite naturally into the identification of appropriate intervention strategies. However, where the focus of the contract is limited by time, ability, or other constraints, any single component may be focused on during a specified period. At the end of the contract period, another component of family life may be the focus of concern; this second focus, however, requires that the client and clinician negotiate a second contract with its own identifiable parameters.

During this phase of the contract, the client and clinician must decide specifically what is to be observed, assessed, or evaluated. Following this phase, which generally takes from one to three meetings, the methods to be used must be discussed.

**Methods of data collection.** Ways in which data about the client are collected include direct interview, observation, paper and pencil tests, health history forms, scales and attitude questionnaires, and tape recordings. The means for collection of data may depend on the specific focus, which is discussed previously, and will most certainly determine the way in which the data collected will be used and analyzed. The methods of data collection depend not only on the focus of the contract but on the overall nature of the contract as well. Where the nature of the contract is prevention and learning, the scope, focus, and methodology may be quite broad. In our clinical situation, such methods include extensive history taking, family interview, observation of family interaction and communication, assessment of emotional atmosphere, evaluation of decision-making attributes, and a determination of levels of productivity and conflict management. Tools include attitude questionnaires, simulated family activities, role enactment, analysis of family photographs and family memorabilia, and completion of tasks that elicit specific areas of concern. Where couples are involved, tools are used that draw out areas of agreement and disagreement. Where children are involved, tools for developmental assessment and screening are included along with a pediatric neurological assessment. Although every effort is made to work with the family as a system, if the family is a blended family or a one-parent family, it is often necessary to interview and observe subgroups within the family system as well. A holistic assessment, whether of individual or family, includes a thorough knowledge of physical, social, and emotional health; tools are used to provide a wide range of information and clinical data.

Where the focus of the contract is more limited, as in crises, problem solving, or evaluation for the purposes of school, hospital, or court referral, the nature of the contract, the scope of the contract, and the range of methods used must of course reflect realistic constraints: for example, emphasis on a delimited problem. Although the focus on problem is antithetical to systems intervention, frequently social systems are not as interested in how the family interacts and communicates as concerned about a specific management problem of a family member in the immediate social system. Where problem solving is emphasized, it is often possible for the clinician to agree to perform the evaluation and consultation in exchange for a specified number of visits with the entire family system. When the family or family member is referred and has previously been labeled a "problem," the clinician's role in the family is frequently taken by the family to be an extension of the system requiring the consultation or evaluation. A previous contract between the clinician and another social system may retard the development of trust and mutual respect between the clinician and the family. Where possible, we prefer that clients be self-referred or at least initiate the first clinical contact themselves. Clients are assisted in as much self-direction and control as possible within given constraints. The data gleaned and the results of clinical interactions will reflect the nature of the interpersonal relationship between client and clinician as well as the methods used to collect the data.

How the information will be used and analyzed is an equally important issue that must be discussed at the outset of the clinical relationship.

**Data handling and use.** This refers to what happens to the information that is collected during the period of clinical involvement with the client system, in this case the family. Where the focus is on prevention and learning, the information is generally compiled, recorded, and used in the educational setting. If the materials collected are to be shared with other colleagues, students, or instructors, the family should be made aware of this at the outset. If the data are to be used in research, in study, or in public forum, the family must give written as well as verbal consent. It is not possible to provide agencies, professionals, or other groups with the information collected without the written consent of the family member and without specifying at the outset who is to have access to the information. If possible, the family system should be informed of the nature of the report and evaluation being forwarded to other professionals. We make it a general policy to make reports available to the family and individuals involved in the clinical process. The family may have a specific interest that grows out of the material collected; these interests form the basis of a second and often a third contract. Most families are open and eager to learn about themselves and to help clinicians and students in particular in the process of interview, assessment, and evaluation.

When the materials are collected and compiled, it is possible to begin to identify, with the family, possible outcomes and feasible intervention strategies.

**Outcomes and intervention.** What is to be done with what is learned about the family process, including any proposed changes, interventions, or evaluations, is considered outcome and intervention. For the student operating under the constraints of academic calendars and course requirements, the first set of outcomes might be to observe, assess, and record the dynamics of a particular family or set of families. A second set of outcomes might be focused on the change that an identified family seeks to make in internal dynamics or external relationships. The outcomes desired must be generally agreed on at the beginning of the contract, so that clinical student and family have a common set of expectations regarding the scope and duration of clinical involvement. For the more sophisticated clinical student and the more experienced clinician, the intervention phase may occur simultaneously with the entry, or intake, phase. Making a telephone call and beginning the intitial phases of contract negotiation may in and of themselves, constitute significant clinical intervention.

Where little is known about the particular individual or family system, and the nature of the contract has been vaguely stated in terms of learning more about family dynamics, outcomes may also be stated quite generally. Regardless of the nature of the particular family, desirable learning outcomes are: enhanced understanding, increased sensitivity and awareness, development of mutual respect, display of trust and confidence in one another, increased knowledge about family as system, a positive encounter with a representative of the health care team, and increased skill in interviewing, observing, assessing, and evaluating family as a system. Where clinical contact is primarily through an academic setting, the contract is written with student learning needs as primary. Where clinical contact is primarily through consultative settings, the contract is written from the standpoint of the need of the referral source. Where the contact is initiated in a service setting or by the family, the contract is written from the standpoint of clinical needs of the family, with the family's need for self-knowledge and change as primary elements of the contract focus.

As the clinical student increases in clinical sophistication, the focus can be expanded to include a wide range of assessment and intervention strategies. However, it should be noted that the best intervention is preceded by thorough history taking followed by assessment and observation. Thorough history taking together with detailed and careful observation are often the primary assessment tools necessary, not only in learning about family dynamics but in identifying strengths, weaknesses, communication contradictions, power struggles, emotional abuse, and so forth, as typified by a specific family system.

The need for specific interventions is often suggested by the findings or lack of findings when interview and observation data are compiled and recorded. The nature of intervention is influenced by the purpose of the contract (prevention, learning, problem solving, health education, consultation, or referral), and by diagnostic information made available through contract implementation.

Contract implementation includes, in addition to outcomes and intervention strategies, the identification of mechanisms for evaluation of the clinical process and agreement regarding termination of the contract. Termination is contingent on contract fulfillment. One of the most important components of clinical intervention is some measure of effectiveness, by which the clinical process may be terminated.

**Evaluation and termination.** This refers to the aspect of clinical contract in which participants formulate and articulate objectives related to outcomes and interventions, including an agreed-on rationale or date at which the clinical contract is to be terminated. The decision to be made as to when all elements of the contract have been fulfilled will largely depend on the elements agreed on initially: length of commitment, scope of involvement, range of questions to be asked, scope of data collected, use and handling of data, and desired outcomes. Generally, the evaluation phase is reached and termination begins when the data have been collected, compiled, and shared with the family. Where change is desired and the clinical student has the ability and time to commit to working with the family, a second contract based specifically on desired change and identified outcomes must be negotiated. Where there is to be no follow-up contract, the family must be informed of alternatives, such as referral to another health professional, student, or agency.

Because of the complexities of family dynamics, the first contract should be limited, either by goals or by time. This assures that both the clinical student and the family will know beforehand: (1) how long the student and family will be working together, (2) the expected date of completion, or (3) the number of visits that will be made. Because of the tendency to want to help or provide the family with some assistance, the clinical student must adhere to the elements agreed on in the contract. Where the contract is primarily a learning contract, the length of time will probably be set by academic calendar and course requirement. Both the family and the clinical student should be aware of the time and action constraints. Where the clinical contract is primarily one of change or problem solving, it is still desirable to set a deadline when goals will be evaluated and the contract either renewed or terminated. Where progress is being made, more elaborate goals may be agreed on; in such instances, the contract is an evolving one, with periodic dates set for examination and evaluation of the clinical process.

The process of evaluation is necessary in order that the clinical student as well as the family have some means of charting the clinical course. Evaluation components will be related to focus and agreed-on goals and may be stated in terms of behavioral objectives, time deadlines, number of visits, desired outcomes, frequency of contact, or a combination of these. The process of termination is equally important; for many clinicians, it is the most difficult of all phases of the clinical contract. Termination means that when the outcomes agreed on (number of visits, goals, behavioral changes, and so forth) are reached the contract is terminated. Termination often comes when needs become apparent and possibilities for change seem the greatest. In all fairness, however, where an agreed-on outcome has been reached, the particular contract has been fulfilled. The termination phase may be preceded by copies of the reports and a series of recommendations, such as the continuation of the clinical process, or may simply follow an agreed-on number of visits or date at which the contract will be considered by both parties to be concluded. It is not advantageous for the clinical student to pursue the contract on an informal basis through continued home visits, letter writing, or hospital visits unless this is an understood part of the contract from the beginning. It is advisable for the clinical student to conclude the contract completely at a given time in order to avoid personal extension into professional endeavors and making promises to the family that the student is unable to fulfill.

## Clinical contract

A clinical contract is a vehicle where by clinician and client can exercise their individual rights and perform their mutual responsibilities in the clinical process. In the contract, clients are viewed as active, responsive, and responsible. Clinicians are viewed as resources, guides, educators, and facilitators. The clinical student is viewed as a budding clinician, whose educational and professional development is enhanced through the familiarization with and use of an informal or formal agreement in which expectations are made known, outcomes are made clear, and the ways of achieving such outcomes can be collaboratively negotiated between the clinical student and the family system. The elements of a contract include entry, general scope, specific focus, data collection, data analysis or assessment, outcomes or interventions, evaluation, and termination.

The phases of contract completion generally are entry, interview, observation, assessment with goal planning, intervention with goal implementation, evaluation with goal completion, and termination. The clinical process encompasses the completion of the contract from entry to termination and is in actuality an overlapping process, with observation overlapping assessment, intervention overlapping evaluation, and evaluation continuing until, and often after, the final stages of termination. The clinical process itself is a fluid, ever-evolving relationship between the clinician and the client system, with identifiable stages that overlap and complement one another. The use of a contract provides a means of organizing as well as charting the progress and development of the clinical process between client and a specific clinician.

The following four contracts are examples of (1) a general format for contracts, (2) a format for a learner contract used by a clinical student and a clinic family that has agreed to participate in the learning process, (3) a clinic contract drawn up for the purpose of referral and consultation where a health agency has asked for emotional evaluation of the family environment, and(4)a clinical contract drawn up for the purposes of clinical intervention where a tensive client has been referred for a progressive relaxation training program.

**CONTRACT: GENERAL FORMAT**

**Contract:** ________________ **Family** ________________ **Student**

*Entry:* ______________________________________________

______________________________________________

*General scope:* ______________________________________________

______________________________________________

*Specific focus:* ______________________________________________

______________________________________________

*Method of data collection:* ______________________________________________

______________________________________________

*Analysis or assessment:* ______________________________________________

______________________________________________

*Outcomes or interventions:* ______________________________

______________________________

*Evaluation:* ______________________________

______________________________

*Termination:* ______________________________

______________________________

**CONTRACT: SPECIFIC EXAMPLE (LEARNING)**

**Contract:** Learning ___Jones___ **Family** ___Hass___ **Student**

*Entry:* Health system/educational setting.

*General scope:* Family dynamics, with particular emphasis on style of communication.

*Specific focus:* Particular emphasis on social systems dynamics—information processing, decision making, and productivity. Psychological system dynamics deferred to second contract.

*Method of data collection:* Interview and observation—tape recording of dialogue, sociogram of frequency of verbal communication, diagrammatic recording of direction of nonverbal communication.

*Data use:* To compile case study for classroom use and fulfillment of course requirements in clinical nursing of families.

*Outcomes/intervention:*

Increased knowledge of family dynamics, identifying style and modes of social interaction.

Shared findings with family to *validate* and clarify observations.

Presented findings to peers for consultation and evaluation.

Prepared findings and submitted them to professor clinical instructor.

*Evaluation:*

Thoroughness of case study with diagrammatic representations of findings.

Evaluation of accuracy by family, peers, and supervisor.

*Termination:* End of the ten-week interview and observation period, to consist of ten visits, one weekly, to last approximately one to one and one-half hours.

**CONTRACT: CLINICAL/CONSULTATION**

**Contract:** Clinical/evaluation ___Allen___ **Family** ___Wilson___ **Student**

*Entry:* Community health agency referral.

*General scope:* Evaluation of the adequacy of family environment.

*Specific focus:* Potential for emotional or physical abuse.

*Method of data collection:* Interview, observation, physical examination (with particular emphasis on emotional contradictions or incongruities).

*Assessment:*

Physical evidence of unexplained accidents.

History of repeated use of medical facilities; physical and emotional evidence of abuse; evidence of need on the part of parent (educational, emotional, or physical).

Parental history of abuse.

*Outcome:*

Referral to Parents without Partners or Parents Anonymous (abusive parents).
Emotional support for parent.
Medical and health supervision for child.
Maintain family integrity as long as possible where feasible.

*Evaluation:*

Parental willingness to participate.
Evidence of abuse (physical or emotional).
Use of resources and services.
Extensiveness of family and social network.
Decrease in reports and evidence of abuse.

*Termination:* At the end of six-week observation and evaluation; to be referred for medical assistance, parent effectiveness training, and home health supervision.

**CONTRACT: CLINICAL/PROBLEM SOLVING**

**Contract:** Clinical ___Craft___ **Family** ___Smith___ **Clinician**

*Entry:* Self-initiated referral on advice of family physician.

*General scope:*

Assessment of stress and tension level.
Evaluation of client potential for relaxation program.

*Specific focus:* Progressive relaxation for tension management.

*Data collection:* Health and medical history, physical assessment, mental status and psychological inventory, Holmes and Rahe stress scale (with modifications).

*Data use:* In-office evaluation, to be shared with family. To be forwarded to family physician on written request and signed consent of family member.

*Outcomes/intervention:*

Enhanced self-control with decreased emotional outbursts.
Controlled tensive states.
Delimited stress-inducing events and situations through progressive relaxation and meditation.

*Evaluation:* Achievement of outcomes as listed with altered tension state as desired.

*Termination:* Ten-week program to be concluded according to the accompanying schedule.

**Schedule for contract completion.** Ten-week contract: progressive relaxation and meditation.

*Week 1:* Entry—intake interview including vital statistics and family record (names, ages, dates).
Client compiles family tree.

*Week 2:* Health and medical history.
Stress scale and record of critical incidents.
Client takes record home to complete.

*Week 3:* Continuation of Week 2.
Mental status and psychological inventory.
Physical assessment.

*Week 4:* Evaluate assessment data.
Begin training program number 1.
Client begins home practice.

*Week 5:* Training program number 2.
Evaluate progress.
Client practices at home.

*Week 6:* Training program number 3.
Evaluate program numbers 1 and 2.
Client practices at home.

*Week 7:* Practice training programs 1, 2, and 3.
Observe individual progress. Assess response to program.
Client practices at home; observe at home per request.

*Week 8:* Assess alteration in physical tension states.
Observe interaction patterns in response to stress-related events.
Evaluate at-home practice.
Begin termination.

*Week 9:* Client presents self in relaxation program.
Client and clinician evaluate program response.
Discuss any areas that need clarification, elaboration, or continued work. Either begin new contract negotiation or discuss termination process.

*Week 10:* Final meeting.
Review program objectives and at-home responsibilities.
Set up follow-up appointment in six weeks where appropriate.

## SUMMARY

The foundation of the clinical process is the relationship established between the clinician and the client system, individual or family. Building such a relationship is a delicate and painstaking process. As a clinician, the student is a part of, yet separate from, the process. As participant, the student or clinician is affected by and shares with the family their fears, needs, and concerns. As clinical observer and health care provider, however, the student must remain clinically distant from the family process. Such a position is difficult. However, where the client is viewed as an active, responsive, and responsible component of the clinical process, the clinician is able to assume a position of resource, guide, and educator. The responsibility for outcomes is then shared, and the means for achieving clinical outcomes is a collaborative effort between equal partners in the contract. The contract is the vehicle by which the partners in the contract spell out their expectations and their willingness to assume responsibility for achieving goals. The contract can be formal or informal but must include a negotiated understanding of the commitment that each is to make during the period of clinical involvement. The contract is used not only to facilitate understanding but to give credence to the concept that clients can play an equally responsive role in the overall clinical process. The nature of each contract will vary with the needs of the parties involved, the level of ability that each has, and the constraints within which the contract is carried out. However, the overall belief is that all parties to the contract have rights as well as responsibilities and that partners in that contract will exercise their rights and carry out their responsibilities to the best of their abilities at a given time.

## STUDY QUESTIONS

1. Discuss rescue fantasies and their relation to helping others.
2. Discuss the primary basis for the clinical contract. What is the philosophy on which such a contract is founded?
3. How does entry affect whose agent the clinician becomes?
4. Discuss determining factors in deciding the focus of a contract.
5. What determines how data collected are to be handled?
6. What is the relationship between intervention strategies and the scope of the contract?
7. What responsibilities does the clinician have in the clinical process? How is such responsibility determined?

## BIBLIOGRAPHY

Barrel, L.: Crisis intervention; partnership in problem solving, Nurs. Clin. North Am. **9**:5, March 1974.

Bruyn, S.: The methodology of participant observation, Hum. Organizations **22**:224, Fall 1963.

Combs, A., Avila, D., and Purkey, W.: Helping relationships; basic concepts for the helping professions, Boston, 1973, Allyn & Bacon, Inc.

Gazda, G., Walters, R., and Childers, W.: Human relations development; a manual for health science, Boston, 1975, Allyn & Bacon, Inc.

McGregor, D.: Theory X and theory Y. In The human side of enterprise, New York, 1960, McGraw-Hill Book Co., pp. 33-48.

O'Hearn, J.: How can we reach patients most effectively? (paper presented at the 28th Annual Conference of the American Group Psychotherapy Association, Los Angeles, February, 1971).

Sedgwick, R.: The role of the process consultant, Am. J. Nurs.**21**:773, December 1973.

## Chapter 13

# INITIATION AND INTERVIEW

The clinical process, as related to gathering data and making clinical judgments relevant to family mental health, involves five essential aspects: interview, observation, assessment, intervention, and evaluation. The clinical process embodies the clinical skills of listening, reflecting, observing, clarifying, probing, pinpointing, goal planning, decision making in clinical judgments, and use of evaluative tools and techniques. Many of the skills are overlapping, just as the aspects of the clinical process tend to dovetail into one another. Interviewing does not exclude observation, observing does not exclude assessment, and assessments are not made without concurrent observation and evaluation. For the purposes of discussion, however, the aspects of the clinical process will be covered as somewhat independent and sequential; keep in mind, however, the overlapping and simultaneous use of these skills as the clinician becomes more experienced.

The early phase of any clinical process includes an in-depth interview.

## CLINICAL INTERVIEW

### Definition

The clinical interview is the process through which the clinician obtains a broad base of information from clients, including basic demographic and sociological data, family history, social history and critical incidents, and health and medical histories.

### Purpose

The general purpose of the clinical interview is to establish a working data base, that is, a basic framework of information that is added to, clarified, and altered by observations, assessments, and interactions. More specifically, interview is used to (1)identify significant events in the lives of family members, (2) identify critical incidents in the life of the family system, (3) obtain information regarding the family's history (medical, health, and social), and (4) establish the basis for ongoing evaluation of and interactions with the family system. The latter purpose of the interview is an extremely important aspect of the interview process regardless of the scope of the interview.

### Scope

The range of data collected can be as limited or as broad as the question that the interviewer seeks to answer and the reason for which the interview is conducted. A *limited interview* is generally designed to explore one aspect of an issue or problem, to initiate contact with the family, or to provide the student with a practice exercise in interview techniques. In such instances, the interview format is designed to focus on a narrowly identified target, for example, a brief history of a problem, characteristics of the problem, techniques used to approach the problem, and changes now desired. A limited interview can take place in one meeting and is generally defined and specifically structured to focus on one topic or problem. Limited interviews are used as an intake procedure to determine which member of a clinical team might best work with a family; to identify needs that require additional consultation and referral; to assist the family in making immediate decisions; or as a practice session for the student clinician. A practice interview is generally focused on the way in which interviews are carried out instead of being concerned with specific content or collection of data. The limited use of interviews for student learning is desirable and legitimate as long as participants in the process are aware of the purpose behind such interviews.

A *goal-directed interview* is set up with some specific goal in mind: problem solving, obtaining medical or health history, collecting sociometric and demographic data, establishing a basis for referral, or exploring a specific aspect of family dynamics such as communication or use of space. In contrast to a limited interview, the goal-directed interview generally assumes contact beyond one limited meeting. A goal-directed interview may focus on any aspect of family or individual dynamics, depending on the situation that prompted the interview contact. Management problems, school problems, unresolved grief, marriage conflict, personal unhappiness, divorce and separation, recent widowhood, and a variety of other issues prompt people to seek consultation and evaluation.

An *extended interview* is designed to encompass a wide range of data that can be used for various purposes by several different professionals. Extended interviews may be used for prevention (education, early detection) and understanding (communication, interaction), as well as in problem solving (conflict, disharmony) and planned change (behavior management, consultation). Where intervention is to be carried out over a period of months, the extended interview is conducted simultaneously with observation and assessment. Thus, the extended interview may last from a minimum of three sessions of one to three hours to a maximum set by the contract established by the family and professional. Although it is more likely that a limited or goal-directed interview will be conducted with a help-seeking family, the extended interview may be used with both help-seeking and non-help-seeking families. Health as well as lack of health may be assessed through the extended interview. Families interested in self-learning, students engaged in examining family dynamics, researchers interested in evaluating communication modalities, and therapists working with specific family systems will all find the extended interview necessary in their endeavors. With a broad base of information professionals can refer, consult, and evaluate without each having to personally conduct individual interview sessions. The method for conducting the interview may be limited or broad.

**Method**

The method whereby the interview is carried out has two basic components: the procedures that are actually used to collect data and the process in which the tools and techniques are employed. The procedure for conducting the interview will be partially determined by the outcomes desired (learning, prevention, problem solving, change) and the nature of the contract that has been established between the family and the clinician. Paper and pencil questionnaires, audiotape recordings, videotapes, and role playing are all tools and techniques employed by professionals to collect and record interview data.

Tools are available that have been designed to collect information of a very specific nature as well as to collect data of a general nature: for example, health and medical histories, social histories, family histories, and health and environmental surveys. Tools are designed and selected by clinicians according to personal interest, family need, and professional ability. Variations in tool selection, similarities as well as differences, can be found within and across professions and disciplines. The effectiveness of the procedures depends on the way in which the interview is conducted.

The manner in which the interview is conducted and the attitude of the interviewer and interviewee are as important as the tools that are used to carry out the interview. An air of acceptance and receptivity on the part of the interviewer will go a long way in enhancing a sense of confidence and cooperation on the part of family members. The family must be assured privacy and confidentiality; the clinician must be able to depend on the family for honesty and factual reporting of information. The family must expect a certain amount of probing from the clinician; the clinician will come to accept a certain amount of resistance to such probing from most families until a degree of trust, confidence, and mutual respect is established within the clinical process. As a participant observer, the clinician will experience a sense of being pulled close to the family through the family's reporting of events and experiences that have been harmful, helpful, painful, and joyous. Although the clinician will feel pulled close, a sense of distance will be maintained as the family and clinician keep in mind the nature of the clinical relationship that exists between the family and the clinician as observer, learner, problem solver, or change agent.

As an educated professional, it is the clinician's responsibility to guide the interview and consequent relationship that is established. As a sensitive individual, the clinician will use sensitivity and personal awareness as tools to facilitate a process and not to establish personal relationships or foster intimate encounters with individual family members. Given the intense, close working relationship that exists between the mental health professional and the client, an air of receptivity balanced with professional distance and education objectivity is essential not only to making sound clinical judgments but to assisting families in becoming functional, independent, and self-reliant. The atmosphere established during the interview process will tend to carry through the entire clinical process.

## INTERVIEW PROCESS

The process of interviewing families can be identified by the following stages: (1) initiation, (2) initial contact, (3) conducting the interview, (4) summarizing impressions and observations, (5) concluding the interview, and (6) setting up the next step of referral, assessment, continuation of the interview, or termination.

### Initiation

"Initiation" refers to the way in which the family becomes known to the clinician. The family may be the initiator, as might be an agency, professional, lay person, minister, friend, or clinic. The initiation of the interview process is revealing not only of family dynamics but of the family's involvement with and reliance on other systems. Self-reliance, independence, community involvement, and multiagency dependence are all partially revealed by the way in which the interview is begun. For example, a family that initiates the first appointment is generally more self-reliant than a family that comes referred by a court system, mental health agency, school system, minister, or physician. Where the process is initiated by a third party, individual or agency, the third party has some investment and influence on the dynamics of the family system and on the clinical process that evolves. For example, where a family is referred by a school system, the family's progress is assessed by changes in the child's performance in school; this assessment may differ from the level of family effectiveness as perceived by the family or clinician. Where an individual outside the family system initiates the contact, that individual often acts as interpreter, evaluator, and silent spokesperson for the family. As a liaison between family and clinician, the third party must be considered in the interview process as well as in the intervention phase. Where the family can function as its own contractual agent, there will be a greater sense of responsibility and cooperation on the part of the family system. Where the family initiates the first contact, it should be noted who is presented as the problem or reason for referral and who emerges as the help-getter for the family. The help-getter often plays a special role in family dynamics that is negative as well as positive. In a negative sense, the help-getter may have an investment in controlling family dynamics and in being in charge of everything and everyone. The identified patient may be used by the help-getter as a means of gaining self-help and assistance in controlling family dynamics. Or, the help-getter may have been somehow identified by the family as the one responsible for gaining assistance and may, therefore, function as a key person not only in clarifying and interpreting dynamics but in assisting in their change as well. Whatever the unfolding dynamics, the member who makes the initial contact and the member who is identified as being the reason for the referral both play a special role in family dynamics. The astute clinician should observe and identify not only those who initiate but those who follow along, those who rebel, those who remain silent, and those who are absent. Absent and silent members can, through their absence and silence, be particularly controlling and influential in family dynamics and in the clinical process as well. Whereas it is most desirable, particularly in private practice, for the family to initiate and be an equal partner in the clinical process, it is more often the case, especially in community agencies, that the clinician must assume responsibility for making the initial contact with the family. Since it is assumed that most families with whom the student comes in contact will be through community agencies or clinics as opposed to private offices, the initial contact will be discussed in terms of the student's making the contact.

### Initial contact

During the initial contact, it is essential to be clear about the nature of the call, the agency or clinic being represented, and the outcomes expected from the clinical encounter. For example, if the family has been referred as a family willing to be interviewed and to participate in a clinical contract with a nursing student, the family should understand that the clinical interview is for the purposes of clinical practice and learning and service to be delivered is secondary in the clinical contract being established. During the early phases, elements of the contract are negotiated between the family and the clinician. The family should also be given options with regard to length of visit, setting for visits, and duration of the clinical contract. Following the initial contact, which is generally made by telephone, the family should have time to discuss the contact, potential contract, and the expectations that each member has for clinical outcomes. It may be necessary for the student to call twice, one time to make necessary introductions and state the purpose of the call and the ensuing interview and a second time to provide the family with time and opportunity to involve and arrange meeting times with other family members. When time, place, and date can be agreed on, the interview itself may be arranged and conducted.

**Conducting the interview**

The way in which the interview is conducted, that is, in an unhurried, concerned, and interested fashion, is as important as the tools to be used in gathering data. At the outset of the interview, the clinical student will want to outline the purpose of the interview, discuss the role played by the clinician and any supervisors or instructors who will be involved, explain the duration of the visit (or visits), explore any questions or concerns that the family has at the very beginning, and emphasize the continual necessity of checking out assumptions, impressions, and concerns. At the same time, the use of any recorders, observers, or paper and pencil questionnaires during the interview should be explained. Where possible, the family may be provided with a copy of the interview format for their own records and point of reference. Interview formats to be used with families can be very general, including names of family members, health and medical histories, social history, and general impressions. Until the clinical student is comfortable with such an open framework, however, a very detailed format with specific questions should be used. Note taking should be discussed and emphasized as important for accuracy; reliance on memory is not only risky but self-defeating for even the most experienced clinicians. Families can understand and appreciate the need for note taking: family members themselves often take notes and make a point of clarifying dates, names, relationships, major illness, and other items.

The information gained through the interview process is compiled in the clinical record, which contains vital statistics, family history, health and medical histories, social history, and critical incidents. The interview is conducted with that goal in mind: collecting a thorough, detailed framework of information about the family (who they are, where they come from, what they do, what they believe, what has happened to them, and what their plans are for the future). Thus, the interview is goal directed, structured toward information gathering, and time limited in order to achieve the completeness required to assess family mental health.

**Family history.** A family history includes, in addition to names, an identification of the events in the lives of members that have impact on the physical, social, and mental health of the family. While one collects factual information, one can focus on process—on action and interaction—within the family itself.

The family begins by telling, in their own words, something about themselves, as individuals and as a family. It is often sufficient to begin with: "Tell me something about yourselves. Who would like to begin?" The family is provided the opportunity to describe, in their own words, their own impressions of themselves and of each other. As the family begins their descriptions, direct questions are gradually initiated by the interviewer. This provides time for the tone of the sessions to be established. The family should be gently but firmly guided into a specific focus on family statistics: members' names, ages, occupations, religion, social groups, and community involvement. Emerging information must be weighed against factual accumulation for credibility and accuracy. The clinician should avoid the inclination to discuss personal matters or interject comments that will disrupt the flow of information sharing. During this phase of the clinical process, the clinical student, however concerned and compassionate, must focus on the objective: collection of accurate information. Particular attention is paid to the nature of the narrative: for example, evasive, vague, conflicting, or contradictory statements are noted. Vague statements like "We don't get along well" must be pursued through statements such as "Give me an example" or "Tell me what you mean." Highly important to history taking is the ability to document, illustrate, and quantify statements by asking for examples and determining to what extent perception of examples is shared by family members.

**Social history and critical incidents.** Names, ages, birth dates, jobs, illnesses, and major trauma (divorce, death, separation) should be recorded, clarified, and summarized as the information is being collected. Illness, death, and separation are often associated with periods of family turmoil or transitory disorganization. A chronological diagram is a useful tool in recording social history and environmental contingencies.

A series of steps are identified that depict critical incidents in the life of family members, including birth, death, separation, illness, and major accidents. Upward arrows indicate those events that are generally deemed positive and downward arrows those usually deemed negative.

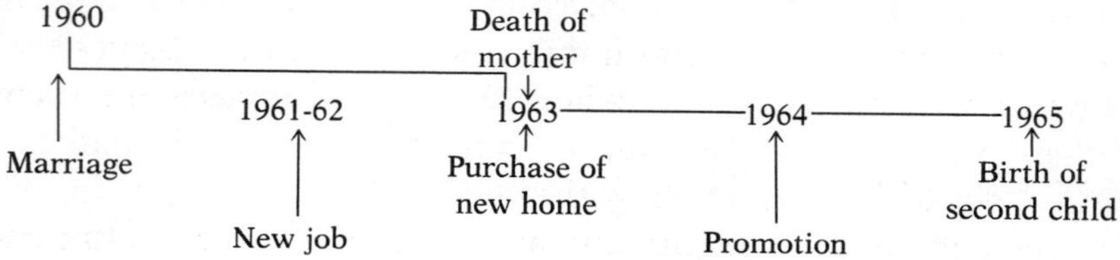


**Social history—significant events**

Note is made of how such events were reportedly handled and what resources were necessary to assist. Reflective listening, that is, listening and repeating back a summary of events, and pinpointing, that is, focusing in on a particular event for clarification and understanding, are valuable tools for the clinician.

Although health and medical histories are generally obtained at the same time as a general social history, such information is summarized separately.

**Health history.** Health history includes a general review of eating, sleeping, and activity patterns of family members. How many meals eaten together, quality and quantity of sleep, and general habits related to work and leisure activities reflect the family's overall attitudes regarding health and illness. Major health problems that result in illness or accident or otherwise require medical attention are recorded in the medical history.

**Medical history.** Medical history includes a review of illness, accident, or injury that has required medical attention, including hospitalizations. Since families are often unable to give a complete medical or health history during an initial interview, space should be left in the clinical record to add, delete, or correct information pertinent to medical history, health history, and critical incidents.

The clinician should assume that the informants, or those involved in providing the information, are as honest and open as is possible for them at that given moment. The family may be prompted, out of necessity or fear, to present a particular image: for example, where the family member is a prominent social figure, there is question of emotional or physical abuse, or there is family dysfunction revealed by individual family member behavior at school or work. However, it is difficult to maintain such an image where there is even one member who strives for emotional honesty and personal authenticity or where the clinician begins to pick up contradictory messages in communication patterns. The clinician must prepare to have to probe such contradictions and support family members when self-disclosures of one or two members begin to erode the social image and psychological facade of others. It is as painful for families to have to face their contradictions as it is for the clinician to have to point them out. For the developing clinician, it is helpful to work with a co-clinician or student partner who can assist and support in the clarifying process, which is essential to establishment of an accurate and dependable data base. It is essential to summarize and periodically repeat back to the family the information and impressions that have been obtained during the interview.

### Summarization and clarification of impressions

The concluding of the interview is accompanied by checking out with the family the accuracy of the information and clarity of impressions obtained during the interview process. Sharing impressions is important since what the clinical student sees and senses may be different from what is perceived by the family. Whereas most births, deaths, and separations cause major family reorganization in time, emotional commitment, use of physical space, and psychological attachments, such life stressors must be examined in relation to the particular family undergoing the experience. One family member may report an episode, such as a family misunderstanding or argument, from one viewpoint, whereas other family members may have a different set of impressions; a clinician may contribute a third view.

Hunches, contradictions, vague messages, and conflicting data must be explored with the family and examined for accuracy and thoroughness. When final impressions are summarized, the interview can be concluded, to be followed by a referral, outside consultation, or further observation. Assuming that students will be following a family or families through the entire clincial process, the final stage of interviewing will include setting a time and date for a follow-up appointment that will include the observation phase of the clinical process.

### Concluding the interview

Terminating the interview process occurs when information pertinent to the family unit has been obtained: (1) family constellation; (2) vital statistics; (3) health and medical histories of individual family members; (4) social history, including school, church, and community relationships; and (5) critical incidents and major life stressors, such as death, separation, relocation, accidents, and births. The interview phase of the clinical process focused primarily on the collection of factual information supplied by family members and significant others. Family process, however, is examined primarily in the observation phase that follows the interview and will be discussed in the following chapter.

## SUMMARY

The family interview is conducted in order to establish a data base which to build for future evaluations and interventions. The clinical record that is compiled through the interview includes the names of family members; vital statistics on the family; health and medical histories of family members; developmental history of the family system; medical problems of individual family members; and critical incidents that have influenced the growth and development of the family system, such as births, death, accidents, separations, promotions, trauma, and physical and emotional abuse; and social and community connectedness through organizations, schools, and so forth. Generally, the clinical record of each family contains information that may be used to construct a profile of the family as a social, physical, medical, and emotional group. The profile gained through the interview is further clarified through the process of observation. When all information desired is obtained, clarified, and summarized, the clinical interview may be concluded.

**Family interview: general format**

*Family constellation:* Names, relationships, generation, maternal and paternal siblings.
*Vital statistics:* Address, phone number, ages, sex, occupations, religion, grade in school.
*Developmental history*:* Developmental progress and lags, birth traumas, handicaps.
*Health history*:* Nutrition, exercise, sleep habits, general activities, environmental characteristics.
*Medical history*:* Diseases, genetic problems, injuries, accidents, hospitalizations.
*Social history*:* School progress, church, neighborhood, clubs, community involvement, relationships at work, extracurricular activities.
*Critical incidents*:* Births, deaths, separation, illness, accidents, traumas, promotions, marriages (gains and losses).
*General impressions and observations†:*

---

*Maternal, paternal, and siblings.
†To be clarified throughout the clinical process.

## INTAKE EVALUATION FORM
## (Adult)

**Rae Sedgwick, R.N., Ph.D.**
**Certified Psychologist**

**Susan Hildebrand, R.N., M.S.**
**Clinical Nurse Specialist**

216 E. Second
Bonner Springs, KS
913-441-3800

Name(s): ______________________

______________________

Address: ______________________

Marital: ______________________

Children (ages): ______________________

______________________

Phone: ______________________

Occupation: ______________________

Physician: ______________________

Insurance: ______________________

Medications: ______________________

Siblings: ______________________

Presenting problem: ______________________

______________________

Describe (onset, duration, context): ______________________

______________________

______________________

History: ______________________

______________________

Similar episodes: ______________________

______________________

Health history (illness, injury, accidents, life patterns): ______________________

______________________

______________________

______________________

Family history: ______________________

______________________

______________________

______________________

______________________

Social history: ______________________

______________________

______________________

______________________

Impressions: ______________________

______________________

**INTAKE EVALUATION FORM**
**(Children)**

**Rae Sedgwick, R.N., Ph.D.**
**Certified Psychologist**

**Susan Hildebrand, R.N., M.S.**
**Clinical Nurse Specialist**

216 E. Second
Bonner Springs, KS
913-441-3800

Name: ____________________

Nickname: ____________________

Address: ____________________
____________________

Age: _____ Birth date: __________

School: ____________________

Grade: ____________________

Siblings: _____ Ages: __________

Parent(s): (M) ____________________
Age _____
(F) ____________________
Age _____

Address: ____________________
____________________

Phone: ____________________

Business phone: (M) __________
(F) __________

Occupation: (M) __________
(F) __________

Insurance: ____________________

Policy #: ____________________

Presenting problem: ____________________
____________________

Similar episodes: ____________________
____________________

Health history (eating, sleeping, toilet training, UCHD, physical handicaps): ____________________
____________________
____________________
____________________

Prenatal (mother): ____________________
____________________

Delivery: ____________________

Developmental lags: ____________________
____________________

*Continued.*

**INTAKE EVALUATION FORM—cont'd**
**(Children)**

Family history: ______________________________________________

______________________________________________

______________________________________________

______________________________________________

______________________________________________

Social history (siblings, school, play behavior and content): ____________

______________________________________________

______________________________________________

______________________________________________

Impressions: ______________________________________________

______________________________________________

**STUDY QUESTIONS**

1. Interviewing can be broken down into components: procedure and process. Which aspect is most influential in establishing rapport and trust? Why?
2. What part do "silent partners" play in the interview process?
3. Elements of the contract are established in the early phases of the clinical contract. What responsibilities does the clinician have in establishing the parameters of the contract? What responsibilities does the family system have?
4. How can family history taken during the interview be used to gain an understanding of dynamics of the contemporary family system?
5. Discuss the contribution reflective listening and clarification of impressions make to assuring clarity of data obtained during the interview.

**BIBLIOGRAPHY**

Allmond, B., Buckman, W., and Gofman, H.: The family is the patient; an approach to behavioral pediatrics for the clinician, St. Louis, 1979, The C. V. Mosby Co.

Bernstein, L., and Dana, R.: Interviewing and the health professions, New York, 1970, Appleton-Century-Crofts.

Burton, A.: Interpersonal psychotherapy, New York, 1975, Jason Aronson.

Breslow, D.: Time-extended family interviewing, Fam. Process **16**:97, 1977.

Fowkes, W., and Hunn, V.: Patient interview. In Clinical assessment for the nurse practitioner, St. Louis, 1973, The C. V. Mosby Co.

MacKinnon, R., and Michels, R.: The psychiatric interview in clinical practice, Philadelphia, 1971, W. B. Saunders Co.

Orem, D.: Nursing; concepts of practice, New York, 1971, McGraw-Hill Book Co.

Stevenson, I.: The diagnostic interview, New York, 1971, Harper & Row, Publishers.

Tapia, J.: The nursing process in family health, Nurs. Outlook **20**:267, April 1972

## Chapter 14

# OBSERVATION

During the period that the clinician is engaged in interviewing family members, it is essential to make observations of the actions and interactions that occur within the family system. The process of observation is an invaluable tool in gathering additional data that support or raise questions about the family system, not only in terms of the information that is being provided but in terms of family dynamics as well.

## CLINICAL OBSERVATION

### Definition

Clinical observation can be defined as a process in which the clinician uses all faculties to see, hear and sense the family's responses, not only to one another but to the environment surrounding the family as well (including the presence of the clinician). Whereas interviewing is used to collect factual information about the family—(names, ages, occupations, illnesses, strengths, social and community memberships, and critical events), observations are carried out that focus on the contemporary setting of the family: communication, use of space, psychological bonding, emotional atmosphere, personal authenticity, patterns of interaction, nature of personal impact on one another, and general orientation.

### Purpose

The purpose of clinical observation is to (1) expand the data base that is begun during the interview; (2) establish a data base with reference to the contemporary family system's communication, bonding, use of space, and general orientation; (3) initiate the early phases of assessment through enhanced awareness of family dynamics; (4) identify particular areas of concern that the family may express through nonverbal actions; and (5) check out impressions, hunches, conflicts, contradictions, or questions that arise out of the interview sessions. Although it may be possible to establish some basic information about the family's attachments, communication patterns, and use of space through the interview, only through observation of and interaction with the family system can interpersonal and environmental dynamics of the family unit be identified and studied. The interview is based largely on the family's self-report; the process of observation is chiefly based on the clinician's perceptions. Through observation, the clinician begins to use what is reported and check it against what can be observed, recorded, and discussed either with the family or another clinician or supervisor.

The scope of the observations will reflect, as does the interview, the intent and purpose of the clinical relationship.

**Scope**

The range of any observation process will depend on what one intends to observe and, in the long run, evaluate. *Limited observations* are generally made during a crisis; the observations made take an account of the severity of the situation and the family's or individual's ability to meet the challenge presented by the event. A brief interview is accompanied by a rather cursory observation with the intention of intervention or referral. Limited observations are generally conducted in cases of extreme emergency, limited requests for information, or immediate problem solving. Limited observations may provide either a hasty, holistic view or a narrower more intensive look at one aspect of family dynamics.

*Goal-directed observations* accompany and follow a goal-directed interview. The clinician examines ways in which problems are solved, medical and health histories and their impact on the contemporary unit, the expression of bonding and its relationship to the family's report of emotional attachments, the use of space, evidence of concern for individual growth and individuation, or some specific aspect of family dynamics as set forth in the original contract with the family. As do goal-directed interviews, observations that are goal-directed assume contact beyond an initial meeting and imply the family's knowledge of and active participation in the observation process. The nature of the observation that is conducted will closely parallel the nature of the interview and consequent assessment and evaluation processes. Management problems, school problems, marriage conflict, personal unhappiness, and social adjustment concerns that prompt individuals and families to seek mental health consultation in some ways shape the scope of the observations to be made. Clinical contracts focused on problem solving, specific behavior changes, or management issues generally involve a narrow, in-depth observation that reveals further information about that one issue or problem.

An *extensive observation process,* associated with long-term consultation or learning, involves an extensive set of observations made concurrently with an extended interview. Extensive observations are carried out to accompany, complement, support, strengthen, or invalidate other data that are being collected through the extended interview. Just as extended interviews are used for prevention (education, early detection) and understanding (communication, interaction) as well as in problem solving (conflict, acting out, bedwetting) and planned change, so observations are planned that augment the overall plan of the clinical contract.

**Method**

The methods employed will be in some ways determined by the extensiveness of the clinical contract itself. Observations can be as general as paying attention to the communication system that typifies any one family or as specific as keeping a record of how many times each member speaks to another family member about discipline or home management.

Observations are geared toward the particular dynamics about which the clinician wishes to obtain current data. The tools used to document observations include audiotapes (with which the observer records information), videotapes (with which one can keep an ongoing record of interaction), paper and pencil diagrams (made by the clinician or co-clinician) that depict the flow of conversation and the seating arrangement, and photographs or sketches of various aspects of any given interaction. The ways in which the tools are used are as important as the tools themselves.

Family members have a right to know that observations will be included as part of the clinical data. In some instances, family members will be able to serve as recorders or note takers as a part of their clinical responsibility and self-learning process; usually, the clinical student will assume the responsibility for keeping a record of any observations. The recording of observations should be done as unobtrusively as possible; however, accuracy and clarity are uppermost concerns. For the beginning student, it is a good idea for two students to take turns, with one interviewing and one observing until comparative ease is felt in simultaneous interviewing and observing.

In general, the observation phase of the clinical process will complement and support the clinical interview and reflect the overall intent of the clinical contract: prevention, understanding, problem solving, or planned change. Regardless of the nature of the clinical contract, the astute clinician always observes on at least two levels, that is, observes what is not perceived, said, or done as well as what is, and, second, seeks through observations to match specifics with the whole. Most intuitive hunches that clinicians develop arise out of the observation that either more is not being said than is being said or that small bits and pieces of family interaction do not fit well with the overall patterns of interaction that can be observed.

What is not said is often implied through gesture, body movement, physical absence from meetings, purposeful and determined silence during observation and assessment sessions, or abrupt changes in behavior in the barometer members of the family. Children are particularly good barometers of family dynamics—shifting positions, making facial grimaces, or attempting to distract the flow of conversation when conflictive or troublesome areas are touched on by the clinician or family members. Barometer members within family systems are generally the more transparent family members, that is, they tend to reveal their feelings, to act out through their own behavior the effect of a situation on themselves; and to disclose, often nonverbally, their fears, anxieties, and personal concerns with regard to the family system. What is not said by the family members outright is often revealed through a family barometer or implied by the actions of one of the family members. Such disclosure by a family member can be observed to occur fairly regularly: the astute clinician may begin to form an organized impression of the relationship between such an individual's behavior and what is going on at the time the change occurs. Hair pulling, teeth gritting, sock twisting, sudden demands on a particular family member, sudden development of a headache or stomach cramp, excessive coughing or clearing of the throat, abruptly leaving the room or changing chairs, and sudden outbursts have all been observed by this clinician to be barometer behaviors on the part of family members. What is not said verbally is often said rather loudly through gesture, body movement, facial expression, or abrupt change in behavior. Such gestures and movements often reveal not only what is not talked about, but point to discrepancies within the overall organization of the family unit.

Where specific observations of individuals, dyads, triads, and interactions do not match up with a holistic view of the family, clinical care must be exercised in investigating the source of the contradiction. One particular family member's dress, actions, attitudes, and beliefs may be strikingly different from those of other members and yet not be a source of contradiction but an indication of that member's attempts at individuation. Where one member, either through action, word, or intent, is consistently at odds with the family system, the result of which is to antagonize, divide, or victimize the entire unit, the individual is suspect as "agent provocateur." Where individuals within the family system are victimized by the system, as is the case in emotional and physical abuse, the family unit itself must be considered as a source of harm. Examples of contradictions between individual behavior and unit action occur when the entire family plans an event and one member is consistently late or fails to appear, when several members are engaged in an endeavor in which family support is needed and one member consistently pulls out at the last minute, when rules are established by the unit and then changed depending on which family member is involved, when emotional honesty is espoused by the family as important but one or two members consistently engage in deception and dishonesty, or when the entire unit agrees on basic beliefs and values and then each goes about in individual ways to destroy or abuse such beliefs. Specific observations are made not only of individual family members but of the family system as well.

## OBSERVATION OF THE FAMILY SYSTEM

Specific observations related to the family system can be made of the following: (1) communication process, (2) use of space and territoriality, (3) psychological bonding, (4) emotional atmosphere, (5) personal authenticity, (6) personal impact of individuals, (7) patterns of interaction, and, finally, (8) the general orientation of the system. These particular aspects are observed because they are the areas assessed in an evaluation of family effectiveness or mental health.

### Communication process

The process of communication itself and the observation of message dynamics can be a lengthy and complex endeavor. Unless the communication process itself is to be the target of undertaking, general observations that are conducted include paying close attention to *who* says what to whom, *how* it is said, and what the *consequence* appears to be. The questions to ask are: (1) What is the language that this family uses to connect with one another? (2) Who is in charge of using whatever language is available? (3) What is the end result?

### Use of space and territoriality

The family's use of space can be observed in their seating patterns, choice of space partners, response to the environment, and general use of the space around and between members. As each member begins to claim a physical location within the room or home, note is made of the impact of such choice on others. The more space demanded by one member, the less available to other members. This holds true of social and intellectual as well as physical space. Family members will tend to locate their spaces around or next to specific family members, and individual members will develop characteristic responses to one another based on that spatial arrangement.

Although it is not always possible to observe the family in a wide range of spatial arrangements, family members often provide sketches, photographs, and life portrayals of the spatial and environmental relationships characteristic of their family setting. The observation of the family's relationship to space is a rich source of data about other aspects of family life. Questions that may be asked in observing the family's relationship to space are: (1) How restrictive and how expansive is their use of space? (2) How often are outsiders included or excluded? (3) How much room does the family take up in the community through membership, participation, or direct confrontation with authority or agencies? (4) How open are the family boundaries as evidenced by members' participation in growth-inducing activities such as education, training, and travel? (5) What kinds of people have access to the family system and for what reasons? The spatial arrangement and relationships are often indicative of the psychological bonding within the family.

**Psychological bonding**

Bonding, or connectedness, can be observed with regard to direction, intensity, and overall nature of the relationships that are established within the family. The direction of bonding is revealed in the establishment of close relationships within the family unit as evidenced through spatial arrangements, verbal statements, physical gestures, and specific actions. Gift giving, granting of special privileges, making allowance for mistakes or rule breaking, differential application of regulations, comments offering support or acclaim of a particular member, and physical gestures of touching, closeness, or confrontation are all indicative of the formation of special bonds between individuals within the family unit. The formation of unique or special relationships within the family involves intensity that can be either positive or negative, restrictive or expansive, and supportive or exploitative. Positive as well as negative relationships have a tremendous influence on family dynamics and on individual growth and development. Restrictive relationships generally involve many rules with a minimum of error allowed; expansive relationships permit rule flexibility and trial and error learning. Supportive or manipulative aspects of connectedness are revealed through comments, actions, and interactions that either encourage or suppress growth, individual as well as group. Psychological bonding is both manifested in and influenced by the emotional atmosphere that is developed and maintained by the family system.

**Emotional atmosphere**

The emotional environment is revealed through family members' conversations and interactions with one another, both close and extended family members. Attitudes, beliefs, and opinions about honesty, personal integrity, acceptance of individual differences, tolerance of mistakes, encouragement in taking personal risks, and promotion of individual identity as well as family membership provide the foundation on which the emotional environment is constructed. The clinical student will want to look for evidence of (1) emotional honesty as well as dishonesty, (2) consistency in stated belief and observed action, (3) acceptance of family members by one another, (4) active listening, (5) emotional reservoirs and "empty cups," (6) abusive or manipulative use of one another, and (7) warmth, compassion, and cooperation. The emotional tenor created in the family system may be cold or warm, close or distant, supportive or manipulative, constrictive or expansive, and constructive or destructive. Although the responsibility for creating such an environment should be shared by the entire system, it may fall to one or two individuals to create, maintain, or alter the mood of the entire family unit. As the emotional atmosphere is observed, each member's ability to be authentic, open, and active in the family system will become more readily apparent.

**Personal authenticity**

Each member will vary in terms of ability and willingness to be open, active, and informative. Fear, expectation, and feelings about the family itself as well as the family's participation in the clinical process may alter the degree to which members will commit themselves to self-disclosure and family revelations in front of others, particularly professional others who have the power and authority to make judgments about the family's integrity, mental health, and social life. Self-disclosure involves self-trust and self-confidence as well as trust and confidence in others. The clinician can facilitate disclosure by others by being open and authentic with the family during the initial sessions. The group experience that the student has had will help the student toward an authentic and full representation of feelings, expectations, and needs. Although it is not particularly desirable that students engage in personal encounters with family members, an air of warm acceptance can assist the family in disclosing information of a personal nature. Self-disclosure and personal revelation can be risky, painstaking endeavors and must be handled with sensitivity, confidentiality, and concern for the impact that such disclosure will have on individual members as well as on the entire family unit.

Being real and assessing one's impact on others and others' impact on themselves make up one of the most important and difficult tasks for the family and for the clinician.

**Personal impact**

The effect that family members have on one another is expressed through action, gesture, comment, silence, and unique response. Individual members differ in their impact on other family members and on family dynamics. For example, individual members differ in their ability to instigate family quarrels, to smooth over family disagreements, to motivate members to action, to influence opinion and judgment, to provide comfort and support, and to initiate behavior or generate ideas. Although individuals within families generally develop characteristic ways of behaving within the family, events and situations may occur that alter those characteristic patterns. Some members will tend to be reactors to the family, whereas other members will tend to be adaptors or initiators, depending on the particular situation.

In observing individual members' impact, it is thus important to note the situation, event, and environmental setting in which the interaction is occurring. Where there are repetitions and stability in interactions and outcomes, patterns emerge that can be observed and recorded.

**Patterns of interaction**

As the clinical student observes family dynamics—communication, use of space, emotional atmosphere, bonding, and social embeddedness—patterns will begin to emerge. Families develop characteristic and habitual ways of responding, acting, thinking, and expressing their feelings to one another and to outsiders. Such patterns are useful in predicting as well as evaluating family effectiveness; even the most dysfunctional of families become predictable in their disorganized ways of behaving. The clinical student will observe that such patterns emerge, not only in terms of family behavior in relationship to one another, but in response to illness, accident, success, failure, death, and other critical incidents that have taken place over a period of time. The identification of such patterns and the elaboration of individual and group responses within such patterns is necessary to obtain a complete picture of the family. In order to identify such patterns, the clinical student must be able to interview in depth, compile a thorough history, elicit the critical incidents that the family has experienced, and observe the family members together in various settings and at different times under varying circumstances.

One characteristic that may be observed to be quite patterned is the family's orientation—to itself, to time, to people, and to goals.

**Orientation**

The position that a family takes in determining what is important and of uppermost concern influences the priorities of individual family members and affects the goals that the family sets for itself as a unit. What is important to a family will be revealed in their investments—financial, social, and emotional—and the care that those investments receive. A family inordinately invested in material gain and social ambition will place more importance on physical and material gain and will highly value admittance to country clubs, social groups, and private schools. Families who place emphasis on emotional development and character building will tend to invest their energies and money in education, creative endeavors, and growth-stimulating activites. Those inordinately invested in individual pursuits will tend to devalue and deemphasize group activity, conformity, and social memberships.

In addition to the family's orientation to itself are the family's orientation to time, its orientation to people, and its orientation to growth.

Families more concerned with the past than with the present or future will display excessive reminiscing, collecting, and hoarding of worn-out articles from the past and failure to provide for current and future needs of members. Some members ascribe to McGregor's (1960) Theory X and others to Theory Y; some invest all their energies in children, whereas others invest all their energies in the adults in the family; some families favor maintenance and others favor growth. Whatever the priority, its selection and use absorb family energy; it manifests itself in an observable and patterned set of behaviors that reveal one aspect of family dynamics.

### Results

The data that are compiled through observations are organized and kept up to date as a part of the clinical record. Where there are marked discrepancies between what is reported by the family and what is observed by the clinical student, a notation is made in the clinical record in order that further observations and data collection can be carried out during the assessment phase. Much of the data collected during observations is somewhat tentative and subject to further investigation and clarification based on ongoing interaction between the clinician and the family members. Observations are continually made throughout the clinical process, and any evaluation or interpretations must be made in light of the possibility that further information will support or invalidate hunches that the clinician may develop at the outset. Although intuition is still one of the best tools that any clinician has, it is a clinical tool that must be constantly honed and tested in order to keep it accurate, sensitive, and flexible.

## SUMMARY

Observations of the family are conducted in order to obtain data regarding the family's pattern of interaction and personal impact, communication process, use of space and territoriality, emotional atmosphere and psychological bonding, and social embeddedness. Impressions formed by the clinician during the interview process are validated or invalidated during the observation process. A profile of the family may be formulated by contrasting and comparing impressions with observations. The profile that is compiled forms the basis for the assessment and intervention phases of the clinical process.

**Clinical record: family profile**

*Interview*

Names:

Medical history: Illness, accident, injury, hospitalizations.

Health history: Growth and development, nutrition, sleeping, activities.

Social history: School, church, peer relations, job concerns.

Critical incidents: Stressors—divorce, death, separation, trauma, moves, changes.

Environmental contingencies: Cultural, physical setting, economic level, housing.

Impressions:

*Observations*

Communication process: Who, how, consequences.

Space and territoriality: Restrictive, expansive; openness to outsiders; individual versus group ownership.

Psychological bonding: Closeness versus distance; support, acceptance.

Emotional atmosphere: Honesty, consistency, active listening.

Personal authenticity: Open, active, informative.

Personal impact: Action, gesture, comment, silence.

Pattern of interaction: Traditional versus novel response, predictability, flexibility.

Orientation: Past, present, or future; child, adult, or mixed; positive or negative.

*Assessment:* (To follow)

## STUDY QUESTIONS

1. Discuss basic differences in focus between conducting the interview and carrying out observations. What difficulties are encountered in carrying out both simultaneously?
2. How might the presence of a second clinician decrease the difficulties encountered in conducting an interview and making observations?
3. What does frequency of verbal behavior have to do with power positions in the family system?
4. How are emotional attachments within the family system reflected in social interaction between family members?
5. Discuss ways in which contradictory evidence is handled in clinical observation.
6. How is the orientation of the family system reflected in expectations regarding individual performance?
7. In what ways is the family's experience with and exposure to significant events and critical incidents reflected in the emotional atmosphere of the family system?

## BIBLIOGRAPHY

Bakker, C., and Bakker-Rabdau, M.: No trespassing! Explorations in human territoriality, San Francisco, 1973, Chandler and Sharp Publishers, Inc.

Halverson, C., and Shore, R.: Self-disclosure and interpersonal functioning, Consult. Clin. Psychol., **33**(2): 213, 1969.

Horowitz, M.: Spatial behavior and psychopathology, J. Nerv. Ment. Dis. **146:**24, 1968.

McGregor, D.: Theory X and theory Y. In The human side of enterprise, New York, 1960, McGraw-Hill Book Co., pp. 33-48.

Mehrabian, A.: Significance of posture and

position in communication of attitude and status relationships, Psychol. Bull. **71:** 359, 1969.

Pearsall, M.: Participant observation as role and method in behavioral research, Nurs. Res. **14:** 37, Winter 1965.

Ruesch, J.: The diagnosis of disturbed communication, In Therapeutic communication, New York, 1973, W. W. Norton & Co., Inc., pp. 74-91.

Sawrer-Foner, G.: Human territoriality and its cathexis, Dis. Nerv. Syst. **31:** 82, November, 1970.

Webb, E., Campbell, D., Swartz, R., and Sechrest, L.: Unobtrusive measures, Chicago, 1966, Rand McNally and Co., pp. 112-141.

Chapter 15

# ASSESSMENT

The information obtained and the impressions formed during the interview and observation can now be organized, examined, and expanded. Assessment is that phase of the clinical process in which clinical judgment on the part of the clinician becomes particularly crucial.

## CLINICAL ASSESSMENT

### Definition

Assessment can be defined as the appraisal or judgment-making aspect of the clinical process. Although assessment is a continual and ongoing element of the clinical process, there must be a period of time in which the clinician makes a concerted effort to organize and evaluate the data obtained, make a judgment regarding dynamics observed, and decide whether additional information, observation, and data collection are necessary before intervention strategies can be designed.

### Purpose

Assessment must be carried out as an integral component of the clinical process in order to determine the adequacy of the data received, examine the need for further information and data, undertake clinical evaluation of family dynamics and individual contribution to family mental health, and formulate appropriate intervention strategies, including referral, consultation, further evaluation, and clinical treatment. The extensiveness of the assessment will vary according to several factors, including the nature of the clinical contract, reason for clinical assessment, adequacy of information received and data obtained, degree of family involvement and participation, level of family effectiveness in the past, individual self-disclosure, clinical ability of the professional, availability of appropriate and useful clinical tools, involvement of outside referral and treatment systems, and time allotted to the overall clinical process. The scope of the assessment will be influenced by these and other factors that may be unique to the family-clinician contract.

### Scope

The breadth and depth of clinical assessment will be determined by a number of factors, including those listed above, the goals set forth in the clinical contract, and the evolving nature of the clinical relationship between family and clinician. Usually, assessment is at least a three-fold process: (1) organization and evaluation of information and data obtained thus far in the clinical contact, (2) examination of and judgment about family dynamics as revealed through the interview and observation phase, and (3) data collection and evaluation of family dynamics through direct involvement of family members with tools and tasks that provide the opportunity to observe and evaluate goal-oriented and task-related actions and interactions of the family system. It must be assumed that information collected during the final phases of assessment will be representative of the ongoing dynamics and system capabilities of the family system. Where there is doubt about the representativeness of such information, evaluation and data collection must be extended to obtain sufficient information to allay doubts and clear up inconsistencies. Intervention strategies will be based on the clinical judgments made about the data obtained and the family dynamics revealed through such data. Such clinical judgments must be made as carefully and systematically as is possible.

### Method

The process of assessment can be broken down into three components that correspond to the scope of the assessment process: (1) organization and evaluation of data already collected, (2) examination of family dynamics as revealed through interview and observation phases, and (3) data collection and evaluation through the further use of clinical tools and family involvement in tasks that clarify, elaborate, or provide further evidence of family effectiveness and individual contribution to family dynamics, such as goal-centered or decision-making tasks.

Specific family dynamics, such as emotional atmosphere and psychological bonding, are examined in the second phase of the assessment process. System compatibilities are explored in the final phases of clinical evaluation and assessment through the use of clinical tools specifically designed for such purposes.

## ORGANIZATION AND EVALUATION OF DATA

The organization of data received is facilitated by categorizing the information and observations into four areas: (1) clinical record, (2) individual members, (3) social network and physical environment, and (4) family dynamics in general.

### Clinical record

The clinical record is the family portfolio that has been compiled thus far; it includes names of family members and vital statistics pertaining to each, health and medical histories of each, social history, and a summary of critical incidents. This information must be examined for consistency, accuracy, and completeness. Facts must check out throughout the interview and observation sessions; dates and incidents must be accurate; and health and medical records must be complete. Where there are gaps, deficiencies, or contradictions, the clinician must explore and probe further with family members in order to assure accuracy of information. Dates are more easily remembered by some family members than others; health and medical histories may have to be obtained from other health and medical sources; developmental information may have to be clarified through school or work records; and critical incidents may have to be further examined for enhanced understanding of their relationship to family adaptation and change. Critical incidents often become clearer as the individual member's contribution to the family is examined.

### Individual member

The individual member's contribution, including physical, social, developmental, and emotional abilities, must be considered in putting together a complete family profile. Individual information is examined for completeness, accuracy, and relatedness to family information. It may be necessary to gather further individual information, to conduct individual developmental screening and health examination, to explore with individual members their perception and recall of certain events, and to determine further one or two particular members' relatedness to the family in general. In going over data obtained, it is not unusual to find that one member has been consistently the focus of discussion, has been repeatedly the source of conflict or disagreement, or has been avoided or left out of the discussions. This point will be noted and further explored in the latter stages of assessment and clinical program planning. Individual behavior is often a clue to the family's relatedness to social networks.

### Social networks and physical environment

The family's relatedness to other social networks, such as school, work, social agencies, church, and cultural or ethnic groups, and the family's relatedness to the physical environment are essential components of the profile that the clinician seeks to construct of the family's ability as an effective social and psychological unit. This information is supplied through social history, review of critical incidents, individual action and behavior, observation of the family's use of personal and intimate environmental spaces, and the family's membership in and use of systems external to their own system. Through the process of interview and during a series of observations, as suggested in the previous chapter, the clinician should be able to develop some impressions about the family's connectedness to other systems, including the environment around the family. If the clinician is unable to develop impressions, for example, of the expansiveness or restrictiveness of the family as a social system, then additional information and observations are necessary. As in the examination of other information provided, the task here is to determine the completeness, accuracy, and consistency of information. Where information is incomplete, for example, where there is a lack of information regarding the home, neighborhood, or community relatedness, this incompleteness can become the focus in the remainder of the clinical contract. Contradictory, inconsistent, or confusing information provides the clinician with an avenue for exploration and for raising questions about specific family dynamics, for example, honesty, self-disclosure, social reclusiveness, or overdependence on outside agencies. Reliance on, excessive use of, or isolation from outside resources and contacts by family members is a reflection of the family's social abilities, sense of self-reliance, and degree of connectedness and of the nature of the boundaries that surround the family.

**Family system dynamics**

The family's general system dynamics are partially revealed through interview, history taking, and observation. The clinician should be able to form impressions or raise questions about the family as a system, particularly as it has been shaped and influenced by history, expresses its social nature through social embeddedness, has been influenced by health and medical events of members, and has been shaped by financial, social, cultural, and physical aspects of the environment. Insufficient information, contradictory information, and lack of relatedness among data become the targets for further data collection and clinical evaluation. Where there is a lack of or discrepant information about the family's ability to function in decision making, information processing, establishing emotional atmosphere, resolving conflict, or being emotionally honest, this may become the goal for intervention: to find out more about and facilitate that particular function within the family system. From the information provided and observations made, two specific areas of family dynamics are examined in some depth, namely, the emotional bonding within the family system and the patterns of interaction within the family and between the family and other social networks.

## EVALUATION OF SPECIFIC FAMILY DYNAMICS REVEALED THROUGH INTERVIEW AND OBSERVATION

Although there are a variety of ways of examining family dynamics within the interview and observation sessions, two particular means may be used easily and quite productively; these are diagrams that (1) provide representative samples of communication and interaction and (2) illustrate characteristic bonding within the family unit. The first diagram is referred to as a "sociogram" and the latter as a "psychogram."

A sociogram is a diagram that depicts a representative segment of an interview or observation session, including seating patterns, frequency of remarks, direction or flow of conversation, and any physical movement within the room by a family member, family pets, or the clinician. This diagram may be constructed during a five- or ten-minute segment of an entire session, simultaneously with the interview sessions, or later while the family is engaged in specific exercises to elicit interactional dynamics. A sample diagram of a three-member family being interviewed in a clinic is shown in Fig. 4.

The diagram provides a quick appraisal, which in this case was remarkably consistent with patterns that continued to emerge throughout the assessment of the family's interaction patterns, with the mother dominating the discussions, the daughter moving restlessly along the periphery of the room, and the father consistently looking out the window. High frequency of comment is often associated with power positions within the family; lack of comment, or silence, is often used manipulatively; and restlessness or

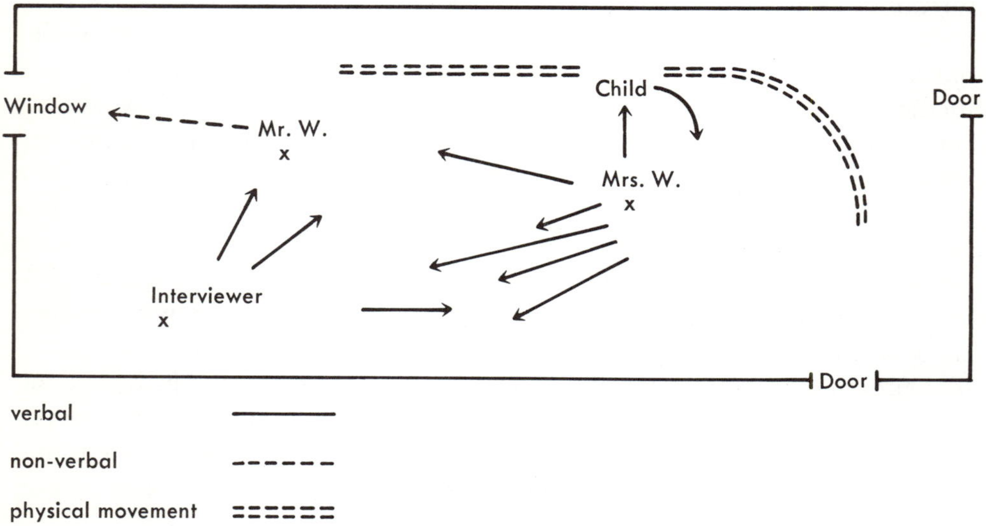


**Fig. 4.** Sociogram.

movement often occurs when topics arise that cause conflict or tension within the family. Just as a sociogram is used to illustrate social relationships, communication, and use of space within the family, a psychogram may be used to illustrate bonding between family members.

A psychogram is much like a sociogram except that the diagram is used to illustrate the apparent attachments within the family. Negative as well as positive bonding may be noted, as may the direction and intensity of such attachments. Emotional attachments are frequently quite intense between children and grandparents, as was the case in Larry's family, discussed in an earlier chapter. In the family presented in the sociogram in Fig. 4, the emotional attachments could be illustrated by the following representative diagram, in which the father is closely attached in a positive manner to the daughter and in a negative and overly dependent way to his wife. The wife is distantly attached to the husband in a mildly positive manner and is strongly, negatively bonded with the daughter. The daughter is strongly attached to the father in a positive manner but equally negatively attached to the mother. The daughter's and father's strong positive attachments to one another and the mother's lack of attachment to the father and strong, negative bonding with the daughter are consistent and recurrent patterns within this particular family, as illustrated in Fig. 5.

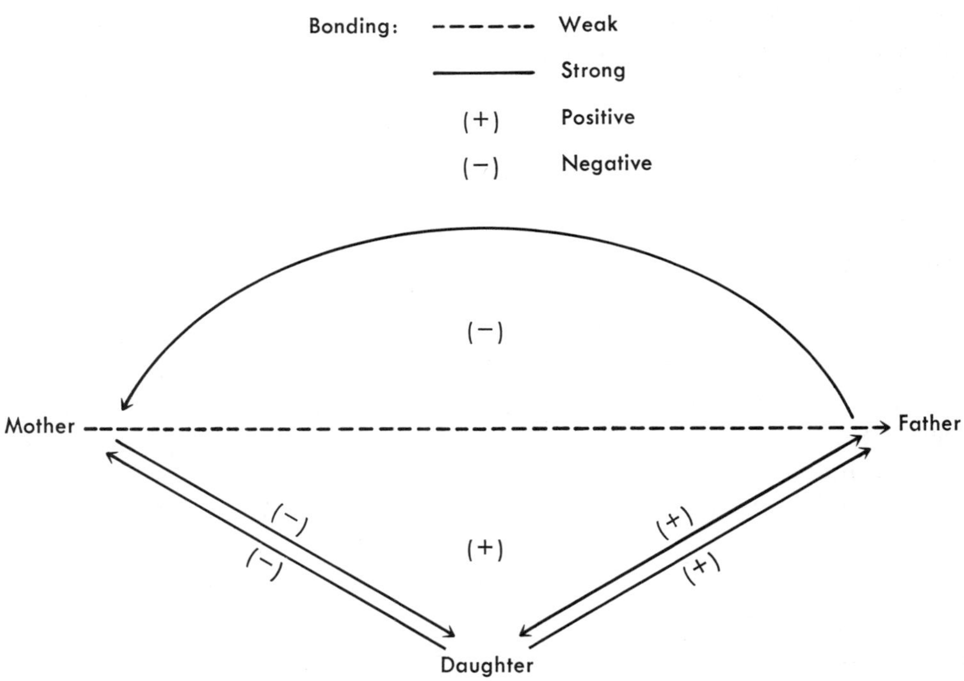


**Fig. 5.** Psychogram.

The mother's centrality in the family is born out in the sociogram as well as in the psychogram, as is the father's strong dependence on the mother and the daughter's lack of assuredness of her position. Not long after this diagram was made, the daughter ran away from home and the father became physically ill, events that were partially predictable from the information at hand. The daughter was caught in a strategic push-pull position between the mother and the father. The father's position was dependent on the daughter's bonding; a break in the socioemotional bonds between daughter and mother had a strong, negative impact on the father, reflected in changes in his physical health.

The sociogram and the psychogram may be used quite productively to explore two very sensitive and crucial aspects of family mental health and consequent effectiveness: namely, emotional attachments among family members and the social communication patterns by which family members send physical, verbal, and nonverbal messages. Although either diagram is only a representative sample of an ongoing, ever-evolving family process, patterns will emerge throughout the clinical process that characterize the emotional atmosphere and the communication process within the particular family system. Sociograms and psychograms may be constructed simultaneously with interview and observation or independently during a session geared specifically to that goal or derived during the remainder of the assessment phase as further information is gathered about family dynamics, focused either on one particular aspect of family life or on general system characteristics revealed through tasks and special assignments undertaken by the family with the assistance of the clinician.

## Clinical tools and family assessment

Clinical tools are designed and utilized in ways that reflect not only the individual clinician's preference but the philosophy underlying the clinical relationship as well. Since client independence, responsibility, and learning are valued in our clinical setting, tools are used that are understandable as well as productive and that require active participation by family members. Whereas a variety of clinical assessment tools are used, for example, Holmes and Rahe's Social Readjustment Scale (stress scale) to determine individual stress levels, Denver Developmental Screening Test to assess child growth and development, Revealed Individual Difference to ascertain couple agreement or disagreement, and physical examination and Health Inventory to establish a data base with reference to individual health, the following tools are used to elicit family interaction. (As will be noted, the emphasis of both tools is self-learning and self-evaluation by the family as a system, as a social unit, and as a psychological environment.) The first tool discussed is the Hanway Family Comparison and Contrast

Exercise and Assessment Tool; the second tool is the Bush Family Photoanalysis Exercise and Assessment Tool. Each tool will be described separately.

**Hanway Family Comparison and Contrast Exercise and Assessment Tool**

This exercise is designed to gather, in a relatively brief period of three to four sessions, a rather large volume of information about the family system. The information is both factual and subjective as expressed by individual family members. The tool is also used to elicit information on how the family operates: uses information, assigns tasks, takes turns, and otherwise functions as a system with a task to perform.

The tool itself consists of a set of 3- by 5-inch cards that the family receives. Instructions are printed on a larger card and read as follows:

A. 1. On the cards which you have received, print the names of all family members, one name to a card.
   2. When the task is complete, that is, listing each family member on an individual card, stack the cards on the table provided.
   3. Now randomly select three cards, by whatever method you desire, and lay the three cards on the table before you.
   4. Compare the three members as to their similarities, for example, physical characteristics, emotional temperament, occupation, unique features; and contrast the members according to their differences, such as religion, attitudes, likes, dislikes, and contribution to the family.
   5. The question to address is: "In what three ways are these family members different and in what three ways are they alike?"
   Replace these cards and repeat the exercise until the family is satisfied that all members have been fairly discussed. Since you may not complete this task in one sitting, a time limit should be established for today's exercise.

B. When you have completed the first part of the exercise, on a separate set of cards, name all family units. Repeat instruction 2 through 5.

C. Select from families within the community in which you live, two most similar to and two most discrete from your own. Repeat the above comparison and contrast exercise, steps two through 5.

As the family engages in and completes the task, the clinician may focus on several aspects: (1) factual information that emerges about each family member that confirms, supports, or invalidates information already received; (2) family dynamics revealed through the exercise itself that have not been previously discussed, pertaining to emotional characteristics, physical abilities, medical problems, critical incidents such as divorce, separation, or criminal activity, religious beliefs, and social connectedness; (3) family system characteristics in information processing, decision making, member assignment, and productivity as manifested in task completion or lack of completion. How the family handles this task will be representative of how the family handles other more complex tasks. Observations are made of who initiates the exercise; how the exercise is initiated by the family; how tasks are assigned, for example, whether each member fills out a stack of cards or whether the family as a group works cooperatively to complete one stack of cards; how much or how little information is given by each member; how much disagreement emerges with regard to the comparison and contrast and how that disagreement is handled; how capable the family is of completing the task with a minimum of guidance; and how effectively each family member is used as a resource.

At the conclusion of the exercise, the family is asked (1) to name the family units within their particular system and to compare and contrast those units and (2) to name four family units within their community, church, or neighborhood, two units being most similar and two being most different, and explore the differences and similarities. The criteria for such comparison are noted: finances, types of housing, kinds of cars driven, schools attended by children, school and social problems, size of family, and religious beliefs.

Selection of families for comparison and the criteria that the family used to measure itself against other family units involve family values and reveal the family's perception of its place in a larger social network. Inability to name any other similar family may suggest social isolation and aloneness. Comparison with families who are obviously in higher or lower socioeconomic categories suggests unrealistic group appraisal and unfair expectation for individual member performance and fit into social groups. Inability to identify areas of differences suggests an unclear or unestablished identity unique to this particular family, whereas overstating of differences tends to occur in families where there is repeated conflict with social systems, school, law, or church and who consequently place themselves on the periphery of society. Appraisal of family and comparing family units with related and unrelated family units enable the family to more clearly identify sources of influence and connectedness with larger familial and social networks. Photoanalysis, the basis of the second tool, focuses directly on the relationships within the family system and the patterns of behavior that develop over time.

### Bush Family Photoanalysis Exercise and Assessment Tool

Photostudy as a diagnostic and clinical assessment tool has been discussed in some detail in other publications and will, therefore, be discussed here rather briefly. The Bush Family Photoanalysis Exercise is designed to provide historical and longitudinal information about family dynamics as revealed in a particular set of photographs and to provide an avenue of interaction for observing the family and assessing family abilities as the group involves themselves in self-examination and study. As a historical tool, analysis of a set of representative photographs that show family members in various settings and under varying circumstances gives the observer some ideas about family patterns. As an immediate participatory tool, photostudy provides the clinician with an opportunity to observe and assess the family as they conduct photostudy of their own selected photographs. As a tool for the immediate elicitation of actions and interactions, the Bush Family Photoanalysis Exercise shares with the Hanway comparison and contrast exercise the purpose of eliciting family process. As a historical and longitudinal reference for family development, photostudy differs in that the behavior, patterns, gestures, and information provided by photographs must be explained and explored in rather concrete and direct ways and placed within a large context of ongoing dynamics within the family system.

The family is instructed in and provided with a guide that aids in the selection of photographs that represent at least six different areas: (1) photographs of individual family members; (2) photographs of family members with friends; (3) photographs of family members with nonhuman interests and love objects, such as hobbies, pets, and pastimes; (4) photographs of family members as units, as couples, and as adults and children; (5) photographs of representative family units, including grandparents, aunts, uncles, and cousins; and (6) photographs that involve unplanned or spontaneous action on the part of the family or individual members. The family selects two or three photographs that represent each of the categories and then examines the photographs for the following content: (1) flow or movement within the picture, such as flow of energy, affection, power, or control; (2) congruence, or consistency, within the picture, including congruence between facial expression, body posture, and activity of the individual or individuals; (3) changes over time, such as hair styles, clothing, setting, or members included; and (4) descriptive information about the picture, for example, feelings evoked, centrality of members, use of touch, use of physical position or posture, general activity level, and general impression about the people in the photograph. Life style, patterns of behavior, and manifestations of power, influence, and conflict within the family may be observed and examined.

If the family conducts their own photostudy, using the guide provided them, the results may be presented during assessment sessions and discussed among members and between the clinician and family unit. During this time, it is possible for the clinician to observe family dynamics, including who initiates the discussion, who has been responsible for the work involved with the study, who fails to show up or participate in the study, who works most diligently to understand and learn from the sessions, and areas in which the family displays greatest strengths and weaknesses. Where there are weaknesses or deficiencies, intervention programs may be developed that focus on the development of necessary skills, such as wider use of resources, and that aim to bolster the strengths already apparent within the family.

## RESULTS

The end goal of these exercises and consequent assessment is not only to determine family effectiveness but also to construct a descriptive profile of family dynamics, to reinforce and encourage strong points, and to shore up and improve on weak points. Even the most effective family has its weak points, and the most ineffective families still have their strong points. As the Hanway and Bush assessment tools are employed, the following categories may be used to divide the impressions formulated during the assessment phase into areas that facilitate planning appropriate and productive intervention: information processing, decision making, emotional tenor, conflict management, and productivity and change.

### Information processing

What kind of information is sought, and how is it used?

1. Are resources used limited or extensive?
2. Is information used in a way that is supportive of what is already known or that challenges that which is being considered?
3. What is the information network within the family: that is, do all participate or do one or two individuals assume major responsibility for information gathering and processing?
4. How flexible is the family in changing their minds or considering an input that might cause them to have to reconsider or reevaluate information received?
5. Are individuals within the family self-reliant, and to what extent is the family as a group independent of outside help and other professional resources?
6. How does the family go about informing itself as to the nature of the task at hand?
7. How is the task accepted, and how much assistance does the family require in performing the task?
8. What is the style of communication used by the family in approaching the task? How important is individual participation in gathering information and carrying out the activities?
9. How is information processing within the family reflected in decision-making abilities?

**Decision making**

How can the decision-making process be described?

1. To what extent is there full participation by family in the task?
2. Are decisions reached by majority rule or by an alternative method such as consensus?
3. To what extent are family activities organized toward completion of the task, or to what extent are family efforts somewhat chaotic?
4. To what extent is the focus of activity within the family on the task itself, and to what extent is the focus on people involved in the task?
5. How satisfied do members appear with ways in which decisions are reached within the family?
6. What is the nature of leadership within the family with regard to decision making?
7. How supportive are nonleader members of those who take leadership positions within the family?
8. How able is the clinician to observe delineated individual responsibilities, for example, agent or victim within the decision making process?
9. To what extent is there individual support of group effort, and to what extent do various members undermine the family's endeavors?
10. To what extent are the decisions that are made implemented in the task itself?

**Emotional tenor**

What is the emotional atmosphere of the family?

1. In what ways can the emotional environment of this family be described: for example, cold or warm, close or distant, honest or dishonest, authentic or manipulative?
2. In what ways can the emotional climate be described: self-centered or other focused, conditional or unconditional acceptance and support, and contradictory or congruent?
3. To what extent is the family able to express tenderness, openness, and regard for each other?
4. To what extent are family members honest, particularly emotionally, with themselves and with each other?
5. To what extent is self-disclosure possible and practiced within the family unit?
6. To what extent and for what purpose is physical touch used by various family members?
7. To what extent are positive statements accompanied by supportive gestures?

8. To what extent is affection used as a means of control in the family?
9. To what extent are emotions used according to age and experience?
10. What opportunity is there within this family for individual expression of feeling, either positive or negative?
11. Is the course of discussion supportive, challenging, manipulative, coercive?
12. Is there an air of openness and acceptance, of warmth, or one of tension, defensiveness, and coldness?
13. How are feelings made known in this family?
14. Who assumes responsibility for caretaking of feelings?
15. Are feelings honored or devalued?

**Conflict management**

How are individual differences handled?

1. What individual differences appear within this family unit (physical, social, emotional)?
2. To what extent are individual expression and uniqueness encouraged or discouraged?
3. To what extent is individual opinion suppressed in order to maintain a facade of group harmony?
4. How able are family members to compromise and cooperate with one another in accomplishing the task?
5. What particular issues, topics, or activities generate tension, conflict, or disagreement?
6. To what extent do family members use tactics of persuasion, coercion, or threat in order to control expression of individual opinion or behavior?
7. To what extent do individuals use persuasion, coercion, or threat to control the family unit?
8. How does allowing for individual expression, opinion, and activity facilitate or hamper overall family productiveness and satisfaction with the task?
9. What is the result of disagreement?
10. Are there individual differences in learning, physical ability, or emotional development that lessen the family's ability to accept itself as a unit?

**Productivity and change**

How adaptable is the family?

1. How able is the family to set goals, divide activities, and take on individual responsibility in accomplishing the task?
2. How does the family go about establishing priorities in accomplishing the task?

3. To what extent do individual pleasure and self-satisfaction override the family needs to accomplish the task and to care for the emotional needs of its members?
4. Are resources used adequately or inadequately in task completion?
5. To what extent are personal needs of members considered in task completion?
6. To what extent is the family influenced by environmental contingencies during task performance (noise, heat, cold)?
7. Does the family rigidly adhere to the task at hand, or is the family able to adapt and allow for altered priorities within the task?
8. To what extent does the level of productivity within the family differ according to individual ability? Does family productivity reflect those individual differences?
9. To what extent has family productivity been influenced by situational demands (divorce, separation, single parenting)?
10. What changes have occurred over the years as revealed in comparing units one with another and in changes viewed in the photographs?
11. What is the greatest need for change and adaptation revealed through these exercises?

Impressions formed based on the above assessment will assist the clinician in identifying strengths and weaknesses of the family and in pinpointing targets for intervention.

**Strengths and weaknesses**

1. Where are the greatest strengths: openness, acceptance, mutual support, strong beliefs, individual expansion and growth, financial and educational opportunity, or ability to listen and challenge one another productively?
2. Where are the greatest weaknesses: genetic deficiencies, social isolation, no strong beliefs, poor work history, repeated reliance on outsiders with no evidence of growth in self-reliance, absence from and increasing abandonment of the unit by family members, or no cultural or ethnic identity?

**Targets**

1. What areas can be identified that need clinical intervention, referral, remediation, or further evaluation?
2. How willing is the family to undergo the effort to achieve increased awareness?
3. How able is the family to bear the pain of self-examination and finding unpleasant or unacceptable traits, interests, or pastimes of members?
4. Given the medical, health, and social history of this family, how much

is the family at risk, that is, how likely is this family to develop problems given their history, the current situation, and the coping strategies that they have described or otherwise manifested?

5. How does the clinician assess self skills in promoting change with this particular family? Is there need to involve others in the intervention strategies, as might be the case where an individual exhibits a learning disability, mental retardation, or criminal activity?

## SUMMARY

As the assessment is finalized, the clinician must make judgments about the data obtained, in terms of accuracy, completeness, and consistency; must evaluate the overall dynamic profile of the family as a social network and psychological environment; must assess and draw conclusions about the family ability to act and interact as a productive and compassionate system; and, finally, must determine appropriate intervention strategies to enhance the network function, the emotional environment, and the system abilities. Intervention strategies will depend on the clinician's assessment and the family's perceptions and participation, as will be discussed in Chapter 16.

Tools have been presented that facilitate the collection of data—historical and contemporary—about the family and that provide for the active involvement of the family unit in the self-evaluation and change process.

### STUDY QUESTIONS

1. Discuss the importance of determining validity of data collected through interview and observation.
2. Discuss the major ways in which information gathered in the family interview differs from data gathered through the family's direct involvement with tasks in the clinical setting.
3. Discuss ways in which the Hanway comparison and contrast exercise can be used to elicit information regarding (a) dynamics internal to family system (b) dynamics that occur between the contemporary family subsystems (siblings, parents, parent-child), and (c) dynamics that occur between family system and other social systems.
4. Discuss ways in which the Bush Family Photoanalysis Exercise and Assessment Tool can be used to provide information about family bonding.
5. Discuss ways in which you would expect ineffective family functioning to differ from effective family functioning.

### BIBLIOGRAPHY

Akeret, R.: Photoanalysis, New York, 1973, Simon & Schuster, Inc.

Beckman, B., and Tauormina, J.: Power relations in families, a social exchange perspective, Fam. Process **17:**423, December 1978.

Erikson, M.: Assessment and management of developmental changes in children, St. Louis, 1976, The C. V. Mosby Co.

Holmes, R., and Rahe, R.: Social readjustment rating scale, J. Psychosom. Res. **11:**213, 1967.

Kaslow, F., and Friedman, J.: Utilization of family photos and movies in family therapy, J. Marriage Fam. Counsel. **3:**19, 1977.

Malasanos, L., Barkauskas, V., Moss, M., and Stoltenberg-Allen, K.: Health assessment, St. Louis, 1977, The C. V. Mosby Co.

Maloney, M., and Ward, M.: Psychological assessment; a conceptual approach, New York, 1976, Oxford University Press.

Sedgwick, R.: Family mental health; a sociopsychological approach. In Kneisl, C. R., and Wilson, H. S., editors: Current perspectives in psychiatric nursing; issues and trends, vol. 1, St. Louis, 1976, The C. V. Mosby Co., pp. 190-200.

Sedgwick, R.: Photostudy as a diagnostic tool in working with families. In Kneisi, C. R., and Wilson, H. S., editors: Current perspectives in psychiatric nursing; issues and trends, vol. 2, St. Louis, 1978, The C. V. Mosby Co., pp. 60-69.

Sedgwick, R.: The use of photoanalysis and family memorabilia in the study of family interaction, J. Corrective Soc. Psychiatry **25**(4):137, 1979.

Strodbecht, R.: Husband-wife interaction over revealed differences, Am. Sociol. Rev. **6**(16):468, 1951.

## Chapter 16

# INTERVENTION AND EVALUATION

### CLINICAL INTERVENTION

The intervention phase of the clinical process is closely related to clinical evaluation that has preceded it and is ongoing. Intervention strategies that evolve and are designed from assessment and evaluation include a number of options, such as referral, consultation with related professionals, goal planning, and change. Whatever steps are taken are designed and implemented during the intervention phase of the clinical process. The following is a succinct discussion of the intervention process. Chapters that follow include specific case illustrations with descriptions and discussions of particular intervention strategies.

#### Definition

Clinical intervention is that aspect of the clinical process in which goal planning and implementation based on previous history taking, observation, and assessment are carried out as a collaborative effort between clinician and client, in this case, the family unit. Although referral to and consultation with other health professionals are often outcomes of assessment, clinical intervention in terms of goal planning and implementation will be the focus of the following discussion. Goal planning involves identifying targets, that is, areas of concern or need, outlining the steps to be taken to meet the need, and carrying out the plan that has been established. Clinical intervention may be generally viewed as a program of planned change whose purpose is to support family strengths, promote skill building in areas of weakness, and encourage individual growth and group expansion, cooperation, and understanding.

#### Purpose

The purpose of intervention, or planned change, is to shore up the skills that a family already possesses, to teach new skills that are lacking, and to enhance the family's awareness of its own resources and sets of choices that are inherent within the family itself. Planned change with a family system is geared toward enhancement of social organization and emotional environment within the family system: that is, to (1) promote a positive emotional environment, (2) achieve a more equitable use of space, (3) encourage the growth of self-worth and personal importance, (4) facilitate positive, growth-inducing emotional attachments, (5) and strengthen the family's productive participation as a social system within a larger social environment. Planned change usually involves alteration in personal attitudes, expansion of personal and family beliefs, examination of family habits and ways of life, acquisition of social skills and psychological tools for self-disclosure and group participation, gaining new outlooks, or exploding myths. The range of activities undertaken will reflect the scope of the clinical contract, the needs of the family, the involvement of health agencies, and the time framework within which the goals must be achieved.

## Scope

The range of clinical activities will reflect the goals established through collaborative efforts of the active participants in the clinical process. Within the participant-observer role that the clinician has maintained throughout the clinical process is the role of educator and guide. Although the clinician may be a skilled observer, trained group leader, and expert in human relations, the clinician's final responsibility is as an educator who teaches the family: about themselves, about dynamics within the system, about consequences of human actions, about the use and abuse of the family environment, and about their own impact on one another and on society. The family's responsibility is to learn and to apply learning in such a way as to enhance choices, activate social and family responsibilities, and assure continued learning throughout the life span of the family. Thus, planned change is a collaborative effort in which clinician and family work together toward common goals that enhance the family's ability as a social system and psychological environment. The family is therefore an active participant in the stages of clinical intervention, which generally include goal identification, development of intervention strategies, implementing change, and evaluating the change itself.

## Method

Intervention can be broken down into three general stages: (1) goal identification, (2) strategy design and development, and (3) implementation and evaluation. The stages are overlapping and interdependent but for the purpose of this presentation will be discussed separately. Intervention begins with the identification of goals to be established.

**Goal identification.** Goal identification involves using the clinical findings and impressions derived through history taking, observation, and assessment to establish targets around which family and clinical energy can be focused for the remainder of the clinical contract. Targets can be generally identified within areas discussed in the observation and assessment phase: communication, use of space, use of resources, decision making, productivity, mutual understanding, emotional support, and so forth. Goals are established within the target areas. Goals identified may include, for example, (1) fostering individual abilities and uniqueness, (2) strengthening emotional support networks, (3) altering family use of individual space or altering individual use or abuse of family space (4) clarifying individual contribution and responsibility within the family system, (5) altering emotional attachments between individual members, (6) fostering conflict management skills, and (7) promoting family productivity in the social and financial environment. Goal identification includes the development of long-term as well as short-term goals. Long-term goals serve to organize the family's efforts in a given direction, for example, clarifying and strengthening message systems, whereas short-term goals, such as spending three hours a week on family-related discussions, serve to guide and motivate the family along the way to achieving long-term goals.

Strategy design and development include statements about long- and short-term goals and a plan for the achievement of those goals.

**Strategy design and development.** The identification of goals is accompanied by a plan for achieving stated goals. *General goals* are broadly stated; for example, (1) enhancing role clarity, (2) expanding use of resources, (3) improving adaptive skills, (4) broadening social networks and support systems, (5) fostering the use of democratic principles in decision making, (6) development of management skills that allow for and encourage individual differences, or (7) promoting a positive emotional atmosphere of acceptance, warmth, and support.

*Specific goals* are stated in simple, understandable terms that focus on perceptible or observable dynamics, such as behavior, actions, or verbal exchanges, and are designed to move the family along to the achievement of general, long-term goals.

The following examples show how specific goals are designed to complement and facilitate achievement of long-term goals. Specific intervention strategies are discussed more fully in the case illustrations that follow.

Enhancing role clarity might be hastened by family members switching responsibilities for one week and recording their feelings, perceptions, and ideas about that week's experience. Expanding use of resources might be accomplished by having each member of the family become an active member in a community, school, or work-related organization for six weeks and report perceptions, feelings, and experiences pertinent to those activities. Improving adaptive skills might involve attending parenting classes, taking a course in stress management, or joining a single parents group where similar experiences are shared. Broadening social support systems might involve taking an active part in community, family, church, or neighborhood activities. Fostering democratic principles generally involves role playing, practice sessions, or group involvement—to test and examine current practices and create new rules of behavior—as does the enhancement of management skills where conflict and individual differences are concerned. Promoting a supportive emotional environment might involve increasing the number of positive statements that members make and assisting one another in activities that are generally role defined or member specific. Activities that would help achieve (aids) or hinder the achievement (barriers) of these goals are examined and a timetable is established for the attainment of specific goals. It is important to remember that the strategies to achieve goals must be tailored to the particular family and to the long-term goals that the family has decided are important to accomplish. Strategy should be designed within a time frame, for example, ten weeks; be focused on one or two general goals, for example, enhancing a positive emotional environment and clarifying message systems; and include a maximum of three specific goals to be accomplished within the time frame. Because barriers and aids often become more apparent in the course of implementation, flexibility must be maintained in altering priorities and shifting goals throughout the remainder of the contract. When the goals are identified and the strategies designed, the plan for change must be put to the test through implementation and evaluation.

**Implementation and evaluation.** Carrying out the plan and determining the effectiveness of implementation are the final stages of the clinical contract. Because change itself is usually difficult for families and because specific problems often prompt families to seek help, intervention strategies are carried out that help families to resolve immediate problems while long-range plans for change are being generated and learning is taking place. Problem solving is directly related to the ability to identify and predict consequences of actions: behavior, words, or gestures. Learning is related to the availability of information and the opportunity to practice in a setting in which consequences can be altered, controlled, or exchanged. An essential component of successful change involves acquiring and practicing skills conducive to change; within the clinical setting, family members can try out new behavior, act on feelings, and attempt emotional realignment with the guidance of the clinician.

One particularly useful structural approach to effective planned change, which I have developed to facilitate family practical skills, is the Family EDIT Strategy. This acronym is derived from a four-step family activity: (1) The family presents an *E*xample of behavior, interaction, or activity that causes concern or conflict within the family unit (2) The family *D*iscusses it fully in the clinical setting, using the clinician as a resource, guide, and facilitator. (3) The family *I*dentifies new ideas, approaches, or ways of handling the problem. (4) The family *T*ries out or practices within the framework of role playing the new behaviors and strategies.

The clinician acts as safety valve, clarifier, buffer, and strategist in assisting the family to explore alternatives, consequences, and changes that best suit the internal needs of and external demands on the family system. When the family has familiarized itself with the tactics of EDIT, the family can then select a series of specific examples to work on during the remainder of the clinical contract, considering long- as well as short-term goals. Practice sessions in the clinical setting are combined with social change attempts in the family setting, with actual work in the home having increasing emphasis.

## EVALUATION

At the end of the specified period of time, it is necessary for the family and clinician to evaluate the process and consequences of the change. Such evaluation may result in the successful termination of the contract or the negotiation of additional clinical contracts with different short-term goals.

Although actual goal implementation is contingent on the goals identified and the strategy designed to carry out the goals, there are several general rules that I ask families to follow:

1. All members affected by the change must be involved to some degree in planning for and carrying out the program.
2. Change strategy must be fair, honest, and directed toward constructive choices for those involved.
3. Change itself must be consistent with the beliefs and values held to be important by the family.
4. Long-term goals must be established in accordance with short-term, specific goals designed to implement more general, long-term change.
5. Change must be consistent with external, environmental, and social contingencies.
6. Principles employed to manage change must be democratic, consensus-oriented, and consistently fair.
7. The final responsibility for implementing change belongs to the family unit, with the clinician acting as resource, guide, educator, and observer.
8. The process of evaluation of the change endeavors must include an examination of adherence to the guidelines and of the appropriateness, effectiveness, and success of the change strategies themselves.

Implementation is accompanied by and concluded with an evaluation of the clinical process by the family and the clinician. Since the family is largely responsible for formulating goals, designing strategies, and carrying out plans for change, the family must be able to engage in self-evaluation, maintain an active role in the clinical process, assume responsibility for self-management, realize interdependent relationships within the family and between the family unit and other social systems, and act as an agent of change.

In assessing the effectiveness of planned change, it may become necessary to assist the family in learning how to make changes and assume responsibility for their own functioning. Many families experience an inability to change because they fail to adhere to the guidelines of including all members, making decisions by consensus, and employing democratic principles and because they rely too heavily on outside resources to make change for them. Such inability need not be taken as a failure on the part of the collaborative efforts of the family and the clinician but must be used as an indication that clinical goals and strategies must be reexamined and redesigned.

In evaluating goals and strategies, it is often necessary to examine the contextual variables and situational contingencies that influence the family system. For example, stresses that the family has experienced may have been overlooked or underestimated in previous assessments and might now have to be considered as barriers to accomplishment of the current stated goals. Situational variables of finances, social and community demands, and job requirements may be prohibitive in the family's efforts to make changes. The change process itself, when undertaken by the family, provides the family and the clinician with ongoing, current data about the family's abilities and the clinician's abilities in a collaborative team and current information about the family as a social system and a psychological environment. As a particular clinical contract is examined and evaluated, enhanced awareness of the dynamics of the family system can be developed and utilized in ongoing clinical contracts or programs for planned change. Following and often simultaneous with evaluation is the termination of the clinical relationship.

As the clinical contract is concluded and the relationship between the family and clinician terminated, each partner in the process will become sensitized to the ongoing and interconnected nature of relationships, including the one between the family and the clinician. Successful change involves terminating, expanding, and altering interpersonal relationships, and the clinical relationship is no exception.

At the conclusion of the time period established in the clinical contract or with the successful accomplishment of stated goals, the clinical relationship is terminated. The family is provided with a written list of options that they may decide to undertake in the future, for example, another clinical contract, referral to another health professional, participation in seminars or family enrichment programs, or maintaining the system in its current status. The need to negotiate another set of goals would be approached in separate clinical contract.

The termination of a clinical relationship is fraught with some of the same difficulties that are encountered and must be mastered in the termination of any human relationship in which attempts have been made to promote emotional bonding, establish honest communication, and create an accepting atmosphere for personal risk-taking and ultimate growth. The clinician and the family members often experience a sense of loss and express a desire to continue the relationship. Separation is a necessary step in the growth process and must be undertaken with the same determination that initiating the clinical contract required. It is often helpful to practice saying goodbye and to discuss future plans that do not include the present clinical relationship. Because the family will tend to follow the lead of the clinician, the primary responsibility for enforcing termination will be the clinician's. The clinician's support group can be a valuable asset in assisting with feelings associated with this stage of separation. The system that has evolved with the coming together of the subsystems of family and clinician is often a positive and challenging experience, one that must be considered as one aspect of the clinician's growth as a professional.

## SUMMARY

Clinical intervention is that aspect of the clinical process in which goals are identified and change strategies are designed and carried out. Stages of clinical intervention are: goal identification, strategy design and development, and goal implementation and evaluation. Families are active members of the clinical team in all three stages of intervention; they are assisted in change endeavors through clinical practice sessions in which the family engages in presenting examples, discussing methods of handling the problem, identifying alternative methods of coping, and then trying out and practicing alternative behaviors, actions, and interactions by means such as role playing, videotaping and active discussion. The clinician serves as group leader, facilitator, buffer, safety valve, and educator as the family practices making changes and undertaking new goals.

As the clinical process comes to a conclusion, the process itself is evaluated by the family and clinician in terms of appropriateness, effectiveness, and general success. As the process is terminated, the family is presented with options to guide their continued development and learning. The clinician and family must assume their responsibility for coping with changing and expanding human relationships, including the clinical relationship between the family and the clinician.

## STUDY QUESTIONS

1. Intervention is largely dependent on clinical activities that include interview, observation, and assessment. Describe the relationship between assessment and goal identification.
2. Discuss ways in which the term *clinical intervention* can be used interchangeably with *planned change.*
3. Discuss the clinician's responsibility in enhancing the family's effectiveness as a system.
4. In what ways can the clinician's peer group be a support to the clinician, professionally and personally?
5. What part do feelings play in the difficulties encountered in working with families who are resistant to change or who demonstrate inability to change?
6. How can the clinician reconcile differences in the case of change strategies desired by the family but considered detrimental by the clinician?

## BIBLIOGRAPHY

Aguilera, D., and Messick, J.: Crisis intervention; theory and methodology, ed. 3, St. Louis, 1978, The C. V. Mosby Co.

Anderson, C. M.: Family intervention with severely disturbed inpatients, Arch. Gen. Psychiatry **34:**697, 1977.

Beal, D., and Dukro, P.: Family counseling as an alternative to legal action for the juvenile status offender, J. Marriage Fam. Counsel. **3:**77, 1977.

Brammer, L.: The helping relationship; process and skills, Englewood Cliffs, N. J., 1973, Prentice-Hall, Inc.

Carkhuff, R.: The art of problem solving, Amherst, Mass., 1973, Human Resources Development Press.

Daitman, R.: Methods of self-confrontation in family therapy, J. Marriage Fam. Counsel. **3:**3, 1977.

Garfield, C.: Stress and survival; the emotional realities of life-threatening illness, St. Louis, 1979, The C. V. Mosby Co.

Hardcastel, D.: A mother-child, multiple-family, counseling program; procedures and results, Fam. Process **16:**67, 1977.

McAdoo, H.: Family therapy in the black community, Am. J. Orthopsychiatry **47:**75, 1977.

Satterfield, W.: Short-term group therapy for people in crises, Hosp. Community Psychiatry **28:**539, 1977.

Tittler, B., and others: A system for tailoring change measures to the individual family, Fam. Process **16:**119, 1977.

PART III

# Theory application in clinical practice

Chapter 17

# A FAMILY WITH AN ACUTE SITUATION

## SITUATION: EMOTIONAL AND PHYSICAL ABUSE

Abuse, physical and emotional, is an increasingly reported phenomenon in the American family. Abuse of children by parents and spouse by spouse and the recently discovered abuse of parents by children represent a serious concern for mental health professionals and for families themselves. As will be seen in the following example, physical and emotional abuse tend to run in families; many abusive parents were themselves abused as children. In most cases, abuse tends to be an outcome of chronic frustration, emotional deprivation, societal pressures, and interpersonal inadequacies and is not necessarily an intentional act designed to harm, injure, or maim. The families that we have worked with express deep remorse, a sense of personal failure, and a general inability to know where to turn or how to handle their feelings and consequent actions. Although there are families in which hurt and violence are intentional and for whom abuse becomes a way of life, the majority of abusive families we encounter resemble the Morse family, which is characterized by a family history of physical and emotional abuse, lack of social and community embeddedness, financial obligations that exceed resources, and interpersonal responsibilities that outstrip emotional reservoirs and experience.

## MORSE FAMILY

Dick Morse, father of five children, was referred to our office by the local juvenile officer as a suspected child abuser. The members of the family include Dick, the father; five children, ages ten months to 13 years; and Joanne, the mother and working wife. Both sets of grandparents are living and well; however, they reside in a distant state. Joanne's family of origin is somewhat sketchy. Dick's family of origin consists of 14 siblings, with Dick a middle child. He spent two years in a home for juvenile offenders, after which he completed two years of high school and was married at age

17 to Joanne, who at the time was a divorcee with two infant children. The two eldest Morse children, ages 12 and 13, belong to Joanne's first husband (later killed in Viet Nam); the three youngest children, ages ten, two, and ten months, belong to Joanne and Dick.

**Presenting situation**

"Suspected child abuse" was reported by a neighbor to the local juvenile officer, who in turn referred the family for evaluation and consultation. During the initial interview, Dick appeared tired, with dark circles under his eyes; he was nervous and cautious, which he manifested in arm rubbing, scratching, and repetitious but halting comments. In spite of the July heat, he was dressed in dark clothes that were rumpled and wrinkled. His hair was unkempt and his shoes dirty. His appearance was that of a person who is depressed or experiencing chronic low self-esteem. (It is important to note not only what people wear but *how* they wear it as well. Dick was dressed in work clothes, but the way he wore the work clothes clearly communicated his feelings about himself and his presentation to the world.) His manner was hesitant but increasingly open and cooperative as the interview progressed. He described himself as "filled with emptiness" and feeling as if the "world fell in on top" of him. He paused several times during the conversation to wipe tears from his eyes, to cross and uncross his legs (mostly at mention of his father and of having married a woman with two small children), to rub the back of his head (when speaking of his sons having robbed him of small change kept in his workbench), and to point to his temple when talking about being reported for child abuse. His overall presentation was one of weariness and futility. He described his relationship with his father as "okay" but stated that his father was absent most of his childhood, working two jobs and leaving discipline to Dick's mother. It was during his father's absence that Dick engaged in stealing, truancy from school, running away from home and became an increasingly difficult management problem for his mother, who finally had him placed in a home for "juvenile deliquents" where he stayed for two years. (Dick has one brother who is serving time for stealing and petty larceny.)

During the initial interview, Dick reported a recurrent incident that happened each Sunday. Dick began Sunday as a "rest day" but by midday had become so caught up in thinking about bills, kids, and job that he became increasingly "homesick and alone." On each occasion he retreated "someplace alone" to try to "pull himself together"; however, he was unsuccessful. He concluded this narration by saying, "I guess I need as much help as the boys." Dick believed his own experience in the boy's home was helpful to him; however, he worried that his own sons would turn out badly as evidenced by their current behavior. His worries were extensive and real: home maintenance, financial security, marital instability. His worries were contradicted by his stated beliefs, for example, that he and his wife had a good relationship because, although he worked days as a maintenance man and she worked evenings as a nurse, they "had frequent discussions and family meetings," in spite of his statement that "we never see each other." In spite of financial concerns and marital conflict, the couple was planning a two-week vacation, taking the three smallest children and leaving the two oldest sons with Dick's brother. The first interview, filled with contradictions and inconsistencies, ended with Dick, the sole informant, requesting another consultation and evaluation session to include the entire family; a subsequent meeting was scheduled for the following day.

The above information was obtained in approximately 30 minutes, during which time observations were made, a family history was outlined, the beginnings of a clinical relationship were established, the need for continued meetings was identified; and a time was agreed on for a subsequent meeting, the goal of which was to meet and hear from all family members. It must be emphasized that this information was obtained from one family member. Thus, the data are incomplete; they can in no way be considered complete family data. Information from any individual member represents an individual viewpoint and a single opinion. However, a wealth of information may be obtained in a relatively short period of time from an individual family member. The process used to obtain the information is described below.

**Interview**

The interview was preceded by Dick's and my meeting in our reception room, where Dick was seated with his arms folded across his chest, eyes fixed on the floor in front of him. As I called his name, he looked up, rose slowly, and extended his hand in greeting. He accompanied me to our family therapy room. Dick chose a two-seater couch close to my desk and sat tucked in one corner. (The room is designed, except for my desk, which is used for writing and as a barrier when distance is needed, to resemble a living room, with couch, two-seater, end tables, hanging plants, oil paintings of familiar landscapes, and volumes of reading and resource material.) I began the session with "Tell me what brings you here," and Dick responded by forcing back tears and rubbing his head. Below is a portion of the exchange that followed:

DICK: "She" (pointing toward the window, across the street from which is located the offices of the juvenile officer) "gave me your name and number and sent me over."

CLINICIAN: "M-m-m" I sat back and waited, sensing his reluctance, which seemed mixed with a strong need for help.

DICK: "The neighbors turned me in for child abuse." Long pause as though he were thinking about something. "They said I locked a kid in a room upstairs," wiping tears. "Nobody even bothered to look to see that we don't even got any doors on the rooms."

CLINICIAN: Shaking my head, I felt myself sighing as I began to sense the load that he carried.

DICK: "I don't know how to handle these kids; they steal from me, they use foul language." Long, thoughtful pause. "They're going to be j. d.'s for sure." He crossed and uncrossed his legs. "I don't know what to do." He hung his head as though someone had shamed him.

CLINICIAN: "You have other kids?" I wanted to direct conversation away from his sense of futility and provide him with a subject of discussion about which he might talk more confidently and thus gain some composure. (It is important for clients to maintain a sense of self-command, particularly when the whole world seems to be falling down around them.)

DICK: Looking up from his lap and laughing. "Five altogether."

CLINICIAN: "Tell me about your family." I could feel the tension lifting.

DICK: "Well," drawing a deep breath and sitting up straighter. He then related some family history: that he had been the middle child of 14, had spent two years in a home for boys, and was what he considered a "juvenile deliquent." He ended by saying, "I don't know what to do."

CLINICIAN: "Tell me a little about yourself—your work, your interests, your marriage. I noticed you haven't mentioned a wife." I also noted to myself that reference to family elicited family of origin information; this led me to believe unresolved relationships existed within that system. I tried now to direct Dick's thinking to his current situation.

DICK: "I work as a janitor; my wife's a nurse" (later identified as a nursing aide). "We don't make much money. We have all our money tied up in credit companies." He then related how much went for various things, their various work schedules, and discipline problems with the kids.

CLINICIAN: "You have a lot of responsibility." I was trying to read between the lines and apparently hit on target; he seemed to wilt under the observation.

DICK: Putting his face in his hands and weeping. He then talked in mumbled tones about his own past, his father's recurrent absences, being sent away to a school, his brother being in prison, buying bikes for his kids and them breaking them up, his oldest son taking the baby's pants off in front of a widow next door and exposing his "thing" and generally unloaded a big emotional burden of frustration, desperation, futility, poverty, and depression.

## Observations

While Dick gathered himself together and gained some control over his emotions, I made mental sketches (sociogram) of the preceding conversation, which had been dominated by Dick's concern about his inability to control his children and direct his life in a more productive fashion.

**Sociogram.** During the 30-minute conversation Dick directed his comments either to the floor or to a point somewhere in back of my head; his gaze rarely involved eye-to-eye contact. He was physically restless, crossing and uncrossing his legs, fidgeting with his shoelaces, rubbing the back of his neck, pointing to his temple with thumb and forefinger, and wiping his eyes with the back of his hand. His body language confirmed his verbal expressions of futility, despair, anger, and frustration. While I concluded my mental notes of his actions and behaviors, I gathered my impressions of the emotional attachments within the family.

**Psychogram.** Dick's primary attachments with his family of origin are strong, with frequent references to his father's absence, his mother's inability to manage him, his parents' having given over custody of him to a boys' school, his brother's being in prison, his "Sunday homesickness." His psychological bonding with his wife and children was less obvious to me. When I remarked on this vagueness to Dick, he revealed his wife's previous marriage and the fact that "his" sons really belonged to "someone else." Dick described his relationship with his wife in distant but supportive terms. The descriptions of his children were somewhat contradictory: for example, "I don't know how to handle them . . . foul language . . . tearing up toys . . . making demands"; however, "they fill up empty spaces . . . they help me through rough times . . . at least they're something to do . . . ." The upcoming vacation was to involve visits to Dick's parents, leaving the two oldest children with a brother and taking the three younger children along. As the preliminary session drew to a close, I began to form my impressions.

### Assessment

During this preliminary session an attempt was made to obtain a family history, gather relevant data about what appeared to be an acute situation, assess the previous coping strategies used by this family, and evaluate the possibility of successful clinical involvement.

The following factors were considered: (1) Dick's helpseeking behavior was prompted by a social crisis that required the intervention of judicial authorities; (2) Dick's family history included repeated social family problems requiring the assistance of outside resources (juvenile officer, police, credit agencies, loan officers, mental health professionals); (3) Dick's family of origin presented some unresolved and potentially conflictive areas of need; (4) Dick's present family make-up was that of a blended family (involving children from previous marriage) with failure experiences in the areas of discipline and parental supervision; (5) Dick's present family contained two working parents, with no provisions for outside help in child care; (6) Dick's family did not attend church, did not belong to any social or community groups, and was generally viewed by the neighbors as "troublesome, noisy, and trashy"; and (7) Dick's coping mechanisms had been depleted and he was emotionally drained, exhibiting subtle suicidal gestures and remarks. Based on the factors considered, the family's effectiveness is tentatively described in the following sections.

**Information processing.** It appeared from Dick's descriptions that the family unit relied heavily on Dick's brother and Joanne's sister for assistance, advice, and support, all of which seemed somewhat inadequate. Information sought tended to support previous beliefs and ways of life; it was not until the neighbors reported the family to a juvenile officer that outside help was sought. Coercion by outsiders was necessary for Dick to seek assistance or advice. Dick's description of family history would lead one to believe that he had primarily functioned as a loner, somewhat outside the mainstream of events. How his current family reached out and used resources as a unit was not clear.

**Decision making.** Although Dick briefly referred to periodic discussions with his wife, decision making appeared disorganized and based on immediate need or demand. A "head in the sand" approach in planning for the future was reflected in putting off disciplining or talking to his kids until forced into confrontation by their stealing and acting out. Whether or not Dick reached out to his family or co-workers for assistance or example is not clear but is doubtful; it appeared that decision making was generally authoritarian and unilateral on Dick's part. There was no apparent pattern to decision making, and decisions made seemed to require more energy than this family demonstrated in Dick's description. An overriding concern would be to evaluate this family's outlook for the future and examine plans, if any, for their moving toward future goals.

**Emotional tenor.** The emotional atmosphere was a mix of previous experiences with families of origin that were conflictive, troubled, and lacking in support and acceptance. Dick seemed distant from his children, from his wife, and from his work. Emotional distance, fatigue, futility, and despair were reflected in Dick's personal behavior and orientation.

**Management of conflict.** Allowing for individual growth and expression had been hampered by the rapid expansion of the family. Housing had been difficult to obtain; physical accommodation of individual members had been limited, with family members sharing the same living and sleeping territory. Both parents had to work to support the family group, which allowed little time for coupling or parent-child interaction. Disagreements appeared to have been handled in a physically and emotionally abusive fashion. Conflict in the past had led to family fragmentation and individual rejection by the system. The basis supplied by the family of origin was weak and ineffectual in providing Dick with knowledge, experience, or motivation in managing conflict or even promoting normal growth and development.

**Productivity and adaptability.** Although both parents worked, it had been necessary for the family to seek loans, extended credit, and financial assistance in order to pay bills and keep a roof over their heads. Adaptability had been shown to be lacking by Dick's rather rigid ways of handling affairs within the home setting.

**Strengths and weaknesses.** The strength in this situation was Dick's interest in and need for a family unit to fulfill his sense of connectedness with the world. His need to be closer to his own parents was both a strength and a weakness. His reluctance in seeking consultation was balanced by his expression of personal depression and need for help, as a person and as a father. His family history of law breaking, antisocial acts, and sibling conflict was balanced somewhat by his awareness that with help people can and do change. Another strength or weakness to be considered would be the part that his wife and children choose to play in the consultation and evaluation sessions to follow.

This was a particularly high-risk family: an early marriage immediately following a two-year placement in a boy's home reflected a need for emotional attachments on Dick's part that prompted his finding a "ready-made family" (Joanne and the boys). Dick was inadequately prepared to deal with his situation as a result of several factors: (1) his own inadequate parenting repertoire; (2) emotional underdevelopment as a result of experiences in family of origin that did not allow or encourage emotional growth, bonding, and expansion; (3) narrowed orientation, namely work, as a result of early life experiences and a family life dominated by frequent moves and job changes; (4) inadequate emotional reserves due to rapid expansion of present family, inadequate emotional experiences, and minimal opportunity for spouse-spouse bonding; (5) inadequate social bonding and present family's distance from possible sources of social and emotional support; (6) limited productivity in spite of both parents being employed; and (7) little adaptability as evidenced by reluctance to change or adopt new methods of parenting, disciplining, and emotional bonding. Although these impressions are tentative, they serve as a basis for ongoing evaluation and assessment. Intervention at this point was based on immediate problem solving: reduction of tension, enhancement of Dick's self-control, and provision for the safety of the children.

### Intervention

General clinical goals are to: (1) promote emotional development and expression of feeling in age-appropriate ways, (2) facilitate social bonding and network interdependence within the community, and (3) encourage management skills on the part of the parents—personal, financial, and emotional. Specific goals would be to: (1) provide the father with an opportunity for ventilation and expression of feeling and a means of support and recognition of his sense of futility and desperation; (2) refer the family to

Parents Anonymous, a self-help organization; and (3) engage the family unit in ongoing evaluation and consultation sessions.

**Evaluation**

During the first session, specific clinical goals were met by providing an environment in which Dick could feel free to confidentially reveal fears, angers, and desperation and in which his strong points of caring, hard work, and concern for his family could be supported. The family was referred to Parents Anonymous, and an appointment was made for the following day for the entire family. Because of the suspected child abuse and concern for the safety of the children, home visits had been made previously by juvenile authorities and would be continued through Social Rehabilitation Services (SRS), as mandated by state law. General goals that serve as an organizing framework are reminders of the long-term needs of this family, presently expressed by a father experiencing acute stress. As a matter of priority and because of the father's pivotal position within the family system, the primary concern was to defuse the father's anger, support his caring nature, and provide him with a sense of choice in working with his children and of coping with his own desperation.

Contact with the family was made through the father, demonstrating both his pivotal position within the family as decision maker, protector, and lone leader and his own personal needs for assistance toward self-control and expression of feelings in appropriate and nondestructive ways. He presented himself with halting authenticity, largely as a result of the potential explosiveness of the situation and his immediate inability to control his emotions. In acute situations such as this, emotional boundaries are often fluid, permitting self-disclosure and the revealing of intimate material that otherwise might be guarded, hidden by generalities. As indicated in the verbal exchange presented, a clinical effort was made to assist in restoring emotional boundaries by not letting Dick's sense of despair and anger run away with him, while encouraging the expression of these feelings by providing an environment of support and comfort. A fine line must often be drawn between giving comfort and providing control, between encouraging emotional expression and verbal self-disclosure and preventing the client from being engulfed in an emotional explosion that will later be regretted. Dick expressed repeated concern over his own inability to control his children, his own sense of desperation and anger, and his unresolved feelings of anger and resentment toward his own parents. Although the safety of his children is certainly at the forefront of clinical endeavors, Dick's safety and emotional liability must also be considered. Joanne's apparent distance and lack of connectedness in this marriage, seen in her absence from the initial session, must be considered as a possible indicator of her relationship to Dick, to child rearing, and to family connectedness in general. From the initial session with Dick, this family appeared to be a high-risk, socially disconnected, emotionally immature, moderately productive family with minimal investments in family dynamics, except as prompted by outside authorities.

The abusive child or parent in such families often becomes the outlet for family tension that results from frustration, interpersonal inadequacies, and emotional turmoil. Abuse is not an isolated circumstance but represents a phenomenon that occurs within a larger context of system inadequacies, regardless of social status, religious belief, or cultural background. Just as the abusive individual must be considered within the context of family dynamics, the abusive family must be considered within the context of a larger environmental setting: community, neighborhood, and social network.

## SUMMARY

The example of the Morse family demonstrates techniques used in interviewing and observing and points out factors that may be considered in immediate problem solving. With an in-depth interview and thorough history taking accompanied by systematic observation, clinical intervention evolves that is directly related to the current situation. Although Dick's motivation for seeking help was "child abuse," it could have just as easily been excessive drinking, wife beating, or acute depression. The method of coping with frustration, stress, and personal sense of failure was learned in his own family of origin, characterized by emotional abuse, physical indifference, personal rejection, and inadequate emotional bonding. Ongoing clinical involvement will depend on success in establishing a sense of bonding between professional and family network and beween the family network and supportive social networks, such as Parents Anonymous. As demonstrated in the following examples, which represents long-term consultation, detailed history taking, and extensive intervention strategies, facilitating a family's social connectedness with similar social networks can be a strong, positive element in helping the family cope with stress and work toward eventual change.

### BIBLIOGRAPHY

Bybee, J., editor: Violence toward youth in families, J. Soc. Issues **35**(2), 1979.

Gil D.: Violence against children, Cambridge, Mass., 1970, Harvard University Press.

Gil D.: Primary prevention of child abuse; a philosophical and political issue, Psychiatr. Opinion **13:** 30, 1976.

Kempe, C., and Helfer, R., editors: Helping the battered child in his family, Philadelphia, 1972, J. B. Lippincott Co.

Kagan, J.: Understanding children; behavior, motives and thought, New York, 1971, Harcourt, Brace, Jovanovich, Inc.

Martin, H.: The abused child, Cambridge, Mass. 1976, Ballinger Publishing Co.

Ounsted, C., Oppenheimer, R., and Lindsay, J.: Aspects of bonding failure; the psychopathology and psychotherapeutic treatment of families of battered children, Dev. Med. Child Neurol. **16:** 447, 1974.

Paulson, M.: Child trauma intervention; a community response to family violence, J. Clin. Child Psychiatry **4:** 26, 1975.

Savion, A., and Sanders, R.: Working with abusive parents; group therapy and home visits, Am. J. Nurs. **73:** 482, 1973.

Wolkenstein, A.: The fear of committing child abuse; a discussion of eight families, Child Welfare **56:** 249, 1979.

Wright, L.: Parent power; a guide to responsible childrearing, New York, 1978, Psychological Dimensions, Inc.

**Chapter 18**

# A FAMILY WITH A LONG-TERM SITUATION

## SITUATION: LABELED CHILDREN IN MALADAPTIVE SYSTEMS

Children are often the cues that stimulate families to seek outside help. A child is often an index of a dysfunctional family system as well as a barometer of a dysfunctional or maladaptive social system, such as a particular school. These children may be labeled by family members as "behavior management problems" and by social systems as "learning impaired," "troublemakers," "juvenile delinquent," or "hyperactive." These labels are often employed by families and school systems to relieve themselves of any commitment to individuals and to deny the active part they play in the overall dysfunctional situation. As labeled individuals, these children and adolescents bear the burden of systems that are unable to resolve conflict, provide for or accommodate individual differences, and alter their patterns when confronted with the need for change.

It has been our experience that the "learning disabled" child serves the purpose of family and system scapegoat, a vehicle for the release of psychological and social tension that cannot be resolved, incorporated, or otherwise managed by the faulty system. Families with such children are often families "on the way up," seeking a better way of life, reaching for higher social status, and grappling with norms and expectations with which there is inadequate skill and lack of previous family experience. The child with special needs—emotional, social, physical, or intellectual—may throw a wrench into an already vulnerable system on the brink of outstripping its own emotional, financial, physical, and social resources. The family itself represents a "weak link" in a social system whose goals include intellectual development and superior social performance on the part of all members, regardless of the needs, interests, or abilities of individual members.

The Lyndon family is a family with a problem child, in this case a learning disabled child, whose patterns are representative of other families with problem children. These patterns can be summarized as follows: The "learning disabled" child is often a boy; the family's current social status is a notch up from that of previous generations; the family's goals and priorities are geared toward material gain, social status, and "keeping up with the Joneses"; underlying emotional tenor is characterized by deceptive communications, social facades, and unrealistic individual and family expectations.

## LYNDON FAMILY

As will be observed in this clinical example, families in less acute situations are able to provide a wide range of information, and the clinician is able to engage in observations that are more descriptive of ongoing dynamics as well as geared toward immediate problem solving as in the previous example. With all family members present, history taking can be geared toward eliciting individual information (developmental, medical, health, social) and group interaction (information processing, emotional atmosphere, and so forth). Comments enclosed in parentheses highlight clinical impressions made, questions raised, or clinical gesture as data were being collected and observations being made. Individual as well as group information is presented.

The following information was obtained during interview and consultation with the Lyndon family, who had been referred by a Diagnostic Center for Learning Disabled Children. The Center's recommendation included the establishment of behavioral management programs for the learning disabled child. As with the Morse family, the Lyndon family came for consultation chiefly as the result of strong recommendations by an outside resource. Their initial reluctance became evident the opening minutes of the first session.

### Initial session

The family entered the therapy room in the following order: oldest son, age 13; father, age 38; mother age 30; second son—the learning disabled child—age 10; and the youngest son, age 4; whom the mother later reported was "hyperactive." The family seated themselves; the eldest son and father sat at the far corners (distance) of a couch opposite my desk, the mother sat across the room in the corner of a two-seater, closest to my desk (support), and the second son plopped down beside her. The youngest child bounced up on the couch between his brother and father; his older brother patted him warmly on the leg (caretaking). The father folded his arms across his protruding abdomen; the mother held her hands tightly in her lap, smiled and frowned nervously (tension). The eldest son sat with one leg casually up over the seat cushion (relaxed) and his arms extended on the arm and back of the couch; he occasionally played with the curls on his youngest brother's head. The second son sat with his head tucked in his arm (embarrassed or shy) and his legs drawn up close to his body; the mother seemed not to notice that he was sitting next to her (self-absorption). All were dressed casually except for the mother, who seemed a little overdressed (individual difference? need for recognition?). I began the discussion.

**Interview**

Since the family had filled out forms before the session, I checked the folder, opened it to the family names and laid it across my lap. "Now let's see if I can guess who you are (setting a mood of informality). You must be Karl," I nodded in the direction of the eldest child, who smiled impishly. "And you must be Ralph," I nodded at the youngest child who sat next to his big brother. Ralph smiled and said, "I be four." "That's a good age to be, Ralph. I know it's going to be very hard for a busy little boy to be quiet when others are talking, but I know you'll try, okay?" (Positive strokes.) Ralph answered "okay" and ducked his head behind his brother, apparently either shy or unaccustomed to positive recognition and inclusion. I moved on around the room, "And you must be Bob?" The father nodded and swallowed (uncertainty). "I appreciate your coming straight from work like this when a cold beer and a shower would probably feel so much better." Bob laughed and uncrossed his arms. I moved on around the room: "And you must be Bobby." (Patterns begin to emerge.) Bobby blushed and squirmed around in his seat. Just as I turned to speak to the mother, Ralph jumped up from his place on the couch, ran over, and sat down beside his mother. "You must be Linda." The mother laughed nervously and twisted her hands in her lap. Linda looked at the floor and then smiled at me: "I remember you from our church group, you spoke at our women's meeting." (Pattern—seeking support and alignment.) There is a concern in the mother's eyes that she does not express and which, for the moment, I do not probe. We move on into the session. (Clinical impressions made during the interview are contained in parentheses throughout the case material.)

CLINICIAN: "Tell me what brings you here." I spoke to no one in particular, providing open-ended leadership and allowing opportunity to test family consensus about the "problem." I looked around the room waiting for someone to speak.

MOTHER: "We don't really know. We thought Bobby was supposed to come and then we found out the whole family was supposed to come. We've never been to a family therapist before." Linda sat back and folded her hands in her lap.

CLINICIAN: "I understand that Bobby has been to the Diagnostic Center and that he has a learning problem, but I wonder how the other members of the family have been affected by Bobby's situation. What affects one member of a family often has direct impact on other family members and vice versa. Family therapy is directed toward trying to better understand how a family operates and how members affect one another." I paused to let the family think about what I had said. No one spoke, so I proceeded. "It would help me in helping you if I knew more about your family; unless you" (glancing around the room) "have any questions, we can start." No one had a question. "Good, then we can get started." I turned to the folder and took out a blank sheet of paper. "I need to keep notes to be sure we get things down right; we may have to correct some information as we go along, but my keeping notes will give us something to work from." (Eliciting factual and familial information at the outset gives the family an opportunity to relax and be less problem centered; it also gives them something to discuss with which they are familiar, thus permitting them to feel less uncertain and nervous about the beginning session. Providing the family with an opportunity to "tell what brings them" often elicits a wealth of information. However, when no one feels particularly compelled to discuss immediate concerns, either the concerns are not so immediate or an effort is being made to "cover up" and protect the family or an individual within the family from exposure. In this family, there was a little of both.) The following information was obtained during the initial interview and subsequent sessions.

**Family history**

*Father.* Robert, age 38, employed as an electrical maintenance man. Robert's father died six months previously; his widowed mother was living and well. Robert was a middle sibling of four children. Relationship with his parents was distant and somewhat detached, with greatest similarity to his brothers and sister. He reported no physical attribute, trait, or attitude in which he resembled either parent or grandparent; however, both he and his father were "poor students" and had "bad tempers."

*Mother.* Linda, age 30, housewife, part-time baby-sitting service. Parents were living, with minimal health problems or medical needs. Linda was an only child. Relationship with parents was described as "close and protective," with Linda living a "sheltered, comfortable life." Reported character resemblance to mother, attitude and physical resemblance to father. Maintained close daily contact with her mother by telephone; maintained close contact with her father through eldest son, who "spends all his time with his grandfather."

*Karl.* Age 13, firstborn of Linda (she was 17). Karl was adopted by his current father, with whom he shared a "bad temper." Karl differed from other family members in academic achievement, social interests, and closeness to grandparents.

*Bobby.* Age 12, second-born of mother, firstborn of father, to whom he bore physical resemblance and with whom he shared "problem learning." Resembled mother in being "a worrier" and "not paying attention." Spent little time with grandparents, no time with his father, and some time with his mother.

*Ralph.* Age 4, third-born child. Resembled his mother in physical appearance and "bounciness." Ralph was closest to his mother and grandmother.

**Medical history**

*Father.* Recurrent headaches, resulting in seven months of lost work; continual fatigue. No medical explanation found for the headaches (suspect stress related physical illness).

*Mother.* Hysterectomy two years before for "bleeding"; no other hospitalizations; currently taking Valium prescribed by the family physician. (Family physician did not recommend therapy or psychological consultation and had not scheduled follow-up.)

*Children.* No medical problems, hospitalizations, or recent visits to medical personnel.

*Grandparents.* Paternal grandfather died within previous six months. Maternal parents both hospitalized for "falls, lightheadedness, and stroke-like symptoms" within the last two years.

**Health history.** Health history, like medical history, reflected a highly stressed family, responding in a physical as well as an emotional way.

*Father.* The father reports no health problems, sleeps well, eats well, is somewhat overweight, eliminates well, does not appear tired or in poor health; however, he reports recurrent, apparently unexplained headaches. (Headaches may be related to unresolved grief over the loss of his father; could also be a response to chronic, unresolved marital conflict or a coping mechanism related to financial, social, and family stress.)

*Mother.* Describes herself as being a "worrier." She takes Valium to sleep at night. Roller coaster weight gain and loss since hysterectomy; appeared tired and described feeling "drained."

*Children.* Karl—active in sports, trim, and alert. Robert, Jr.—slow, sleeps long hours, "eye problems," and overweight. Ralph—no naps, fussy eater, "overactive."

**Social history.** The family as a group did not attend church, belong to any social groups, or engage in neighborhood or community activities. The mother infrequently attended church, and the father worked episodically; however, the children regularly attended school or preschool. The mother reportedly had one or two close friends; the father did not associate closely with anyone at work. Karl attended school, was active in sports, and had several friends; he described himself as an average student. Bobby had problems with school, was in a special class, and had trouble getting along with his friends. Ralph attended a free, church-affiliated preschool that he "liked a lot" and was able to name two or three friends in his class. The family lived in a relatively well-to-do neighborhood and belonged to one of the elite social clubs in the area, in spite of repeated financial troubles and lack of social connectedness. (Social striving with inadequate social background or financial means is probably a source of continuing stress.)

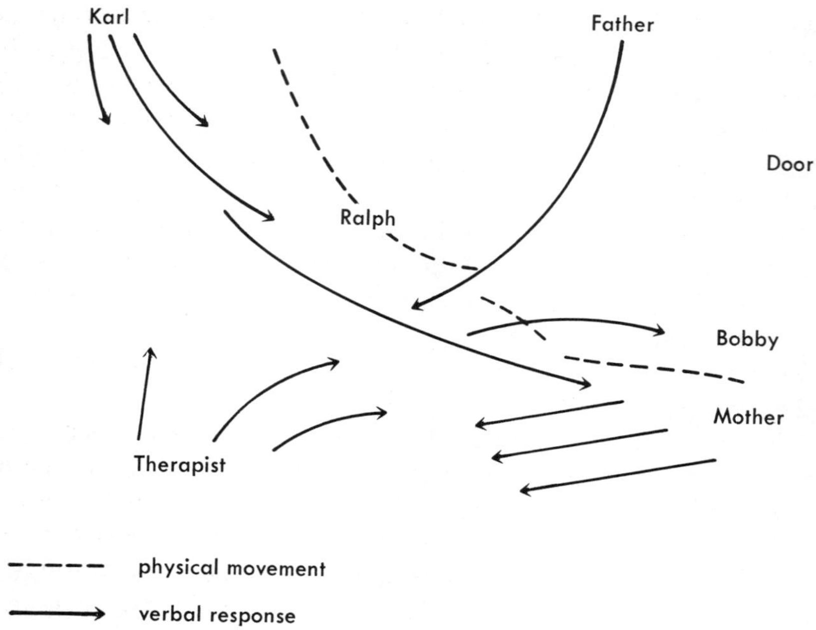


**Fig. 6.** Sociogram.

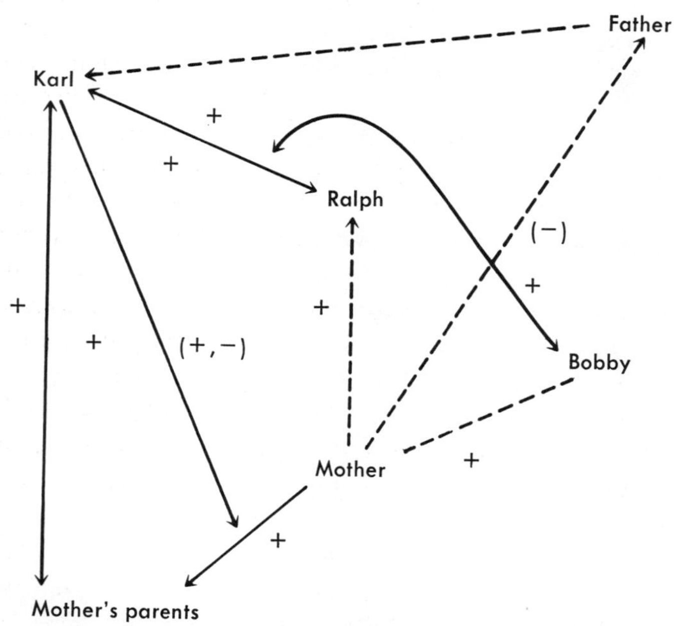


**Fig. 7.** Psychogram.

**Critical incidents.** Critical events, illnesses, changes, or trauma in the previous two years included: (1) two moves, each time to a bigger house and a better neighborhood; (2) the mother's partial hysterectomy; (3) the father's loss of six months of work because of "sinus infections"; (4) the paternal grandfather's unexpected death because of a coronary; (5) beginning of maternal parents' physical health problems; (6) beginning of Bobby's "trouble in school"; (7) Karl's "bad temper" as he reached adolescence; and (8) Ralph's starting preschool and being "overactive."

### Observation

The primary and most active informants were the mother and the eldest son; a representative sociogram appears in Fig. 6.

The most frequent comments were made by the mother, usually to the therapist; by Karl, usually to the mother or Ralph; and by the therapist, to individual family members. Karl assumed a source-resource position in the family, with the mother often turning to Karl for support and clarification. Bobby and his father assumed bystander (victim) postures, and Ralph moved about the room restlessly when areas of disagreement or conflict emerged (index). Individual contributions were primarily activities of victim and index, with an occasional member becoming a transitory or inadequate source and resource.

A primary relationship emerged between the mother and eldest son, who was born before the mother's marriage and was, in fact, son of another man; a representative psychogram appears in Fig. 7. This information is being witheld from Karl by the mother until the "right time." Karl's close relationship with his mother's parents served as a link between his mother and her family of origin. The mother maintained a protective, but emotionally distant, relationship with her two younger children and a mutually deceptive relationship with her husband. The father maintained a distant and illusive emotional relationship with the family. Karl attempted a close, nurturing relationship with Ralph, a protective relationship with Bobby, and a bantering relationship with the mother. In Karl's presence, the family functioned as a unit; in his absence, the family functioned as separate individuals going in separate directions. (Karl was reportedly "hard to manage" and "easily provoked," and the entire family "feared his violence"; these reports all indicate his inappropriately powerful and responsible position in the family and his need for supportive bonding with his grandparents.)

### Assessment

**Information processing.** The family's use of resources was generally limited, extensive only in terms of social service agencies. Like the Morse family, the Lyndon family had required the assistance of credit agencies, loan companies, and welfare. Unlike the Morse family, the family also made the rounds of mental health agencies in the area. The relationship, however, had been passive, with the family assuming a helpless, directionless (victim) attitude. Although the mother's family of origin served as a source of advice and support for her and the eldest boy, the father's family had a more distant, less active involvement with this family.

**Decision making.** There seemed to be a pattern in decision making in which the mother or eldest son was involved as primary agent and the father as silent partner. The eldest son seemed to function as father or husband in the father's absence and as mother in the mother's "emotional" absence; however, this pattern shifted and changed often. As the area of decision making was discussed and observed further, the father and mother revealed a previously made decision to "stay together," with the mother and the father assuming rigidly defined roles. The mother's frequent use of mental health and social services was apparently an attempt to replace the lost spouse and decision maker and seek support for her own needs. The father remained an aloof, often emotionally absent member of the family, with the mother relying heavily on her family of origin for support. "Problems" became the avenue of continued contact and bonding with mental health professionals, who became a "second family" for this mother. (Clinical intervention was ultimately directed at assisting the family unit to find and become a part of a supportive social network in which both parents could participate and experience a sense of belonging.)

**Emotional tenor.** A primary bonding existed between the mother and the eldest son, partially as a source of support for the mother but also as an attempt to maintain family secrets and assure linkages with the mother's family of origin. The family unit contained many secrets, and much energy was spent in an attempt to keep the skeletons in the closet. The two most troublesome deceptions were the eldest son's heritage and the parents' hidden decision to stay together in a contradictory and dishonest relationship. In order to maintain the facade of marriage, the mother often lied to the children, to her parents, and apparently to herself. The eldest son held a powerful, manipulative position as far as the mother was concerned, but he did not know why. Furthermore, he lacked the emotional experience and social skill to successfully occupy such a power position. His frustration, fear, and inordinate responsibility resulted in temper outbursts, assaultive acts, and threats to parents.

In order to "keep a roof over her head and food on the table," the mother had developed a manipulative, dishonest, and contradictory position within the family, as had her spouse. Caught in the middle of the struggle between mother and father were the eldest son and the two younger boys, one diagnosed as having learning difficulties and the other described as hyperactive. The eldest son alternately played the role of other spouse, father figure, mother, and tyrant, whereas the younger boys played the role of troubled, helpless, confused children in need of healthy, decisive, and loving parents. The father played the role of distant ruler, with the mother assuming a position of being helpless and vulnerable. Overall, the emotional atmosphere was contradictory, confusing, and lacking in authenticity. Learning and emotional development in this family setting were hampered by confusion, lack of clarity, inadequate role modeling, and contradiction. The emotional tenor was reflected in the family's overall inability to manage conflict and promote positive individual growth.

**Conflict management and individuation.** In response to the comment, "Let's talk about how each of you is similar to as well as different from each other," the eldest son quickly replied that he had trouble in math; Ralph said that he liked school; Bobby just shrugged his shoulders (a response characteristic of him); the mother said she was a worrier; and the father said he thought his working made him different from everyone else. No one mentioned Bobby's school problems or home management, which the Center had reported was the prompting event behind the family's need for therapy. (It should be noted that the mother and "learning disabled son had made the rounds of all mental health centers in the area in an effort to "correct Bobby's school problems." In response to the comment, "Let's talk about Bobby's school problems," Bobby shrugged his shoulder; Karl reported that Bobby has always been different, to which Bobby gave a shocked and animated response; the mother said the school didn't have adequate teachers; and, after a long pause, the father related his own problems in learning, which he attributed to having moved several times in the school year. The father completed the eighth grade, but his reading and learning skills are questionable. It was not until the family sessions that Bobby learned that his father had had a school problem or that kids had also taunted his father about being "dumb and stupid." The similarities betwen the father and the "troubled" boy were striking but often dismissed or played down by the mother as being "unimportant." The family's inability to permit, manage, or encourage individual development and the inability to handle arguments, disagreements, and behavioral problems of all three boys were founded on an emotional atmosphere that was inconsistent, contradictory, and primarily dishonest. The entire family had adopted an attitude of "if we ignore it, surely it will go away," despite extensive help-seeking behavior on their part. The inconsistent and often contradictory messages within the family were exemplified by two comments made by the mother. The first comment was made during a telephone conversation in which the mother sought to cancel an appointment with the following excuse: "I'm not about to come into therapy and have things found out that will lose me a roof over my head and food on my table." She was willing to do anything, including sacrifice the emotional welfare of her marriage and her children, in order to avoid exposure, confrontation, and "opening up old wounds." On another occasion, the mother called to reschedule a canceled appointment, saying: "We need therapy, because to help the problem child we first have to find the problem in the family." As the emotional tenor vacillated between open and closed, honest and deceptive, so the level of productivity and flexibility tended to alternate between success and failure.

**Productivity and adaptability.** The family's financial, social, and emotional productivity alternated between marginal success and potential failure. Although the father was able to maintain a job for a period of several years, he frequently lost time and wages because of recurrent, unexplained illnesses. On occasions when the financial pinch became severe, the mother took on part-time jobs, which she dropped when the father's work became more steady. The family responded to repeated stress and frustrations with illness, physical complaints, behavioral disorders, and school difficulties. Potential for change was limited because of the unwritten contract between the mother and the father to stay together no matter what, with the resultant interactions geared toward maintaining secrets, withholding information, and maintaining social and personal facades. The family's initial tentative, off and on commitment to therapy was a characteristic pattern with regard to other social, family, and financial responsibilities. Productivity was somewhat limited by the father's narrowed sense of accomplishment, which he did not want exceeded by his family (children as well as wife). This family maintained a commitment to sameness, oneness, and lack of change in spite of help-seeking behavior that involved a number of different agencies.

**Strengths and weaknesses.** When one considers that this family had survived, however ineffectively, a series of stressful circumstances, namely financial stress, physical illness, joblessness, marital instability, and parental loss, one wonders if there is not an emotional reservoir in the family that has not been fully tapped. The family's inconsistent but recurrent need to divulge information suggested a potential strength in the direction of being more open and self-disclosing. The father's physical, episodic presence in the sessions was a potential asset in facilitating the parents' taking a more active role in the process, thereby relieving the eldest boy of responsiblity in fathering the family. Fostering adult responsibilities, sexually, socially, and psychologically, was essential. The strong belief in deception and secret keeping was perhaps the family's major weakness. The investment in deception was accompanied by a strong belief in stereotypical roles and functions for family members. In spite of the belief in sterotypical myths, however, there was a lack of role clarity and an assignment of responsibility that was inappropriate in terms of age, sex, and experience. Children were assigned parenting roles, adults were given child roles, and parents neglected their spouse obligations. Goals for intervention were designed that focused on altering weaknesses and bolstering strengths.

Although there is little doubt that Bobby had learning deficiencies, his learning was further hampered by conditions within the family system. Attention was directed toward those situations within the family that were of greatest concern: emotional dishonesty and intolerance of individual differences.

## Intervention

General clinical goals were: (1) generating and supporting a communication system within the family that was consistent, based on logical and understandable rules, and as emotionally honest as possible within the limits of this family; (2) establishing skills for management of conflict and allowing individual differences; and (3) enhancing a stable and lasting financial productivity in line with material goals and social ambition.

Specific clinical goals, designed to complement and facilitate the accomplishment of long-term goals, were to: (1) establish a system of priorities in which an awareness of consequences of selective priority setting would be developed; (2) generate emotional realignments that would provide age and development appropriate experiences for individual family members; and (3) develop adult autonomy and social network bonding. Strategies involved in working toward goal accomplishment are summarized below:

### Intervention strategies

| General goal | Specific goal | Strategies |
|---|---|---|
| Honest communication | Priority setting | Discussions centering on rules and family boundaries. Examples of topics are: discipline, use of leisure time, spending money, expression of feeling. |

### Priority setting and developing awareness of consequences

*Questions*

1. What is the rule regarding ______? (Use of leisure time, spending money, disciplining children.)
2. How did the rule come about? (Who was involved; did a specific incident prompt the rule making; are rules made prior to events or do rules evolve?)

3. What happens when rules about ______ are broken?
4. How important is this rule compared with other rules? List the five most important rules or priorities for the family.

*Exercise.* "Let's develop a new rule (or establish a set of priorities) about ______ and practice changing the rule through group debate. The conditions are that:

1. Each member must speak up and have a say.
2. The rule must be logical, understandable, and serve a purpose.
3. We debate the rule until *all* members are satisfied—no rule by majority vote and no speaking for others.

*Questions*

1. How did this exercise compare with at-home practices?
2. What were your feelings during the exercise?
3. Which is more important—making rules or setting priorities, carrying them out or punishing rule breakers?
4. How would you like to change your contribution to or participation in this exercise?
5. How honest were you during this exercise?

This and similar exercises are designed to help the family look at itself and listen to itself while working together, particularly to decide what is and what is not important. Being honest can be a risky business, particularly in a family heavily invested in secrets. Conflict is often avoided in order to maintain secrets and protect family boundaries; the second set of strategies was designed to enhance awareness of the consequences of such practices.

**Management of conflict and individuation.** Exercises and experiences were designed that would promote emotional realignment, which would help the family explore issues of being different and encourage adult awareness of and need for individual experiences and expression. Since emotional bonding grows out of social bonding and network experiences, the couple were encouraged to take a "weekend together" in their recreational vehicle, with the children going to the home of the grandparents, where those bonds could be strengthened. Each child was helped to gain an appropriate peer group network—ball team, Scouts, or preschool—in order that social and emotional boundaries and bonds could be expanded.

Parents were encouraged to join an ongoing "couples group" where similar issues could be explored and adult peer support could be found. Since many couples also had children who were "different," issues of discipline, relationships with school officials, expectations for performance, and personal disappointments could be explored. Couples within the group used the Hanway comparison and contrast exercise to explore their similarities and discuss their differences. Finding many similarities helped individual couples within the group to experience a sense of belonging and support. Common characteristics included such things as having a child who was "different," experiencing sexual and marital difficulties, having financial problems and social difficulties, and feeling inadequate. EDIT strategies were used by the group to practice alternative ways of handling similar problems. A sample EDIT exercise is described below. Group support and encouragement aided in the couple's growth in autonomy and a recognition of their interdependence.

**EDIT exercise**

CLINICIAN: "Tonight we're going to practice problem solving using EDIT strategies, which all of you have used before, so I'll just summarize the directions: Find one *example* of a situation at home that you would like to improve or need to handle; *describe* the situation to the group; group members generate *ideas* for handling the situation differently; and then, we'll *try out* the various methods to see which works out best."

Group members form a circle while waiting for volunteers. One couple volunteer to discuss a problem with the school system, which had recently asked the family to remove their child from the school.

**Example.** The couple received a letter from the school asking them to remove their son from the school because of "inability to manage him, even in special education class."

**Description of event**

GROUP MEMBER: "What did they say he did?"

FAMILY MEMBER: "Punched another kid in the nose." Folded hands in her lap and stared at the floor; other family member folded and unfolded the letter.

CLINICIAN: "It seems to me like we need a little more information; could one of you fill us in on the background details?"

FAMILY MEMBER: "Like what do you mean?"

GROUP MEMBER: "Like how'd your kid end up in special ed. classes in the first place?"

FAMILY MEMBER: "Same kind of letter, telling us we had to put him in special classes." Waves letter and nearly shouts.

GROUP MEMBER: "You mean you didn't sign no letter of agreement or nothing?"

FAMILY MEMBER: "Well, yeah we did sign a letter, but we didn't know what it meant."

SEVERAL GROUP MEMBERS: Nodding in agreement and voicing support. "Yeah, that happened to us." "Yeah, us too; they said they had to have at least six kids in special ed. to qualify for federal funding. . . . We're all guinea pigs, that's what it is."

CLINICIAN: "Since many of you seem to have had similar experiences, how would you go about handling this situation?"

**Ideas**

GROUP MEMBERS: "You don't have any choice, you have to do what they say."

"You could refuse . . ."

"I'd sue them. . . . It's their responsiblity to make kids mind."

"I don't understand why they're kicking him out just 'cause he punched a kid."

CLINICIAN: "I wonder why no one has mentioned a meeting with the teacher and other school officials."

FAMILY MEMBER: "Are you kidding?"

GROUP MEMBER: "Well, we agreed to try different ideas. Why not?"

FAMILY MEMBER: "Because we're not talking about your kid, we're talking about mine, that's why not!"

GROUP MEMBER: "We could be talking about my kid."

GROUP MEMBER: "Or ours—we all have kids in that school."

GROUP MEMBER: "That school don't care about us and our problems."

**Try it out**

CLINICIAN: "Let's test your belief that your opinions don't matter, that your kids are guinea pigs, and that no one cares. How could we go about testing those beliefs?"

GROUP MEMBER: "I went to that school for a meeting once and they really ganged up on me—teacher, school psychologist, principal—all using language I never heard of and telling me what a mess my kid was causing. I wouldn't go there." Began crying.

GROUP MEMBER: "Let's have them come to us."

GROUP MEMBER: "Come to us."

GROUP MEMBER: "Yeah, we've had meetings with ministers, Scout leaders, and neighbors when we've had a problem, why not with the school?"

CLINICIAN: "How would you go about that?"

GROUP MEMBER: "Write a letter or make a phone call. Like they did to us and demand a meeting!"

CLINICIAN: "What happened to _______family when the school *demanded* . . .?"

FAMILY MEMBER: "Made me mad as blazes . . ." "Made me feel awful . . ." "Made me pig-headed."

CLINICIAN: "Resistance breeds resistance. What else might be done?"

GROUP MEMBER: "How about a meeting here? We could elect a delegation to set up a time and date." (No one volunteered.) "Would you act as our go-between?"

CLINICIAN: "Yes, I could do that, provided the group comes up with an agenda and each member agrees to contribute thoughts and feelings."

GROUP MEMBERS: Agreed to put together a list of concerns and questions.

CLINICIAN: "Before we spend the last half hour putting together a list of concerns for our meeting with school officials, let's discuss what each of you learned from this exercise."

**Processing or discussing what's happened**

GROUP MEMBERS: "Guess we all feel pretty helpless."

"And mad, real mad. Demands don't get us where we want to go."

"Scared."

"Scared?"

"Yeah, alone, different. It makes me scared."

"We have each other."

"We care about each other."

"We can stand by each other."

"Let's make our list!"

CLINICIAN: "Are we all ready to spend the remainder of the time making a list?" (Nods.) "Good, let's get started. Who has the first suggestion?"

Social autonomy and interdependence were encouraged through the group experience; financial autonomy was facilitated through a permanent part-time job for the wife. Through added employment, family financial burdens were eased and a sense of individual competence was initiated. With a sense of financial independence, emotional honesty carried less of a risk of losing financial security. Long-term financial management problems created a need for full-time employment and budgetary management education.

### Evaluation

This family, like many families who experience long-term, recurrent stress, benefited most from becoming part of a social network in which problems could be shared and a sense of belonging could be found. Having a commonly shared supportive network in some ways made up for the differences in family history, like experiences, and personal expectations of the adult couple. Through the Hanway comparison and contrast exercise the couple discovered greater similarities between themselves and other couples in similar circumstances than differences; they also found a greater sense of camaraderie and shared experience than was possible with their respective families of origin. The social network developed into a familylike group with shared experiences and similar hope for the future.

The social network of parents became a sounding board, a source of social and emotional support, and a testing ground for ideas (regarding different rules and so forth) and strategies. Although the network's encounter with the school system was not altogether successful, the group did learn that their views, beliefs, expectations, and concerns were of greater importance than they had previously believed. In order to have their view represented and alternative programs considered for their children, one member of the network decided to become a candidate for the school board. Through association with a supportive social network, the adult subunit became a stronger component within the family system. As more emphasis was placed on adult-adult bonding, less energy was available to continue the inordinately strong and constrictive mother-child bonding.

As each of the children became involved in expansive social network experiences—athletics, Scouting, and preschool—avenues for self-expression, development of social skills, and interpersonal growth were opened. The development of social skills was accompanied by growth in emotional strength and self-confidence, so necessary for individual autonomy and self-reliance. As each child grew, his social peer group within the family became stronger, an element essential for later parent-child separation. With social and interpersonal strength increased in the peer subunits in the family, group activities could be engaged in with less risk of coercion, intimidation, or manipulation by a disorganized social system.

## SUMMARY

Progress was not made in this and similar families without incident. As is characteristic of families where inappropriate emotional bonding exists between individual members, such as emotional attachment between mother and child exclusive or mother-father or father-child bonding, alteration in bonding sends a resounding shock wave throughout the tightly bounded, often socially isolated, family system. Essential to the absorption of the shock is assistance for each member in developing a social support system that can provide emotional acceptance, growth, and recognition *not* available in the family. A struggle often ensues between the family system and competing social systems; competition often develops between the inappropriately bonded adult and other adults or children who threaten to realign that bonding. Such struggles often erupted in this family's growth and development.

Emotional honesty and open communication with the family will require long-term effort: the habits are strong, generational role modeling is lacking, and emotional skills continue to lag behind social investments. As long as this family (and families in similar situations) makes social status and material gain a greater priority than emotional maturity and character development, there will be individuals within the system who will never measure up and will, by their individual differences or deficiencies, threaten the goals of the family system. As long as society places greater emphasis on performance and conformity than on human potential and individual worth, there will be families who threaten the overall social system, resulting in society's need to label, categorize, and otherwise contain the "imperfect" family.

### BIBLIOGRAPHY


Breslow, D.: Time extended family interviewing, Fam. Process **16**:97, 1977

Chinn, P.: Child health maintenance; concepts in family-centered care, ed. 2, St. Louis, 1979, The C. V. Mosby Co.

Corey, G., and Cole M.: Groups; process and practice, Monterey, Calif., 1977, Brooks and Cole.

Despert, J.: The emotionally disturbed child; an inquiry into family patterns, New York, 1970, Anchor Books.

Holt, J.: How children fail, New York, 1971, Dell Publishing Co.

Jacobs, A., and Spradlin, W.: The group as agent of change, New York, 1974, Behavioral Publications.

Lewis B.: Group silences, Small Group Behav. **8**:109, 1977.

Moustakas, C.: The child's discovery of himself, New York, 1976, Ballantine Books.

Ryan, W.: Blaming the victim, New York, 1972, Pantheon Books.

Skinner, B. F.: Beyond freedom and dignity, New York, 1971, Alfred A. Knopf.

Tolsdorf, C.: Social network, support, and coping; an exploratory study, Fam. Process **15**(4):407,1976.

Weiskott, J., and Cleland, C.: Assertiveness, territoriality and personal space behavior as a function of group assertion training, J. Counsel. Psychol. **24:**111, 1977

Weiss, G., and Hechman, L.: The hyperactive child syndrome, Science **205:**1348, September 1979.

Wogan, M., and others: Influencing interaction and outcome in group psychotherapy, Small Group Behav. **8:**25, 1977.

Wunderlich, R.: Allergy, brains, and children coping., St. Petersburg, Fla., 1973, Johnny Reads, pp. 21-30.

Chapter 19

# FAMILIES WITH A LIFE PHASE SITUATION

## SITUATION: EFFECTS OF ENVIRONMENTAL CONTINGENCIES ON PHYSICAL AND MENTAL HEALTH

There is increasing evidence to support the observation that physical health and emotional health are strongly related, with changes in one area of health bringing about or being accompanied by changes in another.

## HAWTHORN FAMILY

Mary Hawthorn, an 80-year-old widow, is illustrative of that observation. She came to our office on the recommendation of a dermatologist who believed her skin disorder was psychosomatic, that is, that the physical condition was due to her emotional state. All attempts at medical treatment had been unsuccessful.

### Presenting situation

During her initial visit, Mary appeared tense, replied to questions tersely and picked at her white handkerchief, with which she repeatedly dabbed her forehead. During the interview tiny beads of perspiration trickled down her forehead, this in spite of the air-conditioning in the office. She was clearly upset. She was bothered by itching from a rash that apparently covered her entire body except for her face and hands. It was only after we had worked with Mary for approximately three to four weeks that the nature of her nervousness and terseness became understandable. We agreed to work with Mary, provided that she see another skin specialist, who would be responsible for prescribing medication to relieve her itching and who would monitor her medical condition: the extensive scaling, rash, and itching. The physician to whom we referred Mary specialized in working with the elderly and did not automatically assume that certain conditions, such as depression and psychosomatic illnesses, were inherent in getting older. Although we believed that there might be some relationship between her life situation and her physical condition, we felt it was important to have her medical condition monitored and evaluated during the period of consultation and evaluation. She agreed, reluctantly, to our plan, which included a visit to the medical specialist and an in-depth interview and observation period of three weeks with us. Our contact with Mary was as follows:

| | |
|---|---|
| *Week one* | 1. Appointment and visit with dermatologist, with whom we would consult closely. |
| | 2. Initial interview with Sedgwick-Hildebrand, Health Associates, to include a health history and medical history. |
| *Week two* | 3. Continuation of interview, including family history, social history, and critical incident record. (The order of history taking was reversed in this case to give credibility to Mary's physical problems and to determine her apparently deteriorating health status.) |
| *Week three* | 4. Observation to include home visits, keeping of daily activity logs by Mary, and initial clinical assessment. |

### Interview and observation

The stated purposes of the contract were to explore and assess the sociopsychological components of Mary's physical condition, to examine the impact of Mary's social and family relationships on her physical health, and to assist in making changes that would promote an optimal level of holistic functioning, which included focus on physical, social, and emotional health. The tools to be used in the clinical contract included an in-depth interview, a nursing examination of physical health status, and clinical observations of Mary in our office and in her home. At the outset of the clinical relationship, it was decided to postpone use of any standard psychological tests until their use could be justified by information revealed through interview and observation. As it turned out the tests were not necessary. The information obtained through interview, observation, and home visits is summarized below.

**Family history.** Mary was the youngest of three siblings; an older sister was in fair health and an older brother was in poor health. The older sister was a widow, lived in her own home, was able to care for herself in spite of cataract surgery on both eyes, and maintained telephone contact with Mary on a daily basis. Mary's older brother lived with and was cared for by his wife, who was in fair health. Neither of Mary's siblings had children, and the older brother also kept close contact with Mary by telephone. Mary's parents were described as warm, supportive, caring people; no evidence contradicted this description. Mary's own husband had been a successful businessman; their only son maintained an active and productive law practice. The relationship between the mother and son was supportive but periodically strained because of differences between Mary and her son's wife. In order to minimize conflict, the son had lunch with his mother twice monthly and called her on the telephone on a regular basis. Mary had one grandchild, who was single and following a course of premedicine studies at a college in the east. Mary saw the granddaughter on holidays; the granddaughter made it a point to call Mary on her birthday, on holidays, and on special occasions. Their relationship appeared warm and mutually supportive. As determined from history taking, the family history in and of itself did not pose particularly problematic or troubled areas. The medical history was also not particularly revealing of areas of vulnerability.

**Medical history.** Mary's medical history was not particularly revealing, except that the skin rash had been present for more than a year, during which time Mary had felt herself becoming increasingly irritated, weepy, and nervous. The itching accompanying the skin rash was of such intensity that Mary had trouble sleeping at night, for which a family physician had prescribed a "mild sedative." (The "mild sedative" was Valium, one of the most frequently abused prescription medications.) After the family physician treated her for several weeks with sedatives, he referred Mary to a colleague who treated Mary for more than a year with "ointments, balms, baths, and mild sedatives." At the end of a year, he determined that her problems must be due to aging or "something emotional." After her first visit with us, we recommended that she visit another skin specialist, an idea that she found particularly objectionable because of her experiences over the past year, which she identified as unsuccessful. Although Mary had experienced medical problems requiring medical intervention in the past, her recoveries were consistently uneventful and noncontributory to her present situation. Her last medical visits were two years before the onset of her skin rash and one year ago. Her pattern of coping with medical problems before this particular incident had been excellent. Mary's health history was as noncontributory and unremarkable as her family history and medical history.

**Health history.** Until one year ago, when Mary developed a skin rash, her health habits were sound. She slept well, ate well, exercised regularly, traveled a moderate amount, and met with friends regularly. As her rash progressed and lingered, in spite of medical attention, Mary's otherwise light and outgoing mood became sullen and withdrawn. As the months wore on, she slept less and less and gradually lost her appetite. Because of the creams, balms, and ointments that she was required to apply several times daily, she was unable to keep a social calendar. Her health habits continued to decline and her mood became despondent. A decline in health habits was accompanied by a decline in social involvement, as seen in the following summary.

**Social history.** Until approximately a year ago, Mary was active, involved, and social, with interests that included a garden club, a book club, and community groups. She was an officer and leader in several clubs and kept an active roster of social appointments. Her social network included friends, social acquaintances, club members, and business associates. Although her social network was progressively smaller because of death and disability among friends and colleagues, this in and of itself did not appear to be a source of unresolved feeling, fear of her own aging, or symptom-producing concerns. However, in the last year Mary had begun limiting social engagements, saw her son less often, and did not entertain friends or acquaintances on a weekly basis as had been her custom for the past several years. This change in behavior was what led friends and physicians to suspect that Mary was "depressed." There were several critical incidents within the last two to three years that might lead one to suggest that loss, grief, aging, and being alone were responsible for Mary's change in behavior.

**Critical incidents.** Within the last two years, there had been a considerable decline in the health and medical status of both Mary's brother and sister, with her sister being less and less able to visit with Mary in her home as a result of cataracts that prevented the sister from driving. Within the last two years, Mary's granddaughter had changed schools, from a college nearby to one in a distant state, making their visits less and less frequent. Within the last two years, Mary had lost two very close friends and one brother-in-law through death; these events narrowed social and family networks. Although these events were sources of grief for Mary, she described herself as "one who confronts life and its realities—none of us wins all the time and none of us lives forever." Critical incidents may have contributed a certain amount of sadness to Mary's life and certainly prompted her need for continued social and emotional adjustment, but the patterns of loss and diminishing did not coincide with the appearance of or seem to contribute to the continuation of her generalized skin disorder.

**Assessment**

During the interview and observation, Mary was cooperative, kind, and open with us. She invited us into her home and as the days progressed into her family circle. She was communicative; a sociogram would depict her as engaging in two-way communication, initiating as well as responding, and as being consistent in her verbal and nonverbal messages. A psychogram of family bonding would show warm, mutually balanced regard between Mary's siblings, between Mary and her son, and especially between Mary and her granddaughter. Her relationship with her daughter-in-law was strained but no more so than other mother–daughter-in-law relationships where the husband is an only son. The progressive diminishing of family and social circles cannot be eliminated as a source of sadness, but Mary functioned broadly, using a wide source of information; was capable of productive, sound decisions with ample follow through; exhibited warmth and emotional authenticity with self-disclosure; avoided conflict by creating situations within which conflict could be avoided (a weakness); and maintained a productive, involved, and active life, except for the changes of the last year and a half.

The strengths, or aids to change, in this situation are many: Mary's involvement with family and friends; the extensiveness of Mary's social network and the use of the network, which is supportive and positive; Mary's financial and social stability; Mary's embeddedness in a family that was warm, nurturing, but realistic in terms of individual need; and Mary's persistence in seeking resolution of her problem. The weaknesses, or barriers to change, are: the long-term, unimproved nature of Mary's medical condition and our inability to pinpoint family, social, or emotional components that significantly contributed to Mary's physical condition. There was clearly no path to take other than to reevaluate our data base and probe more deeply into Mary's life as an individual.

**Intervention**

Our clinical intervention became essentially one of continued assessment, probing more deeply into Mary's life, analyzing habits and patterns of behavior that might coincide with changes in her physical condition. The initial interview and observation period, scheduled for three weeks, was completed in less time, leaving the remaining weeks of our original contract to broaden our data base and to examine in more detail Mary's relationship with her environment and her life style itself. Mary agreed to this added dimension of our clinical contract. The following intervention goals were established: (1) to expand our original data base to include information and observations of Mary's life style, including daily habits and routines; (2) to teach Mary how to keep a daily log that included not only her habits, but observations of the appearance, change in, or lessening of her rash; and (3) to conduct the remaining sessions in Mary's home at different times of day so that patterns throughout the day could be observed in representative segments. Of particular interest were any changes in patterns, habits, or environmental factors that might in any way contribute to Mary's physical condition and consequent emotional vulnerablility. There is probably nothing quite so debilitating as a chronic condition that does not change in spite of individual effort, professional intervention, and financial investment; we therefore made a commitment to Mary to use our resources to fully investigate the problem, and we made a commitment to ourselves to become problem solvers as well as system analysts. To focus specifically on the problem was necessary in order to eventually work our way around in the system to locate contributing factors, a strategy that is sometimes difficult for the pure system clinician to accept.

**Evaluation**

Within a little more than a week, we began to hear Mary report via her daily log and we began to observe a cyclical pattern to Mary's skin rash. As we completed our inventory of the house and environment, noting any changes—additions, deletions, or experiments—within the setting, we began to notice a correlation between what Mary wore and the condition of her skin. Since her clothing varied from day to day and the rash did not vary accordingly, it had to be something more constant. It took us nearly two full weeks before we were able to discover the relationship between a fabric softener used in the dryer and Mary's skin rash. There were times those weeks when Mary became discouraged, depressed, and frankly irritated with our strategy. There were times when Mary's despondency overtook her and she expressed feelings of futility, that all our efforts might not be worthwhile. In spite of the longevity of the problem and the emotional toll this took on Mary, within six weeks after the fabric softener was eliminated from her life style, the skin rash was completely gone and Mary was like a new woman.

Had we not had Mary keep a thorough daily log and completed a home and environmental survey with emphasis on locating changes within the last year, it is questionable whether Mary's problem would have ever been solved. At the outset we did not know what the interrelationships were—social, physical, family, stress, aging—between Mary's physical condition and her emotional health. With Mary, we found no correlation between significant others and symptoms, no correlation between food irritants and symptoms, and no social events that corresponded with appearance of the rash. We did not find factors within the family, her emotional state, or her social network that contributed in a causal way to her skin rash; what we did find were strengths in her family history, strengths in her individual pursuits, and support in her social network that assisted her on the road to recovery. As it turned out, a particularly consequential relationship had been established between Mary and her environment, a finding that has been repeated on a number of occasions. Examples include the hyperactive child whose activity is triggered by food allergies and the asthmatic construction worker whose temper flares on days in which he works in asbestos.

As Mary's skin condition improved, her mental outlook improved and she became more socially active, an avenue that had not been cut off despite the longevity of her problem. We learned system change can come about through problem solving and that it is not necessary to identify emotional liabilities in order to make clinical interventions that promote mental health.

Mary Hawthorn was clearly an agent, a self-directed individual who, in spite of a chronic physical disorder and emotional strain, was able to maintain a semblance of order in her life and who ultimately was able to fully restore the balance in her overall health. She originated in a family system that produced creative, enduring, and successful individuals who could at the same time maintain a sense of belonging and togetherness, so essential to family life. Mary's sense of social and psychological space was expansive and included friends, extended family, social acquaintances, and business associates, with whom she was able to initiate and maintain productive relationships. Although these relationships were weakened during a chronic physical problem, the social bonds were quickly restored and continued on for several years. Mary's family adjusted to change—social, technological, and political. All family members were active discussants on topics related to change and its implications for their respective lives, such as inflation, gas prices, retirement, and aging.

Mary's persistence in obtaining help and her ability to respond positively can be attributed to strongly positive contributing factors: family, social network, and individual strengths that fostered self-esteem, allowed bonding with strangers who became like family, and promoted holistic healing, including physical, mental, and social aspects. Mary's situation can be compared and contrasted with Areva Wick's; Areva is clearly a self-defined victim and the factors contributing to her situation differ substantially.

## SITUATION: INDIVIDUAL DIFFERENCES
## WICK FAMILY
### Presenting situation

Areva Wick was referred to our office by a nurse on a medical-surgical ward of a local hospital where Areva had been hospitalized for the third time in less than six weeks. Each hospitalization was prompted by an "acute attack of pain," the basis for which could not be medically established. Each attack involved pain; however, the center of the pain alternated between head, neck, throat, and chest. Our initial contact took place while Areva was still in the hospital, included her and her husband, and focused primarily on brief introductions and gathering of preliminary sociometric data necessary for our records. Areva and her husband were friendly but cautious and responded only to direct questions. During the initial visit, plans were made for Areva and her husband to come to our office where interview and observation continued. A summary of the clinical record follows.

### Interview

**Family history.** Areva was a 75-year-old mother of seven and grandmother of 20 or 25 children and the wife of Harry, an 80-year-old retired railroad worker. Areva's immediate family included her husband and a son with whom she and her husband resided. Six other children and their respective children were widely scattered geographically and maintained infrequent contact. Areva herself was the youngest and only remaining survivor of a family of five. Her parents had a stormy and conflictive marriage; Areva was literally kicked out of the family home at the age of 16. After that time she saw her father only once and never saw her mother again. Her mother died when Areva was 20. Areva's relationship with her siblings was distant, except for one brother with whom she had contact two or three times a year until his death several years ago. Areva married immediately following her mother's death. Harry was the youngest child and only son of parents who were now deceased. Harry's relationship with his family, except for one sister, had remained distant and fraught with conflict—arguments, blaming, fault finding. Harry, like Areva, had very little to say that was positive about his family. This present family network consisted basically of Areva and Harry, with their son David being a distant but supportive member.

**Medical history.** Areva's long history of medical problems included hearing deficits, "heart pain," cataracts, diverticulitis, "foot problems," arthritis, and "pains in the head." She was currently being seen by an average of three medical professionals per month and some months more than once, often weekly. These visits continued in spite of the fact that each physician had told her that there was "nothing medically to be done for her." Harry had no medical complaints and other than to have his eyeglasses checked did not see any medical personnel on a regular basis. Their son David, on whom they are financially dependent, has no reported medical problems. Areva's physical complaints, often without medical basis, were emotional cues or signals that had gone unheeded. Her emotional needs were personal as well as family related; they grew out of loneliness, aging, chronic social and financial deprivation, lack of a supportive family network, and a set of life experiences filled with loss and rejection.

**Health history.** Areva is a heavy-set inactive woman who complains of an inability to sleep, poor appetite, chronic constipation, and feelings of depression and despair. Her husband, however, stated that he "sleeps well, eats good, and never had a problem with his bowels." Despite his statements of good health, Harry was observed on several occasions to be eating what he called "mints," which were, in fact, antacids. Their son, somewhat overweight, stated that he had good health habits, and there was no evidence to the contrary. Areva's self-disclosure through physical complaints was in marked contrast to Harry's inward and undisclosing nature.

**Social history.** Areva's social network was limited to one or two friends whom she contacted by telephone. She described herself as a woman who spent a lifetime raising kids and "never had time to make friends." She stated, "I wouldn't know what to do with a friend if I had one anyway," to which Harry responded in characteristic fashion, "Boy, is that ever the truth!" Over the years, the couple had stopped going to church, and Areva had totally eliminated volunteer and social activities that she had undertaken for a period of years after their children left home. Harry still maintained his circle of "cronies" from the railroad and took a "night out with the boys" nearly every week. Their son, single and very quiet, spent long hours working at a service station or engaging in activities associated with the National Guard. Whereas Harry maintained his social network of cronies and David maintained his social network of buddies, Areva had only a small, and inactive circle of friends.

**Critical incidents.** Over the past several years the Wick family had lost a significant number of family and friends through death, divorce, and separation. With each loss, Areva had become more isolated and increasingly preoccupied with physical complaints. Neither her husband nor her son seemed able to relate to or relieve her grief and suffering; both had become tired of listening to her complaints and were willing to pay for her hospitalization, psychological care, or spiritual counseling in order to "set her straight again." Areva had clearly been selected as the "patient"; the family was unable to see her problems as a reflection of faulty interpersonal dynamics within the family or as a result of diminishing family and social networks. As the unresolved and unmanaged critical incidents in this family accumulated, the family's psychological distance increased and Areva's physical complaints intensified (which came first is not clear). Unresolved grief centered around: (1) Areva's not having seen her mother prior to the mother's death and being blamed for the mother's death by one of the mother's sisters; (2) the loss of a son following a long, involved battle with cancer; and (3) the loss of a grandson in a car accident within the previous year. Other concerns include and are affected by diminished physical capacities, advanced age and inadequate planning, fear of dying, and chronic family squabbles and misunderstandings. It is notable that when the family was asked about any events—death, accidents, job promotions, divorce, and so forth— that might have influenced this family either positively or negatively over the last five years, only Areva responded with a list; both the husband and son simply shrugged their shoulders. Areva was both an index and the victim of an inadequate and poorly functioning family system.

### Observation

During the interview and subsequent data-gathering sessions, Areva was the primary informant, pausing at times to weep openly or fight vigorously with her husband. Areva and Harry sat at opposite ends of the couch and often interrupted or corrected one another. Harry sat with his arms extended along the back of the couch; Areva's physical posture reflected isolation, despair, and depression. She sat, head down, hands folded in her lap, shoulders slumped, and spoke in broken, halting sentences. The electricity and conflict between the two of them were evident whenever Harry would try to interject a comment. David, their son, came for one session, waited in the reception room, and was never heard from again, except on occasion when he would telephone for a "report on his mother's condition." Areva often attended sessions alone, making Harry "stay in the car." From outward appearances Areva and Harry were bonded in a strongly negative but highly dependent relationship, while David played arbitrator and distant resource, particularly a financial resource. The emotional attachment with the rest of the family was virtually nonexistent, except for Areva's strong emotional hold on and unresolved feelings for deceased members.

**Assessment**

By the data collected, the family appeared socially and psychologically fragmented, with Areva maintaining emotional control but receiving little emotional support. The family's network resources were limited, except for Harry's and David's resources, which were used for individual pleasure. Each member made decisions independently of other members; Areva responded to this with anger, frustration, and emotional outbursts. The emotional atmosphere was nonsupportive, self-directed, and counterproductive in terms of individual growth and family interrelatedness. The emotional atmosphere in this family reflected the emotional atmosphere in which each of the parents was reared. Conflict was always on the surface in this family, with frequent arguments and infrequent physical assaults on one another. There was perhaps more individuation in this family than there was family connectedness, except for Areva, who responded to the needs of each individual member with an ache, pain, or angry feeling. She alone was so embedded, first in her family of origin and second in her present family, that she could identify no like, dislike, or uniqueness that she believed was entirely her own. Harry and David, however, acted more as independent agents, with Areva responding to their independence like a victim who has been "left again." Productivity in this family centered primarily in David, with Harry contributing part of his railroad pension. As a family, they had been unable to support one another through life changes, loss, separation, and aging. The only photographs that this family was able to produce during the photoanalysis were of Areva as a child, Areva's mother, the couple's dead son, and the dead grandson. As a general rule, this family lived in the past and continued ongoing struggles with the past. Intervention centered primarily on the past and its unresolved consequences and on Areva's needs for nurturance and approval and secondly on the long-term goal of restoring or promoting a more positive bond between Areva and her husband.

### Intervention

Short-term goals were to engage in activities that relieved Areva's emotional pain, namely, a review of the historical events of loss and separation that had led to years and years of anger, fear, a sense of abandonment, and mistrust of intimate others. Because of Areva's, and to a lesser extent Harry's, longstanding mistrust of others and fear of separation, a decision was made to contract on a week-by-week basis for several weeks and to work toward a clinical contract that would be more specific when members could contribute more actively. One of the ways in which Areva extended the initial contractual agreement was by making Harry wait in the car, thereby preventing his actual involvement in planning. She eliminated David altogether by setting appointment times that conflicted with his work schedule. Not until she had had "her day in court" did she allow Harry and David back into the therapy sessions.

Long-term goals focused on restoring a positive relationship between Harry and Areva and facilitating a more accepting relationship between David and his parents. Specific goals were as follows: (1) that Areva come each week with a list of resentments, hurts, and disappointments that she had harbored over the years and that those resentments be discussed until resolved; and (2) that Areva engage in a weekly activity of her choosing, such as having her hair done. General goals were to: (1) include Harry in discussions at least once a month and (2) build a social network for Harry and Areva that might include senior citizens, church, or neighborhood groups.

### Evaluation

During the initial sessions, Areva and Harry were distant and self-protective. However, as Areva began to explore old, unresolved resentments, disappointments, and sorrows, tentative trust developed and cooperation was possible. As the exploration of resentments progressed, the topic settled more and more on aging and eventual death. Clinical contact evolved into exploring Areva's and Harry's feelings about aging, separations, and eventual death. One conversation is partially revealing:

THERAPIST: "Areva, what bothers you most about getting older?"

AREVA: "Dying." She leaned forward and held her head in her hands; she began a gentle rocking motion.

THERAPIST: "Tell me about your mother's death." (I had gathered information regarding the significance of her mother's death in earlier sessions.) I got up out of my chair and went to sit down beside her, forcing her to sit closer to Harry.

AREVA: After a long pause. "What bothered me most was there was never anyone to hold me anymore." Areva rocked herself and sobbed quietly.

THERAPIST: "I wish I had a chair to rock you; let me comfort you by putting my arm around you." Areva continued to cry quietly and I slipped my arm from around her and put Harry's arm around her instead, helping him to reach out and comfort her. She didn't notice that Harry and I had exchanged supporting positions. Areva began talking about her mother, good memories and bad memories; words and feelings flowed like a river suddenly set free from its banks.

THERAPIST: "Our time is nearly up. Harry, you and Areva sit here for a time together while I finish some paper work in the next room. Areva, it's important for Harry to feel close to you and for you to be close to him." Areva became suddenly aware of Harry's arm around her and she stiffened. "What is it, Areva?"

AREVA: "He'll only leave me." She hung her head and sobbed. "And I can't stand anymore leaving."

THERAPIST: "Let's ask Harry about that; you're speaking for him."

Harry was as afraid of leaving and being left as Areva was. Such fears only served to further isolate them from contact with other people—a social network that might have been potentially helpful to them. As individuals, their life experiences had not contained success experiences with emotional attachments. Lack of emotional attachments and a limited social network, particularly for Areva, only served to further enhance feelings of loneliness and alienation. Their life style was characterized by limited information seeking, decision making that centered primarily on seeking solutions to "Areva's problems," emotional bonding that was cautious and lacking in commitment, communication patterns filled with conflict, and an overall fear of and resistance to change. Lacking skills in emotional interdependence and social connectedness, this family turned to and relied on pain and physical problems as a predominant language in which to express needs and manifest fears.

## SUMMARY

In moving emotionally closer to Harry, Areva had the simultaneous task of preparing for their eventual and, in her mind, final separation. Her reluctance was partially based on a life filled with abandonment, sorrow, and separation, events that created within her feelings of sadness, anger, and despair. Lacking the skill, education, and family atmosphere in which to explore and express her feelings and work through fears, her pain was expressed in physical pain. Her emotional pain eventually translated in real, demonstrable physical change—change that might have been avoided had this individual and family been able to secure psychological understanding and support.

Coping with diminished social networks, lessened physical energy, and preparing for death are tasks that many aging persons face on a daily basis. For them, the process of disconnecting represents as important a need as does the process of being connected in the first place. Physical needs are often the cue that causes them to seek assistance in understanding, working through, and preparing for death. Where physical ills are treated independently of emotional needs and where the individual is treated apart from the significant other, feelings of futility, abandonment, and separation are reinforced. The struggle that the aged face in preparing for death is often similar to the tasks that adolescents confront as they prepare for adult life. The events that surround their struggles are largely responsible for their success or failure.

## BIBLIOGRAPHY


Bell, J.: Disengagement versus engagement; a need for greater expectations, J. Am. Geriatr. Soc, **26**(2):89, 1978.

Bengton, V.: The social psychology of aging, New York, 1973, Bobbs Merrill Co.

Coleman, J.: Life stress and maladaptive behavior, Am, J. Occup. Ther. **29**:169, March-June 1973.

Dohrenwald, B.: Life events as stressors, a methodological inquiry, J. Health Soc. Behav. **14**:167, June 1973.

Ford, C., and Long, K.: Group psychotherapy of somatizing patients, Psychother. Psychosom. **28**:294, 1977.

Garrison, J., and Howe, J.: Community intervention with the elderly, a social network approach, J. Am. Geriatr. Soc. **24**(7):329, 1976.

Kiely, W.: Stress and somatic disease, A.M.A. **224**(4):521, 1973.

Mazar, M.: Psychiatric disorders in general practice, the experience of an island community, Am. J. Psychiatry, **124**:609, 1967.

Molmquist, C.: Physiological aspects of depression, Am. Fam. Physician **11**:89, May 1973.

Pinkerton, P.: Symptom formation reconsidered in psychosomatic terms, Psychother. Psychosomat. **23**:44, 1974.

Rahe, R., Mayer, M., Smith, M. and others: Social stress and illness onset, J. Psychosom. Res. **8**:35, 1964.

Schwab, J., and others: Psychosomatic medicine and the contemporary social scene, Am. J. Psychiatry, **126**:11, 1970.

Sedgwick, R.: Living after death, the role of the survivor (unpublished paper presented at continuing education seminar for registered nurses, sponsored by Sedgwick and Hildebrand, Health Associates, September 24, 1979).

Spear, F.: Pain in psychiatric patients, J. Psychosom. Res. **11**:187, 1967.

Chapter 20

# A FAMILY WITH A LIFE STAGE SITUATION

## SITUATION: MAJOR LIFE CHANGES—ADOLESCENCE, DIVORCE, BLENDED FAMILY

Change, whether preparing for life or death, does not come particularly easily at any stage of family life. It is during rapid growth and emotional development of individual members that the family system receives one of its greatest tests, that is, the family's ability to endure and support change—individual or system. When rapid change in the family system is coupled with intense individual change of one or more members, individual behavior within the family system may take a dramatic shift: cooperation turns to rebellion, trust turns to suspicion, and loyalty to family gives way to allegiance to peers.

## STANTON FAMILY

In the following case, Ebbie Stanton experiences her first years of adolescence just as her parents decide to separate and divorce. Within one year, Ebbie loses her grandmother, with whom she had been able to share openly and freely, and her mother remarries. Ebbie's new father is cold and distant, bringing with him into Ebbie's family unit another teenager, who competes for privileges and wins, chiefly (in Ebbie's mind) because he is a boy. Ebbie's mother forms a strong alliance with her new husband and stepson, leaving Ebbie in charge of herself and her three younger siblings. As Ebbie's despondency grows, suicide becomes her only viable option. She was referred to our office by a local minister with whom she had discussed her despondency and plans for suicide.

### Presenting situation

Ebbie Stanton was brought to our office by her father, whom the mother had called on receiving a call from her minister. The minister had found Ebbie walking along a country road, crying, and talking about kill-ing herself. The minister took Ebbie to his office and called Ebbie's mother, who wanted to have Ebbie placed in a detention home but instead called Ebbie's father to "do something about his daughter." The father, on the advice of the minister, called our office and brought Ebbie in for consultation and evaluation. At the first meeting, Ebbie was distraught, withdrawn, and sat tucked in the corner of a chair. Her long blond hair hung lifelessly around her shoulders, and her hunched-over figure gave a clear impression of hurt, shame, and sadness. In spite of her reluctance, initial anger, and deep despair, Ebbie was receptive as we talked. Ebbie picked at her arm as we talked, often raising red marks and making scratches. As I asked questions, I noted her behavior.

**Interview**

It was my intent to probe deeply enough to be able to describe the immediate situation, identify resources or strengths within Ebbie and Ebbie's family, and assess Ebbie's potential for continued self-destruction. After I had introduced myself to Ebbie, explained the nature of confidentiality, and explained briefly our philosophy of practice, I emphasized her ability to exercise choice and that I would expect her to exercise both her rights and her responsibilities. She lifted her head slightly.

EBBIE: "You mean I can leave here if I want to?"

THERAPIST: "Yes, I mean that. You may also stay." Ebbie looked back down at her lap and picked at her arm. She got up slowly from the chair and walked toward the door. She stood with her hand on the doorknob and seemed to wait for something. "I want you to stay Ebbie, but I can't promise miracles. I can't even take away all the pain you feel and all the disappointments you've experienced, but I can try to understand. I'll need your help, though. If you stay you must agree to help me. I can't do it alone." All I could hear were muffled sobs as Ebbie clung to the doorknob, wanting to run and needing to stay.

Ebbie did not leave, for which I was relieved and grateful. I knew that for her to decide to work with me meant running the risk of being hurt, and Ebbie had just about had her fill of hurts. I sensed her hurt without ever having heard one word from her mouth; it was evident in body language and social presentation. We spent the next two hours talking about what had happened to her that day, for several days preceding, and for the last several months. Change had come at her from all different directions, and there was no source of support; Ebbie had no one to turn to for reassurance that the whole world was not falling down around her. She came, over the months, to be a trusting and semi-open individual, but not without several stormy sessions and many family quarrels. It was a full six months before all of Ebbie's family of origin, which included three siblings, her father, and her mother, would participate in family sessions.

The following spring, Ebbie's new father and his son began to participate in the sessions. Ebbie's family history follows.

**Family history.** Ebbie was the firstborn child and first grandchild. The family consisted of three children, two boys and one girl, and two parents, each recently divorced and remarried. Ebbie's mother was the eldest sibling of three girls, who recently lost their mother and whose father was in ill health. Ebbie's mother described her relationship with her own mother as warm, supportive, and open; her relationship with her two sisters was not described in particularly warm terms. Ebbie's father was the only son of parents who were both living and well. Ebbie's father, like his father before him, was a mechanic. Ebbie's relationship with her siblings differed from time to time and situation to situation, suggesting a lack of strong peer bonding within the sibling group. Ebbie's greatest and most painful losses in recent months included the severed bonding with her deceased grandmother and fractured bonding with her father, recently divorced from Ebbie's mother. Ebbie's mother won custody of the children because of the father's reported "marital infidelity." Shortly after their divorce, both parents remarried, the father in two months and the mother in six months. A diagram of the family network, including the spouses of each parent and their respective children, follows:

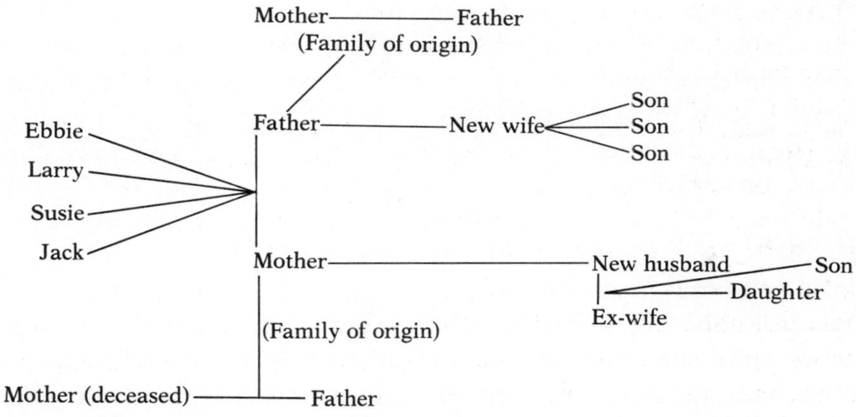


**Family network**

**Medical-health history.** In spite of the high levels of stress that these family units endured in less than a two-year span, their health and medical status was excellent, with the exception of Ebbie, who suffered severe, recurring headaches. Ebbie's maternal grandmother died from cancer; other grandparents were living and well.

**Social history.** The family unit was a fairly isolated group in that major interactional activities were often family centered; however, children all belonged to Scouts, farm clubs, and participated in school activities. All adults worked and spent the majority of their time at work or engaged in work-related activities. Ebbie was often left in charge of the children; this had severely limited her ability to attend or participate in extracurricular activities or engage in relationships with friends.

**Critical incidents.** The critical events that this family network experienced over the last two years can be summarized as follows: death of a significant member, marital conflict between parents that resulted in several fights, separation leading to divorce, custody disagreements resulting in court intervention, and remarriage of adults within the network. The critical incidents that most affected Ebbie were the loss of strong, supportive bonding with her grandmother, with whom she had lived the first five years of her life; learning of her father's infidelity and his being thrown out of the house; the threatened loss of bonding with her father, who referred to Ebbie as "his favorite"; and the increase in child care responsibilities without appropriate experience. Within several weeks after the separation, Ebbie's mother took a full-time job, took the father back to court for more money, began dating a series of "undesirable men," purchased an entire wardrobe, and essentially experienced the grief and separation of divorce through acting out, leaving Ebbie to take care of home responsibilities. In many ways, she began to expect from Ebbie the very behavior that her ex-husband had expected from her: perfection, quiet children, an immaculate house, no friends, no social life, and total obedience to rules and commands set forth by the "head of the family" (which changed several times within a matter of months). As the critical events occurred with increasing frequency and as the demands on Ebbie mounted, her pivotal point in the family became more and more burdensome; she was essentially holding together four family units.

### Observation

During the initial sessions, which she attended alone, Ebbie was quiet and reserved. She responded to questions but rarely initiated conversation. It was not until she shared her diary that she began to open up and reveal her inner feelings. Her writing revealed a sensitive, caring, and frightened girl who thought often about running away or dying. Her inner pain was so severe that only in writing was she able to express herself without fear. Her closest bonds were with her recently deceased grandmother (Ebbie's mother's inability to comfort Ebbie was founded in her own confusion and sense of deep loss). Ebbie was strongly bonded with her father, whose life style the mother found objectionable; she therefore discouraged Ebbie's visits with him. Ebbie's relationship with her mother was strained and often antagonistic; her relationship with her stepfather was out-and-out dislike, distrust, and annoyance. Within the sibling peer group, Ebbie was closest to her next sibling in birth order, and the two youngest siblings were paired. In what ways the parents were bonded was never clear, but it seemed that the mother's marriage was one of convenience and not based on compassion or caring. As the siblings began to participate in the sessions, Ebbie's responsibility became clearer, as did her inexperience with the tremendous responsibility with which she was expected to cope as well as a "seasoned parent." The parents took turns attending sessions with the children; the stepfather attended sessions with his own son and occasionally with his new wife. The father's new wife and her children were involved only distantly.

**Assessment**

Of five ways in which an individual may contribute to family functioning, Ebbie was expected to contribute in all: as resource, link, agent, index, and, finally, victim. She became the victim of a system in which her position would be depicted as a many-sided star, with adjoining units—dyads, triads, or individuals—hanging off each point. She had lost her only sources of adult support in that fluctuating system: first her grandmother, who provided her approval, acceptance, and emotional warmth, and then her father, who provided her with self-esteem, self-importance, and a sense of connectedness. With her two major sources of bonding severed, her sense of disconnectedness became overwhelming, as did her emotional pain. In terms of overall functioning, the family unit expected Ebbie to link mother with ex-husband, father with his parents, and mother with her father. Each subunit within the network took turns giving Ebbie messages to take back and forth and then blamed her when the messages were scrambled. The dynamics of the system can be described as follows.

**Information processing.** Each subunit within the system had its own methods of gathering information, but all depended on Ebbie to serve as the informational link between the units, just as they asked her advice in making decisions. Each unit's information sources were tied to their own primary peer group, with the men taking advice from work, the women from other women or ministers, and the children from their own peer group. Ebbie alone lacked a peer group.

**Decision making.** This network had one of the most chaotic, fluid decision-making patterns I had ever seen. In contrast to the Lyndon family, which had an authoritarian and rigid pattern, this family had a fluid pattern that was totally unpredictable except in its fluidity. One unit would consider a decision, wait for agreement from another member, and then change the original decision. Each adult acted as a separate and single unit, making decisions and breaking decisions, saying one thing and doing another. Messages sent were confused, contradictory, and arbitrary. Finally, each adult settled into an authoritarian, "it's going to be my way or else" approach, and then all the children in the unit began their "you're not going to make me do anything" actions, and the battles raged. Decision-making patterns were reflected in the emotional atmosphere.

**Emotional tenor.** The emotional atmosphere in this network was self-serving, particularly on the part of the adults, and contained numerous inconsistent and contradictory messages, such as: "I beat you because I love you," "I abandon you because I need you," and "If you don't please me, you'll be punished. . . ., however, I will change what it takes to please me so you will never know whether you're right or wrong." Ebbie, in particular, sought authenticity, what she called "being real." She would often say, "There are times when I don't know what's real and what isn't." The emotional bonding in the network was fragile and fluid, with final bonding resulting in the mother's divorce of her new husband, who, according to her, thought more of his children than he did of her. Ebbie's mother demanded 100 percent loyalty; when she didn't get it, she threw the erring member out of the system, physically or psychologically. Conflict was frequent in this family. Where the Lyndon family reacted to conflict by withdrawal, this family charged headfirst into arguments, with verbal attacks and reports of physical abuse, and eventually by-passed each other altogether.

**Conflict management and individuation.** Differences in opinion were not particularly tolerated in this family, and individuals, especially children, were expected to conform to a rather rigid set of rules and expectations. The adults in the family were divided in opinion and attitude, from rigid, authoritarian, highly moralistic standards on one hand to liberal, flexible standards regarding drinking, sexual behavior, and attitude toward authority. Differing ideas were not openly solicited, and frequent arguments occurred over simple discussions of bedtimes, foods to eat at mealtime, selection of friends, and general behavioral expectations in public. The intolerance for differing ideas and opinions and individuality made it difficult for individual members within the system to express differing ideas or develop individual ways of acting, thinking, or behaving. The overall rigidity was reflected in the family's limited productivity and most certainly in its inflexibility in terms of change.

**Productivity and flexibility.** Each adult was generally productive in terms of work; that is, each worked at his or her job at a level that assured job stability and that gained enough money for individual pleasure, pursuit of material gain, and social recognition. However, the overall productivity was not geared toward growth of interpersonal skills, development of strong, supportive emotional atmospheres, or promotion of individual pursuits and abilities. As each member, enmeshed in a rigidly defined system, struggled for individual productivity, the group reacted to reinforce boundaries and a lifelong pattern of inflexibility. When change resulted because of overall intolerance of differences and tightly woven network, as occurred in separation and divorce, family members acted as victims to which something dreadful had happened that had nothing to do with their own actions. Forced change through death dealt this family, particularly Ebbie and her mother, a dreadful blow, one that had taken an emotional toll. One of the positive outcomes of all the change, however, was that the family was forced, because of Ebbie's depression and suicidal thoughts, to take a hard and penetrating look at themselves. Although it was a reluctant look, it was a thoughtful look; this was perhaps one of the family's greatest strengths.

**Strengths and weaknesses.** Within this family network, which was made up of subunits involved in their various levels of system functioning, was the dim awareness that efforts until this point in life had not been necessarily to the benefit of everyone. This dim awareness, despite the reluctance to participate in therapy, represented a ray of hope within the growth potential of individual members and within subunits. Whether the entire family network with its various subunits, could ever achieve a harmonious, mutually supportive relationship was doubtful. The barriers to such a goal were the adults' limited emotional capacity; the heavy investment in maintaining public image and highly moralistic standards; the heavy emphasis on approval and disapproval, with limited emphasis on emotional development and individuation; and fear and inflexibility when faced with change. The greatest potential for growth within the system resided in each individual member, especially in Ebbie and her siblings. Their being pulled back and forth between various subunits, however, put them in a position of emotional power as well as emotional vulnerability. (We often refer to such children as "rubber-band children.") A major effort was directed toward establishing a sibling peer network and toward emotional bonding with an adult or adults within the family who would be capable of offering leadership, resources, skills of agentry, emotional support, and social guidance.

## Intervention

Intervention was aimed not so much at restoring balance, promoting self-disclosure, or facilitating authenticity within the system as at supporting Ebbie as a viable, legitimate individual with rights and privileges. Short-term goals were designed to provide Ebbie with a relationship in which she could experience interpersonal warmth, personal acceptance, and support for a waning sense of human importance. Ebbie was also encouraged to seek out and develop a social network of her peers. Through role playing, practice telephone calls, and impromptu dialog with other teenagers in the office, she began to sense herself as an attractive young woman, desirable as a friend, intelligent as a person, and capable of making sound decisions. As she gained confidence, she gained friends at school and began sharing her writing in a literature class from which she received much-needed acclaim and encouragement. Short-term goals were established within the long-term goals of rebonding Ebbie with her siblings; encouraging her emotional bonding with her father, along with emotional independence from manipulative adults; and reestablishing talking-listening activities between Ebbie and her mother. Implementation of long-term goals required that siblings attend and participate in sessions, that adult subunits be actively involved, and that clinical efforts be directed toward teaching, listening, talking, responding, and caring skills through EDIT, role playing, and individual adult sessions as well as combined adult-child sessions.

Breaking up the network into the subunits that existed within the system provided each subunit with an opportunity for self-exploration, privacy, learning, and establishing credibility as a legitimate social and emotional unit. The following subunits were included in various clinical sessions:

**SUBUNITS**

1. Ebbie
2. Ebbie and siblings
3. Mother, Ebbie, and siblings
4. Father, Ebbie, and siblings
6. Stepfather, mother, and stepbrother
7. Stepbrother
8. Ebbie, stepbrother, and siblings
9. Stepfather and mother
10. Stepfather and stepbrother

**UNITS**

11. Stanton family
12. Burns family
13. Wiley family
14. Adults from Stanton, Burns, or Wiley families

Short-term goals for the network involved strengthening individual units to alleviate fear on their part of being swallowed up by a massive, emotionally chaotic system. As each unit gained strengths and self-confidence, the goal became one of developing and promoting mutual respect, if not mutual interaction, among the units, particularly the warring adult subunits, between which the children served as buffers and linkages. Because of the emotional intensity and lack of toleration for individuation, a major effort was directed toward promoting distance between units—distance that could later be shortened through systematically planned and controlled meetings, in which face-to-face discussions could be directed by clinicians. Sample goals, for individuals, subunits, and the network, and the intervention strategies used to implement those goals are summarized below.

| INTERVENTION GOAL | INTERVENTION STRATEGY |
|---|---|
| *Individual* | |
| 1. Promote individual sense of worth, importance, and competence. | 1. Use interactions, role playing, and EDIT activities in which individual directs and practices listening-responding. |
| 2. Promote age appropriate family and social experiences. | 2. Develop social network of peers and encourage participation in school, social, and community activities. |
| *Subunit* | |
| 1. Promote unit emotional bonding that is supportive, yet allows space for individual growth and expression. | 1. Design sessions to include dyads, triads, and units, in which risk taking (emotional, intellectual, social) is demonstrated by clinicians and practiced by units. |
| 2. Develop communication skills and behaviors necessary for effective communication. | 2. Encourage units to plan once weekly sharing and listening time at home—away from work, school, or social obligations. |
| *Network* | |
| 1. Promote mutual respect and allow for existence of subunits within network. | 1. a. Explore attitudes regarding "togetherness" and "parent authority." b. Balance orientation of work and play. |
| 2. Establish channels of communication, interaction, and bonding that eliminate the children as linkages and buffers. | 2. Have monthly meeting under the guidance of clinician, in which conversation and interaction can be monitored, guided, and altered. |

## Evaluation

Goals that were to be accomplished within the clinical sessions were moderately successful, with the greatest amount of trust, risk taking, and personal growth being demonstrated by Ebbie. There were also goals to be achieved in the homes of each of the subunits: for example, weekly conferences, participation in community and social activities, use of leisure time in individual and family activities, establishment of regular visits between children and parent groups, and specifically designed exercises to promote cooperation, decision making, and emotional honesty. These goals were also accomplished with a moderate amount of success.

As various subunits began to experience themselves more fully, differences became more apparent and more acceptable. Although there was no agreement on several issues, one being life style, there was a general ability to permit the differences. The best policy turned out to be one of "benign neglect," that is, each parental subunit left the other unit alone unless some need arose, at which time a network conference was called. Network conferences, which used the assistance of clinicians, proved to be productive and worthwhile endeavors. Although there was not a great deal of individual change, except on Ebbie's part, there was a general network change in that subunits were permitted their individual life styles and help was consistently sought when network conferences were needed. Progressively, subunits began making their own decisions, with consideration for others but somewhat independent of the need to control or be prime authority for the entire network. Progressively, the various subunits formed bonds: the father and his wife seemed to develop a warm, mutually supportive relationship, in spite of her two children leaving home; Ebbie's mother and the mother's new husband discovered irreconcilable differences that led to a rather peaceful, planned divorce; Ebbie's stepfather chose to live with his young son, who was repeatedly in trouble with the law and who needed a father more than Ebbie; and Ebbie's parents chose to "leave one another alone" and "not to use the kids to carry messages." The parents also decided to bring their differences to therapy rather than settling them in court.

It is of interest to note that, in spite of Ebbie's growth in self-confidence and self-reliance, she returned on two occasions: the anniversary of her grandmother's death and the anniversary of her parents' divorce. Her ability to seek help, without being troubled or sick, is perhaps one of the strongest indicators of her developing competencies and abilities as a growing human being. We believe that the choice to focus on her as an individual, along with expressing concern for the family network, was a good choice, since she alone demonstrated great potential for growth and expansion; however, to ask her to change without altering dynamics within the system would have been to set her up for failure experiences. She had reached a point at which she had the most to lose—her life—which she now believes must be assertively defended and protected.

## SUMMARY

Blended families, that is, family systems that contain members from previous or other ongoing systems are rarely without incident. "His kids, her kids, and our kids" are all elements that must be incorporated, adapted to, or otherwise managed if the current blended system is to function effectively. Each subunit comes to the blended family with differing beliefs, rules, and expectations for performance and interaction.

Adolescence is a period in which rules are challenged and tested and peer groups provide competitive and real challenges to the social and emotional network relationships within the family system. When the social system and family network from which the adolescent emerges are also in a state of flux and there is a concurrent loss of emotional and personal support, behavior within the system will reflect the turbulent and emotionally chaotic atmosphere.

Individual behavior reflects family system stability, level of honesty, and patterns of communication. Ebbie's behavior reflected a combination of events and interacting factors that served to undermine her individual efforts at growth and development while maintaining an integral position in an ongoing family system. In order to change her behavior, it was necessary to alter patterns within and between family networks.

## BIBLIOGRAPHY

Daitzman, R.: Methods of self-confrontation in family therapy, J. Marriage Fam. Counsel. **3**:3, 1977.

Hall, S. E., and Weaver, B. R.: Nursing of families in crises, Philadelphia, 1974, J. B. Lippincott Co.

Kaplan, S.: Structural family therapy for children of divorce; case report, Fam. Process **16**:75, 1977.

Laing, L.: The politics of the family and other essays, New York, 1972, Vintage Books, Inc.

Madanes, C., and Haley, J.: Dimensions of family therapy, J. Nerv. Ment. Dis. **165**:88, 1977.

Rhodes, S.: A developmental approach to the life cycle of the family, Soc. Casework **58** (5):30, 1977.

Sane, D.: Reestablishing communication between parents and their young children following a distributive life crisis, J. Clin. Child Psychol. **3** (1):52, 1979.

Sedgwick, R., and Hildebrand, S.: The adolescent at risk; crisis, the delicate balance. In Howe, J., Nursing care of adolescents, New York, 1980, McGraw-Hill Book Co., pp. 281-304.

Speck, R., and Attneave, C.: Family networks, New York, 1974, Vintage Books.

Strelnick, A. H.: Multiple family group therapy; review of literature, Fam. Process **16:** 307, 1977.

Thies, J.: Beyond divorce; the impact of remarriage on children, J. Clin. Child Psychol. **6** (2):59, 1977.

Wallerstein, J., and Kelly, J.: Divorce counseling; a community service for families in the midst of divorce, Am. J. Orthopsychiatry **47:** 4, 1977.

Wright, L., and L'Abete, L.: Four approaches to family facilitation; some issues and duplication, Fam. Coordinator **26:** 176, 1977.

Chapter 21

# CLINICIAN INTERVENTION STRATEGIES

## the nurse as a change agent

The contribution that the clinician makes to the clinical process has been described throughout this book: participant observer, equal partner in a contract, listener-learner, group leader, diagnostician, individual with a unique family history, educator, and skilled therapist. The philosophy underlying these skills and activities is one of partnership between the client and the clinician; effectiveness can best be reached through the mutual efforts of those involved in the change process. As a partner in the clinical process, the clinician engages in activities that are geared toward facilitating change: in physical space, in emotional climates, and in family practices. Thus, the clinician is often a change agent.

A change agent helps others make changes in their lives that facilitate their becoming more efficient problem solvers: independent, responsive, and responsible. One of the primary focuses of clinical intervention is to assist families with change which often requires that the family alter its own organization to accomodate, integrate, or otherwise manage change, whether that change is in response to stress, loss of family members, job and career changes, children leaving home, death, divorce, or separation.

### SOCIAL CHANGE AGENT IN THE FAMILY

Clinical intervention with the family takes a variety of forms, as shown in the preceding chapters; however, the underlying thrust is primarily toward helping the family make changes in family organization (communication, interaction, territoriality). This may be accomplished by a variety of means, all of which include direct observation of family dynamics and participation in the unfolding of family life. Descriptions of family life that are obtained through interview and record completion are accompanied by direct knowledge of family and individual actions within the family system. The more direct knowledge the clinician has of the reality that the family faces, the more able the clinician is to assist the family in establishing choices and gaining control of the management of everyday and long-range affairs.

Where such knowledge and direct observation of the family system are limited, as was the case with Dick Morse, clinical intervention is limited to assisting individual members in coping with their own perceptions and responses to specific situations commonly shared by the single parent: making decisions alone, establishing rules and carrying out policies without the assistance of another adult, living with feelings of uncertainty about one's own needs with regard to job and home. An important aspect of identifying choices and gaining a sense of control with regard to long-range management is membership in a network that is supportive of individual endeavor while offering group connectedness, as illustrated in the Lyndon family.

Fostering the family's participation in a social network of peers aids the family in feeling more a part of their environment and provides them with a supportive group, often experiencing similar situations. Membership in a group provides the family with a wider set of resources, gains it added sources of information, and provides it an arena for idea sharing and skill building. The Lyndon family's participation in a social network aided not only their dealings with everyday problems but provided them with avenues for long-range planning. A group is often far better equipped to challenge ideas, test attitudes, and follow through with decisions than any one family or couple alone. The clinician's assistance is often vital: encouraging the family unit to become part of a larger group, teaching the family how to be group members, initiating the first meetings of the group and bringing various family units together, demonstrating communication and decision-making skills, and teaching group skills of leadership, followership, decision making and cooperation. As the group becomes more adept, the clinician assists family members to take on more and more group responsibility, with the group finally continuing on with only intermittent consultation with the clinician.

Social connectedness is important for families not only in the support that is available but in that the group setting provides an arena for practice and learning. The clinician acts not only as a consultant to the group but functions in an educational and leadership capacity as well. Tools and techniques are used, such as the EDIT strategy, that provide families with an opportunity to take a look at their own interactional patterns and receive information from non-family members and other group participants about those patterns. The change agent acts as a resource who can bring to the group tools, techniques, strategies, ideas, and support for trying out new ideas and new behaviors. The group may be composed of unrelated family units or of various subunits within a larger family system, as was the case with the Stanton family. With the Stanton family group and with the Lyndon social network, there were several principles that guided clinical intervention; the most important are summarized in the following section.

## PRINCIPLES

### Directing discussion

Conversations within the family must be directed *between* members. In the early stages of therapy, family members often talk *about* other family members as though they were absent from the room. Complaints are often directed *to* the clinician *about* some family member, as was the case with Areva Wick, who discussed her husband rather than talking to him about her feelings. The clinician redirects such discussions with comments such as: "Let me hear you tell __________ how you feel about him. Carry on a discussion as you would at home." "Please speak to one another directly, like I am talking to you now." "Face each other and say it directly." Saying it directly involves another important principle: encouraging each family member or individual group member to "speak for oneself."

### Speaking for oneself

Each member speaks his or her own feelings, thoughts, or ideas. In the Lyndon family, the mother often assumed that she knew other member's hidden thoughts and frequently spoke for other members. Such actions on her part not only decreased the potential for individual participation but put her in a central position for blame. Second guessing another's thoughts encourages silence and misunderstanding; speaking for another creates artificial lines of power and authority. Family members are encouraged to speak for themselves by comments such as: "One of the rules that will guide our discussions is that each family member must speak for himself or herself." "Bobby, please tell me about your problem with your reading teacher. Mrs. Lyndon, I know this will be difficult for you, but please let Bobby tell his own story." "Every family member will get a turn: I will take the responsibility of seeing that each member gets an equal chance to speak." As each member takes a turn speaking, the clinician demonstrates the use of silence and listening as important ingredients of effective communication.

### Silence and listening

An air of receptivity and the use of silence for reflection and learning are important components of effective communication. The clinician demonstrates active listening through questions that elicit additional information and enhance understanding; the use of nonverbal gestures and cues that indicate attentive regard, such as head nods and eye contact; and the rephrasing and summarization of major issues and ideas presented to assure mutual understanding of the interaction and communication. Comments such as: "Tell me more about ___________." "I could understand better if you could provide me an example." "Let me repeat my understanding of what you've said to see if we're on target." "I'm not sure I'm following you; tell me again and I'll stop you when I get confused." While active listening is used and demonstrated, the use of silence is noted and commented on.

Silence is used by family members in a variety of ways: to avoid painful issues, as a means of withholding information or approval, as evidence of shyness or boredom, as a time of reflection, as a means of establishing personal space and privacy, or as a time out to gain new understanding. Silence can be useful and powerful. Silence may be used to manipulate or encourage interaction. Clinicians and family members together can explore the *meaning* of silence with regard to a particular situation through comments such as: "We've been sitting here quietly for 15 minutes now. I wonder what each of you was thinking (or feeling, wondering, doing) during that time." "How does the way silence is used in this group (setting, situation) compare with the way silences (withdrawal, clamming up, going to one's room, having one's private spaces) are used at home?" "It's hard for me to sit here quietly while you struggle with your confusion; how can I help?" Silence and active listening are accompanied by the exploration of the meaning or purpose that the identified "problem" has for the family.

**Seeking the purpose of the problem**

The identified problem serves a purpose in the family. One of the primary purposes for problems in the family is that the problem itself serves to unite the family against a common enemy. However, the family may be united in such a way as to hamper their effective solution of the problem. The problem itself is generally a manifestation of a larger dynamic issue within family interaction and communication. Allison's nightmares were the cues that prompted the family to seek professional help. The child's nightmares served to unite the family in an effort to dispel the nightmares. However, major disagreements emerged between the parents as to how best to handle "Allison's problem"—arguments that reflected wider issues of marital conflict and discord. Allison's problem drew attention away from the parents, making it difficult for them to focus on their own marriage relationship.

The purpose that any problem serves may change from time to time. Allsion's nightmares served at different times: to bring her closer to her father; to bring the couple closer to each other; to bring the couple closer to each of their respective families of origin; to assist the family in seeking professional help, first for Allison and finally for themselves; to provide Allison a power position in the family; and to provide Allison's mother with an outlet for her own frustrations and disappointments. It can be seen that positive as well as negative purposes are served by the same identified problem. Exploring the meaning of the problem may be facilitated by comments and observations such as : "I notice that you spend the majority of time discussing ____________'s problem." "How much time do you spend at home discussing problems?" "If you did not have ____________'s problem as a link between you, what would hold you together?" "Let's pretend for a moment that ____________'s problem is solved; what would you like to spend your time discussing or doing?" "What purpose could this problem be serving in your life?" "What are you getting out of being afraid of _____ (riding in cars, disciplining a child, saying no to a spouse)?" "What would happen if you never solved this problem?" "Have you noticed that when we get close to finding a solution to the problem, you seem to recreate it somewhere else?" "Let's see how many ways we can assign a name to the problem that this family is having." An essential component of problem solving is the ability to focus in on a problem, identify the consequences of the problem for the entire family, and design solutions that involve an awareness of what each member may be getting out of the problem in the first place. Part of understanding the purpose that a problem serves for any family unit involves deemphasizing the person believed by the family to be *the* source of the problem.

**Deemphasizing the identified patient**

Deemphasizing the identified patient means taking the attention off the person blamed for the problem and redirecting the family's energy toward the family unit, social network, environment, or community as the target for change. Bobby Lyndon was the cue that brought his family to the attention of school officials and mental health professionals. Although he had been identified as "the patient" and had been chiefly blamed for "causing trouble," the family itself was involved in the creation of an emotional climate that was not conducive to effective individual action and behavior. The social system around the family unit also demonstrated a general inability to incorporate individuals and family units that deviated to any extent from the social norm. The family and the social system were part of the problem as well as part of the solution.

Identified patients must be assisted in moving from victim positions; family units must be encouraged in their growth toward agentry and responsibility. Family units like the Lyndon family must be assisted in assuming agent functions, just as individuals, as in the case of Mary Hawthorn, must be helped to view themselves in relationship to a larger system. Comments that may be used to deemphasize individual blame or responsibility include: "Although Bobby is the one having difficulty at school, each of you has something to say about how this family get along and are affected by one another. I'd like to hear from each of you." "Each of us has our own way of letting others know how we feel. What signals does this family use to let feelings be known?" "Each family has its own way of assigning individual responsibility. Tell me how each of you carries out his or her responsibility in this family." "How did __________ get selected as the patient?" "Where did __________ learn to take on the sick role?" "How does this family go about __________ (making decisions, drawing up rules, punishing rule breakers, earning a living, preparing for change, reacting to disappointment, having an argument, expressing warm and affectionate feelings)?" "Show me how you (individual member) react when someone gets in your space (ask two members to sit on the same cushion or share the same coffee cup)."

Asking and assisting the family to explore its own internal dynamics often leads to identifying one or more members who currently serve as resident family therapist. Just as the identified patient is deemphasized, the resident family therapist must be assisted in giving up such tasks to the professional. Removing the resident family therapist from that position provides that individual with time and energy to commit to other endeavors, such as personal growth needs, and provides the family with added options of looking at itself as effective and with growth potential.

**Defusing the resident family therapist**

Redirecting the energies of the family member who has taken on the task of identifying, analyzing, or treating the identified problem or patient is important. Just as each family usually has one person who gets blamed for creating the family problem, there is usually a member who acts as the resident family therapist. Ebbie Stanton was identified as a "patient" in need of professional help. Her mother, although initially refusing to attend sessions, "knew exactly what was wrong with Ebbie." Not only did she "know what was wrong," but she also knew exactly what it would take to "straighten her out." Ebbie's mother was clearly the resident therapist.

In another situation, an elderly woman called to get help for her daughter and the daughter's son, both of whom live with the elderly woman. However, as soon as the first session began, the elderly woman began directing the discussions by interrupting, arguing, and correcting. She demonstrated very clear opinions about what should and should not take place in the sessions. When the mother and son were seen alone, the grandmother interrupted the sessions with telephone calls. When home tasks were assigned, the grandmother would alter or change the plans according to her ideas about what the family needed to do. A power struggle developed between the elderly woman and the clinician until the elderly woman's own needs (sadness, depression, unresolved grief) were addressed and she became a full member of the family sessions. Individuals, as well as family members, often serve as armchair therapists who give advice or render opinion with little or no knowledge about family dynamics or clinical intervention. Schoolteachers, ministers, neighbors, club members, drinking buddies, spouses, in-laws, or distant friends are often found standing on the sidelines directing the family's efforts while the family unit is attempting to seek professional help elsewhere.

Although such assistance is often well meant, it adds to confusion, creates uncertainty, and may even undermine the family's efforts to gain self-control and assume responsibility for its productivity and change. The family must be assisted in making decisions about how to grow, who is to assist in their efforts, and in what ways the family can best use the resources and expertise available to them. Defusing the resident family therapist entails refocusing the family member's energies on personal needs, building trust relationships between clinician and family unit, and enhancing natural abilities of family members to be sensitive, concerned, and problem solvers. Comments and observations include the following: "I notice that __________ (family member) has strong ideas about what is wrong with this family and what it would take to correct the problem. How does that compare with your (indicating other members) perceptions?" "How long have you been assuming the responsibility for identifying and trying to remedy family (or name an individual) problems?" "How much time does that leave you for your own personal needs?" "I notice that (schoolteacher, minister, neighbor) is often mentioned in your family discussions, particularly as one who gives advice to this family. Let's discuss the role that __________ plays in your family (or in family therapy)." Identifying the purpose of problems, deemphasizing the influence of the identified patient, and defusing the resident family therapist are all essential components of breaking old patterns and making way for new ways of interacting.

**Breaking old patterns**

Breaking old patterns involves assisting the family in altering its own organization in ways that widen the set of options and permit greater self-control and management on a long-term basis. Larry and his grandfather, from an earlier example, had a good emotional relationship. However, that relationship, had deleterious effects on Larry's school work, until the family could be helped to alter patterns of interaction in such a way that positive emotional bonding could be directed in a more productive fashion for Larry. Ebbie Stanton's family had developed a longstanding habit of using one another for self-gain, in ways that were not age and experience appropriate. The Lyndon family had a longstanding practice of self-concealment and other deceptions that encouraged emotional dishonesty and created confusion and uncertainty for the family members. Areva Wick clung to unresolved grief, anger, and despair until there was little room in her life for the living members of her family.

Breaking old patterns involves a knowledge of what those patterns are, where they came from, and what effect such patterns have on family interaction and personal development. It may be necessary to assist the family in completing the unfinished task from the past in order that family energy may be directed to the present and future. Dick Morse's unresolved anger and other unfinished business with his own father hampered his ability to father his own children and cope effectively with feelings of anger and separation. Ebbie Stanton's unresolved grief over her grandmother's death and unresolved grief and anger over the dissolution of her parents' marriage made repeated demands on her physical and emotional health.

It may be necessary to explore the effect and consequences of naming, particularly where the naming process carries with it self-fulfilling prophecy or expectation. Bobby Lyndon was named for his father; he was remarkably like him. Children who acquire labels early in life (dumb, silly, tuffy, four-eyes) often take on those labels and incorporate them into identity development. The same thing occurs with families: troublemakers, losers, and winners are tagged by the community or neighborhood they live in.

An examination of the use and abuse of family space may be needed. The Anders family redesigned their home to make more space, with little or no regard for the intrusion into their son's territory. He left home in search of his own place. Donald was territorially deprived and exhibited his deprivation by attacking other children, an inappropriate but often used space-expanding behavior of children. Each family member must have territory, personal space, and room for privacy.

Evaluating the styles and patterns of communication within a given family is necessary. Toby came to our office and displayed unusual nonverbal messages, which, however, became very understandable when the communication within his family became known. To change his message patterns, it was necessary to intervene in the patterns of communication within his family system. Families know they communicate; they are not always aware of the pattern or organization of who says what to whom, in what manner, and with what impact, as Toby so clearly indicated to us by his behavior. Communication often reflects the underlying emotional tenor.

Understanding the emotional tenor in any given family will aid the clinician in knowing how the family allows or encourages individual growth and provides for and accommodates conflict and disagreement and will assist the clinician and family in changing emotional bonding and creating climates more conducive to expansion. To alter bonding, it is necessary to know what the bonding is. Breaking old patterns must be accompanied by the possibility of replacing old ways with better ways.

As demonstrated in earlier examples, several means exist to facilitate breaking old patterns and preparing ground for new ways of interacting and communicating among family members. Families themselves need to be assisted in assuming an active, positive posture with regard to their own futures. The use of a contract helps family members to recognize their equal partnership in the clinical process. Ebbie Stanton had the option in her contract to leave; she also had the option to stay, but the choice was hers. Choice and the feeling of self-determination can be enhanced by the clinician's strong belief in and insistence on the family's right and responsibility. A clinical philosophy that entails client rights and focuses on health as well as illness is essential to implementing a contract in which the client and clinician are equal partners. Few families totally lack an aspect of health, no matter how grossly ineffective in that area they may appear at any given time.

Tools and techniques employed in the clinical process reflect the underlying philosophy of the professional. Observation, assessment, and intervention strategies may be employed that permit and encourage the family's active participation: the Hanway comparison and contrast exercise requires active knowledge and participation in identifying family members, naming family units, and comparing similarities and differences between individuals and across units; the Bush family photoanalysis requires the family's active and ongoing participation in the location and examination of photographs that describe a portion of the family's life; Personal Space Maps are surveys that individual family members conduct of living space (physical, social, emotional) available and used by the family; and Family Art Drawings are sketches that the family as a unit undertakes which require cooperation and participation of individuals within the family as the exercise is being completed. The more active and involved the family can be in learning about itself, the more able the family will be in designing and implementing long-range goals and making changes in family organization that are lasting.

From the outset of clinical contact, the family is involved: in history taking, observations, assessment, intervention, and evaluation. The need for change that becomes evident as the clinical record is compiled becomes the target for contract development between the client and the clinician.

As targets are identified and options discussed, the family practices by means of EDIT strategies, making strides in altering old patterns. Practicing changes, role playing, group discussions, and family exercises that provide the family an opportunity to try out new behaviors and gain understanding and awareness of their impact on one another, with the skilled guidance and direction of the clinician, are an essential part of breaking old patterns and establishing new avenues of interaction. The clinician serves as facilitator and change agent: offering encouragement, teaching skills, and supporting the exploration of options.

## SUMMARY

The clinician makes a valuable contribution to the family's efforts toward becoming a more effective system: through more efficient problem solving, greater emphasis on creating emotional climates conducive to emotional growth, and enhanced social skills in terms of community and environment. As a change agent, the clinician assists the family to identify the resident family therapist, deemphasize the role of the identified patient, evaluate emotional bonding, manipulate physical territory and alter personal space, construct intentionally designed living photographs, find new family units to relate to, explore new avenues of communication with the family, and establish social and emotional support networks. The efforts of the clinician follow the philosophy that client and clinician maintain a partnership in the clinical process, with equal rights and responsibilities related to skill and experience. Just as the family is interdependent with the environment surrounding it, so the clinician and the family are interdependent components of communities, social agencies, neighborhoods, and social movements.

Mental health and family effectiveness are a joint endeavor—the outcome of interpersonal processes that involve family systems, social networks, and health professionals. None can exist without the other; all have impact on and are influenced by the process that they seek to manage and eventually change.

# INDEX

**Q**



**R**